Eighteenth-Century
ENGLISH SOCIETY

Douglas Hay is Associate Professor of Law, Osgoode Hall Law School,
and of History, at York University, Toronto. He has co-edited and
contributed to *Albion's Fatal Tree: Crime and Society in Eighteenth Century
England* (London, 1975); *Labour, Law and Crime in Historical Perspective*
(London, 1987), *Policing and Prosecution in Britain 1750 to 1850* (Oxford,
1989); and other collections.

Nicholas Rogers is Professor of History at York University, Toronto. He
is the author of *Whigs and Cities: Popular Politics in the Age of Walpole
and Pitt* (Oxford, 1989), and, with Paul E. Lovejoy, has edited *Unfree
Labour in the Development of the Atlantic World* (London, 1994).

Eighteenth-Century
ENGLISH SOCIETY

Shuttles and Swords

Douglas Hay and Nicholas Rogers

OXFORD
UNIVERSITY PRESS

Oxford University Press, Great Clarendon Street, Oxford OX2 6DP

Oxford New York

Auckland Cape Town Dar es Salaam Hong Kong Karachi
Kuala Lumpur Madrid Melbourne Mexico City Nairobi
New Delhi Shanghai Taipei Toronto

With offices in
Argentina Austria Brazil Chile Czech Republic France Greece
Guatemala Hungary Italy Japan South Korea Poland Portugal
Singapore Switzerland Thailand Turkey Ukraine Vietnam

Oxford is a registered trade mark of Oxford University Press

First published as an Oxford University Press paperback 1997

British Library Cataloguing in Publication Data
Data available

Library of Congress Cataloging in Publication Data
Hay, Douglas.
Eighteenth-century English society : shuttles and swords / Douglas
Hay and Nicholas Rogers.
p.   cm.
Includes bibliographical references (p.   ) and index.
1. England—Social conditions—18th century.   2. Great Britain—
Politics and government—18th century.   I. Rogers, Nicholas.
II. Title.
HN398.E5H29   1997
306'.0942'09033—dc21   96–52761
CIP
ISBN–13: 978–0–19–289194–5

12

Typeset by Graphicraft Typesetters Ltd., Hong Kong
Printed in Great Britain by
Clays Ltd, St Ives plc

As the Liberty lads o'er the sea
Bought their freedom, and cheaply, with blood,
So we, boys, we
Will *die* fighting, or *live* free,
And down with all kings but King Ludd!

When the web that we weave is complete,
And the shuttle exchanged for the sword,
We will fling the winding sheet
O'er the despot at our feet,
And dye it deep in the gore he has pour'd.

George Gordon, Lord Byron, *Song for the Luddites*
(Dec. 1816), opening verses

Preface

When Byron wrote of the shuttle and the sword he sought to capture in a phrase the forces arrayed in the industrial and social struggle of the Luddites in 1816. On the one side were insurgent weavers and shearers and framework-knitters; on the other, cavalry regiments stationed in the manufacturing districts. He also hoped (or warned) that swords would eventually be in the hands of the people as well as the servants of the state. 'Shuttles and swords' form the subtitle of this book because they evoke for us many of the issues at the heart of English society in the eighteenth century. Manufacturing industry and commerce, but also military might and the state that deployed it, formed many of the social relations within England. They also created the new empire of Chatham and Pitt, the source of so much of England's wealth and international power.

The phrase also reminds us of the profoundly felt identities of different populations that are so characteristic of the century. 'Shuttles', to a squire or a great landed patrician, meant trade, manual work, the stain on those who were not, and could never be, gentlemen. To a small master weaver, and his journeymen and apprentices, they were the proud symbol of 'the Trade', a skill and a claim to legal rights, against all those outside it. A man like Joseph Arkwright, however, who made his fortune from mechanizing textile processes, wished shuttles of looms could be operated, as spinning-jennies already were, almost without human labour.

Swords, the emblems of gentlemanly status, were still commonly worn in the streets of London in the early eighteenth century. But even when fashion made them less common, they remained an essential element of male formal dress among the upper classes, as long as the duel also remained central to the code of honour. In the eyes of the middling sort they were more likely to be either risible, or to carry connotations of privilege or even tyranny. The labouring poor, increasingly through the century, and especially at the end of this period, looked up at swords in the hands of mounted soldiers and propertied volunteers as the state turned more to coercion. In 1819, three years after Byron wrote *Song for the Luddites*, at least eleven men, women, and children died of sabre wounds or were trampled to death when the yeomanry, directed by the magistracy, attacked the mass meeting for parliamentary reform at St Peter's Field, Manchester. Over 400 were wounded at 'Peterloo', many of them maimed for life. The government congratulated the perpetrators.

A social history must concern itself with power, not only in such extreme settings, but in all the ways in which contending individuals and social groups, with unequal means, deal with each other. At the most visible level, that means constitutional issues, the power of the state, the civil and criminal law, military force. In the 'long eighteenth century' covered by this book, 1688 to 1820, the local state in the persons of the JP and the borough magistrate was particularly important, in sharp contrast to the extreme centralization of government in Britain at the end of the twentieth century. Of equal importance for the social historian are the structured relations of master and servant, husband and wife, officers and other ranks, and a large number of others. This book is written in the conviction that all these relationships were interdependent, and helped sustain and reflect the values of state authority and social power. However, alive within such social relations were other values also, claims and hopes and achievements that circumvented and sometimes subverted power. How they did so, and when and why, is also central to any social history.

One of our themes is that the consensual politics (in the widest sense) of the minimalist state that characterized much of the eighteenth century, was greatly eroded in the period of dearth and revolutionary wars at the end of it. The state then increasingly armed itself against its own population. This transition forces the historian to look for answers to a classic question of early-modern political thought: the achievement of consent to governance by that great mass of people not formally represented in the political process. In considering the issues of consent and coercion in governance of the people, we none the less must remember that coercion and the other forms that power takes do not overtly determine everything people can or cannot do.

Those who wield most power, in most societies, indeed are indifferent to much of what goes on in the lives of their fellow citizens. And it is a common criticism by those who do not like to think about human relationships in terms of power, that much social life is cooperative, peaceful, rewarding, and uncontentious. People in the past, as now, fell in love and married, worked hard at their jobs, loved their sovereign and country, committed no crimes, enjoyed sports and games and food and drink, were surrounded by their families on their deathbeds. However, such a criticism is inapposite. How many people did so, who they were, what were their material circumstances, and how those circumstances changed, are the subject-matter of historical and social explanation. The smell of power is acrid. Sweet histories written in the late twentieth century are like the nosegays on the benches of eighteenth-century courts.

Power defines the limits within which people live and lived their lives, including the length of those lives. The boundaries are not only drawn by force, but also by what is made thinkable: by received ideas of politics, of the state, of the criminal, of the moral or godly or responsible. Boundary ideas, received ideas, hegemonic ideas, what is thinkable, or at least thinkable without prosecution, also change. This book is therefore also about how ideologies have real bite, particularly when a contested one is finally seen off the stage by another.

In the late twentieth century we are in such a period. Both of us were born roughly when one ideology (the bald market economics of the 1930s) was displaced by that of the mixed, prosperous war-and-welfare economies of wartime and post-war governments. We were students in a period when the left denounced the post-war status quo as a conserver of privilege, and we became lecturers as a resurgent right began to argue that that status quo was instead a destroyer of liberty. We are writing when political programmes to demolish the post-war verities, much of local government, and the very idea of a benevolent, redistributive state, all in the name of a neo-classical theory of markets, have taken recent root in the United Kingdom, North America, much of Europe, and Australasia. Those changes have been accompanied, in many of those economies, by a great increase in social inequality in the last two decades.

No student of Hanoverian England can fail to be struck by some similarities, embedded in a very different ground. The last half of our period saw the initial triumph of classical political economy, and we have attempted to identify some of the important points of that triumph, and some of its consequences. In our view it reflected, embodied, and promoted decisive changes in the ways in which the English thought about themselves, and acted towards each other.

The degree of its success, and the degree to which it was implemented, was closely related to the issue of coercion and consent that is our other principal theme. The structure of the book reflects our conviction that these two large changes had interconnected ramifications throughout English life. They reappear in different chapters that describe different areas of social life. In many we find evidence of similar shifts in practices and beliefs, beginning about mid-century and accelerating during the period of the Revolutionary and French Wars at its end.

How well we have fulfilled our intentions is for our readers to judge. In a survey of more than a century the extent of our borrowings from fellow historians of the period is very great. We have indicated some of our main sources for ideas and arguments, as well as evidence, in the list of suggested readings and in some places in the text, but the names of many colleagues are necessarily omitted in a short book such as this. We have identified some of the main points where we differ significantly from others' conclusions, without pretending to summarize dispassionately the many scholarly debates in the field.

As we wrote the book we were sharply aware of the challenges of reducing our conclusions about a great deal of research into a small compass. We have tried to avoid two extremes toward which writers of short surveys are tempted. One approach produces a pastiche of quotation and anecdote which, while conveying much of the flavour of a past society, leaves the reader ignorant of its structures and its workings, and especially the ways in which those changed over time. The other extreme, a schematic diagram of abstractions and vectors, or shifts in linguistic ambiguities, may fail to convince the reader that anyone lived in the past at all: only classes, or hegemonic ideas, or texts.

We are persuaded that our ancestors were as real as their bones in the graveyards and their letters in the archives and the other material legacies of their labour: canals and clocks and chairs and courtrooms and poorhouses. To an even greater extent their ideas also survive. Certainly the issues about which they worried, and argued, and sometimes fought, as individuals, and as opposed interests—unemployment, poverty, markets, crime, public disorder, new technology, new wealth, war, politics, and love—are with us still. But they dealt with all of them within different limits from ours, and in terms of organizing ideas that are often like our own, but sometimes so different that it is only with difficulty we recognize the vivid immediacy they had 250 years ago.

As historians, we hope that we have conveyed much of the Hanoverian England we carry in our own heads, and that we have also given an argument, and evidence enough to make it plausible. We will have succeeded if our readers want to read more widely and deeply in the sources, to create in their minds, or books of their own, other versions of eighteenth-century England to put beside the one presented here.

We are very grateful to John Beattie, James Epstein, Jeanette Neeson, John Phillips, and Adrian Randall for comments on earlier versions. Chris Frank helped with some questions; Mirka Ondrak advised on graphs; Rex Russell provided maps; Deanna Jubas helped prepare the typescript; and Jennine Hurl assisted with the index. At Oxford University Press, George Miller provided encouragement and Rebecca Hunt assistance in the final stages.

D. H.
N. R.

Toronto 1996

Contents

1 Landscapes and Perspectives

Flying into Heathrow before dawn, when the flight-path is over the length of England from the north, the visitor sees first in the blackness below, a gradually sharpening pattern of interlinked ganglia, glowing yellow, dense at the centres, fraying suddenly into fine tendrils at their edges. The dark gaps between the sodium lighting of cities and towns are large, but over Lancashire, the Midlands, and then approaching London, the density of light increases, forming broad swathes of gold. Then from a lower altitude, as the sun rises, the visitor begins to make out roads, towns, rivers, and eventually the intricate patchwork of small enclosed fields next to the new development which has uprooted the hedges and ditches of two hundred years ago. There is a glimpse of Windsor amid the green, then the endless streets of the western reaches of metropolitan London, and the sudden blur of the runway.

England first seen this way seems both small in extent—one traverses the whole country so quickly—and immensely dense in human terms, a density of population that none the less is sharply delineated, in part by post-war planning, into countryside and city, great conurbations on the one hand, and almost-empty farmland and upland regions elsewhere. When we reconstitute in our mind's eye the appearance of eighteenth-century England, we can find some similar contrasts. London was unique: then as now the largest city in Europe. But outside the metropolis the areas of greatest population were very different from those of today. And the difference in scale is remarkable: the crowded country we now know, with almost 50 million people in England and Wales, held little more than 5 million in 1700, and fewer than 9 million at the end of the eighteenth century. The small population, the slow pace of travel (not much faster than in medieval times), and the nature of agriculture and industry made England in 1700 resemble much more the country of several centuries earlier than that of 1800. This chapter provides a quick tour, first of the countryside, then of Georgian London, and then of the Celtic periphery and the wider empire. It is an introduction to some of the themes and changes we discuss in later chapters at greater length.

Industry in the countryside

Landscape paintings, and the imagery of Georgic and pastoral poetry and prose, give us a gentlemanly ideal of the eighteenth-century countryside: one that was peaceful, empty, and profitable, with the odd picturesque haymaker or shepherd. Gentry and aristocracy created such vistas when they could, by changing landholding patterns, by refusing licences to alehouses, or (in the extreme case of the great magnate enlarging his deer-park) by moving whole villages to a discreet distance. But colliers, framework-knitters, and weavers were usually not very far away. Where industry had been long established or was growing quickly in the eighteenth century, resident gentry were fewer, the social texture often markedly different from the conventional image.

The countryside of England today is comparatively unpopulated, a striking contrast to the human density of city and town life. The division was much less marked in the eighteenth century, largely because rural industrial workers, and the commoning populations of open field and forest, were numerous, fecund, and not very quiet. Such 'open' communities were likely to be so in the sense that enclosure (the elimination of the ancient common fields and the rights over them) had not yet taken place (see Ch. 7). They were also open to population growth, both through incomers and through earlier marriage and hence higher birth rates, made possible by the earnings of rural industry. Spinning, weaving, woolcombing, frame-work-knitting, nailing, shoemaking, lacemaking, and a host of other industries were heavily dependent on the labour of such communities. Where extensive common rights coexisted with such wage labour, large and (in the eyes of gentlemen) unruly populations were concentrated. Forest regions in particular (and they were found throughout the country) were in the eyes of authority the 'nest and conservatory of sloth, idleness, and misery'.[1] Such observations were often interested ones: forest and commoning populations were not quiescent labour of the kind of which farmers and gentlemen approved. They preferred that of 'closed' parishes, which were held by a few large owners, sparsely populated, intensively farmed, and subject to constant scrutiny by the landlord or his agent. Often such parishes had been enclosed in earlier centuries.

Some industries were dependent on local resources that peers and gentlemen were only too anxious to exploit: landlords with coal or other mineral deposits gladly sacrificed rents, even sporting land, to their exploitation. (The Pagets of Staffordshire dug coal-pits on Cannock Chase, in the deer-park of their great house: wherever coal could be found.) But industry was found in the countryside primarily because that was where cheaper, underemployed labour was to be found. The textile and metalworking trades, and a wide range of manufacturing industry were found in almost all parts of England. Generally organized either as a putting-out system, with materials advanced on credit to be collected later by the clothier or nail-factor, or as production on the artisan's own account, in both cases it might be only one of the economic activities of the family. Certainly in the seventeenth and early eighteenth centuries dual-economy households were still common, in which agricultural smallholding was combined with weaving, scythe-making, potting, or another of the trades. They became less common as the eighteenth century progressed, as regional specialization advanced and industrial populations grew (and some areas already were like that in the seventeenth century). Recent work has suggested that industry of all kinds was considerably more important at an earlier period than was once thought, because the traditional sources tend to ignore or underestimate by-employments, and because a large part of the workforce, in textiles but also a host of other trades, was female. Women workers were simply not counted in many of the sources historians have used. Many traditional industries (for example, the growing of flax and making of linen) fitted both within domestic economies for home use, and as part of highly organized outputting systems. In most rural industries production was overwhelmingly domestic, carried on in the home; the exceptions were mining, smelting, and a few other industries dependent on a central plant. But the loomshop or large manufactory (factory) was very rare: the few that existed in the eighteenth century were remarkable, and prime attractions for tourists (see Ch. 8).

Parish, county, and nation

We have emphasized industry first, because its organization and development, largely in rural settings, set in motion many of the important changes in English society we describe in later chapters, and because industrial production, particularly textiles, had employed large numbers of people for centuries. But in 1700 probably half of male employment in the country as a whole was still involved in agriculture, a proportion that probably had not differed much for a long period of time. The agrarian social structure is described in Chapter 2, but some other characteristics of England outside London deserve mention here.

The first are some very broad geographic divisions which still characterize the English landscape and shape rural life. There is the contrast between what geographers call highland or upland areas, and the lowlands, a contrast which in agricultural terms was broadly that between pastoral areas dominated by sheep and cattle on higher ground, and arable farming of cereal grains in the more populous lowlands (see Fig. 1). It has also been suggested that another division existed within lowland England, a distinction between 'ancient' or 'original', and 'planned' landscape. This contrast became more sharply defined by the end of the eighteenth century:

On the one hand, as in Essex or Herefordshire, we have the England of hamlets, medieval farms in hollows of the hills, lonely moats and great barns in the clay-lands, pollards and ancient trees, cavernous hollways and many footpaths, fords, irregularly-shaped groves with thick hedges colourful with maple, dogwood, and spindle—an intricate land of mystery and surprise. On the other hand there is the Cambridgeshire type of landscape, the England of big villages, few, busy roads, thin hawthorn hedges, windswept brick farms, and ivied clumps of trees in corners of fields; a predictable land of wide views, sweeping sameness, and straight lines.[2]

Much of this contrast (which has many local exceptions, and ancient origins) was accentuated in the period covered by this book, as the planned countryside of straight lines took its modern form through the legislation and then the physical surveying which obliterated an older pattern of agriculture in the process of enclosure. Moors, heaths, and wasteland receded, or became more obviously marginal, as enclosure proceeded. It should be added that although the restructuring of the planned landscape of the Midlands in particular often occurred in more open countryside than was characteristic of ancient lowland areas, the process none the less was in part a closing-in. Between 1750 and 1850 some 200,000 miles of hedges were planted, at least as much as in the previous 500 years.

But the quotation evokes for us also another set of contrasts, and a related set of developments in eighteenth-century England. Intricacy, particularity, and local practice were immensely important in the social life of the eighteenth century, in a great many ways. Yet at the same time a process of integration and rationalization, in markets, roads, political discourse, and national consciousness, was eroding such differences, slowly and then much more quickly by the end of our period.

As Carl Philip Moritz, a German tourist, travelled through much of England on foot in 1782, he did not often remark on English hospitality, but rather on local suspicions. On the London to Oxford road, enveloped by the dust of the many waggons and coaches, Moritz was repeatedly asked his purposes, for pedestrians, especially strangers, were scorned or held in deep suspicion, since only the poor and vagrant walked. Visitors from other countries often remarked on the suspicion and sometimes outright hostility that both English chauvinism and local feeling could produce: Moritz was hissed through Burton-on-Trent. Earlier in the century even incomers to villages, moving from elsewhere in the same county, were likely to be called 'foreigners'. In part this sense of extremely local identities was sustained by the organization of the poor law, since only those with a 'settlement' in a particular parish (through birth, employment, or a variety of other legal claims) could expect to receive poor relief there (see Ch. 5). The 10,000 parishes of England sometimes coincided with, sometimes overlapped, the similarly small-scale division called the manor, a legal and territorial unit also of medieval origin that was still important because the manor marked out the boundaries of important property rights defined by local custom (see Ch. 6). The pressure which new population might put on local common rights, defined by these boundaries, could also generate hostility to immigrants, unless local industry provided an alternative means of livelihood. At a regional level, the identities of the forty counties of England and Wales (with boundaries largely unchanged for centuries) remained very important, in part because so much local government was concentrated in county quarter sessions (see Fig. 2). The phrase 'the country', in local usage, generally meant the shire rather than the nation.

In both small localities and larger regions, dialects were very marked, and the kind of trust on which commercial and political life thrived was often profoundly local also. Throughout the country credit networks depended largely on local and personal knowledge. Trade tokens and even sometimes counterfeit coin (both necessary because the state coinage was so bad) often defined a particular region, since their acceptance depended on such understandings. Political identities were differentiated locally, but also regionally. In the first half of the century, support for the exiled House of Stuart was concentrated in some counties (Staffordshire, Lancashire, Cheshire), although there was also significant support in London (see Ch. 4). There were regional differences in a range of popular beliefs and accepted practices, from the rites of customary marriages to the strengths of particular religious sects, or the usages (legally recognized) of employment and service.

Developing national markets, as well as national politics, eroded but did not eliminate all such differences, and they created others. In many places local fairs and markets had long served quite small areas, with local customs, distinctive weights and measures, and bylaws that punished farmers or buyers who sought to make bargains outside their regulations. Increasingly they were bypassed by corn-factors buying for the large London and export markets, but they did not disappear. Employers tried to break strikes, and sometimes succeeded, by bringing in workers from distant counties, a reminder both of the strength of local social and trade organization, and of how wider markets for labour and commodities constantly challenged parochial ideas of protection, trust, and power. New regional concentrations of specialized farming or industry (such as East Anglia and what would later be called the Black Country) did not eliminate older identities, at least for many decades, but long before that they had weakened local customs and institutions, generating new ones as they did so (see Ch. 8).

Piking to London

'Piking to the start' was thieves' cant for returning to London from a tour of the provinces. England was a reasonably mobile society. Judging from the parish registers there was a high degree of population turnover, with few families remaining in the same parish for more than three generations. In 1782 only 30 per cent of the married adults in Cardington, Bedfordshire, had been born in the parish. The same was true of many provincial towns even a century earlier. A good deal of this geographical mobility was age-specific, involving young servants or apprentices, and it did not necessarily take them very far afield. The vast majority of migrants, in fact, moved less than 15 miles from their birthplace, especially in the more intensively farmed south. The growth of regional industrial areas was due in part to population growth (closely related to industrialization itself), but partly also to in-migration from neighbouring villages and parishes.

Even so, England became an increasingly urban society in the eighteenth century; it was the fastest growing urban society in Europe, in fact, with about 10 per cent of its population in towns of over 10,000 inhabitants in 1650 and 24 per cent by 1800. Much of this growth came by in-migration, for until 1770 deaths exceeded births in most towns. The most remarkable magnet for the migrant population was London, by 1700 surpassing Paris as the largest city in Europe with a population of 575,000. Arguing from its appalling mortality rate yet dramatic growth, it has been estimated that one in six English men and women lived in the capital sometime in their lives. This meant that more English people had experience of metropolitan life than did the French (2.5 per cent), and the Dutch (8–9 per cent), although the latter's population was significantly more urban in 1700 and still so in 1800.

For Daniel Defoe in 1724, London was 'the most glorious sight without exception that the whole world at present can show, or perhaps ever cou'd show since the sacking of Rome in the European, and the burning the Temple of Jerusalem in the Asian part of the world'.[3] He marvelled at its size and wondered where it would end. This was because London was far greater than the chartered City, whose walls and gates could be viewed 'within a small compass'. It was now linked to Westminster, the city of Parliament, the Court, and from the seventeenth century onwards, the fashionable piazzas and squares, the playground of the social élite. It also spread eastwards, through the weaving districts of Spitalfields to the wharfs and rope-walks of the River Thames, where ships unloaded foreign goods and coals from Newcastle, and southwards into Southwark, the home of breweries, distilleries, and industries like tanning, what were called the 'nauseous trades'. London was a city of government, society, commerce, and manufacture; it was still the major port, the major centre of artisanal crafts and of conspicuous consumption. That was what made it a source of wonderment as well as apprehension.

'When a man is tired of London', said Dr Johnson, 'he is tired of life; for there is in London all that life can afford.' This was the Augustan view of London as the centre of the arts and civilization, the symbol of grandeur, progress, and enlightenment. It was a view reproduced by Canaletto, who imposed order, symmetry, space, and a Venetian grace upon the bustle of London's teeming wharfs, streets, and squares. Yet, as Johnson well recognized, there were darker realities that kept disturbing this sense of civilized order: the degradation of *Gin Lane*; the low-life vigour of the *Beggar's Opera*; the insubordination of London's jostling crowd, who, as Matthew Bramble and less literary stereotypes discovered, paid little court to gentility. In London, the contrasts between wealth and poverty often seemed more threatening and sinister than in the countryside where the gentry felt more confident of their place in the social order. London's conspicuous consumption was a tonic to theft; well-dressed men and women were often robbed in open daylight, their goods rapidly fenced through a network of receivers, their assailants part of the anonymous mass who worked, drank, and lived in the innumerable alleys and courts that abutted the main thoroughfares. London's sanitary problem, moreover, was appalling, despite the efforts of river companies and statutory bodies to pave and clean the streets and provide clean water. Every summer those who could afford to do so left London to avoid the stench of a city that, for all its facilities, seemed out of control. Unlike other provincial towns, most especially spas, where the social élite could enjoy the pleasures of urban civilization in elegant surroundings, the seamy underside of London life kept breaking in. By the end of the century, people were less con-fident about London's urbanity and more fearful of its anonymity and crime, of its unknown rookeries. Some of those grew as a consequence of the speculative mania that had accompanied the making of Georgian London, forcing the poor into the cramped and more populous quarters of the city. Cobbett was not the first to think of London as the 'Great Wen', an excrescence on the body politic, a monster out of control. The same thing had been said by Josiah Tucker, one of the most urbane of Georgian clergymen, who had lived much of his life in the cathedral cities of Bristol and Gloucester. Those cities were both physically and mentally accommodating to those who cherished the urban renaissance of the eighteenth century in a way in which London was not.

A shrinking country

In some important ways the England outside London was becoming smaller in the eighteenth century, especially after about 1760 (see Fig. 3). Canals and turnpike roads mastered the most important routes of internal travel. Highwaymen, if they escaped the gallows long enough, felt their habitat disappearing, and increasingly had to make sure that the gatekeepers on the new turnpikes were well bribed. Topographical artists caught the striking sight of canal boats gliding over remote valleys on viaducts; timetables and guidebooks listed scheduled coach services, and shorter travel times. When Dr Sacheverell was convicted on articles of impeachment in Westminster Hall on 20 March 1710, the news took three days to travel from London to the Shropshire borders; in 1820 the outcome of Queen Caroline's trial in the House of Lords reached the Isle of Skye as quickly. Travel in eighteenth-century England, whether for pleasure or business, was increasingly likely to be by coach rather than on horseback or by coastal vessel. Or it might be by canal: one William Foulds, 'the Little Devil', a notorious Manchester criminal who robbed Matthew Boulton and James Watt's great Soho Manufactory at Birmingham in 1800 (see Ch. 8), escaped on a boat plying the numerous manmade waterways that had threaded the industrializing Midlands since mid-century.

The vast expansion of a provincial press recirculating metropolitan and international news, and feeding the dominant London press in turn, also shrank the political and economic landscape of England. By the time of Walpole (prime minister from 1722 to 1742) most tradesmen, shopkeepers, and small farmers could read, and within twenty years so could about 40 per cent of all labourers and women, making England arguably the most literate nation in Europe. In 1770 the *London Gazette* and many other papers began publishing the weekly returns of grain prices for dozens of markets throughout the Kingdom, and from 1803 *The Course of Exchange* published authoritative prices on the stock market. The victory of the printers, who successfully resisted Parliament's attempt in 1771 to control the publication of debates, was a measure of the new commercial and political importance of the press, the tying-together of provincial and London political culture. When Admiral Keppel (an opponent of the government) was tried before a court martial on capital charges of incompetence and unofficer-like behaviour in the face of the enemy in 1779, the news of his acquittal was rushed from Portsmouth to the London presses within six hours by special courier (see Ch. 11). The mob in London rose instantly to celebrate their hero: they tore down the gates of the Admiralty, broke windows of ministers' mansions, and gutted the house of Keppel's prosecutor in Pall Mall. By the end of the century, caricatures made familiar in the remotest part of the nation the faces of politicians like Pitt and Fox; hitherto only the features of monarchs had been widely known, from the coinage and prints.

Thus a growing public came to share more and more elements of a common perception of the country: an England with a less mysterious landscape, in which common fields and some heaths and wastes were increasingly fenced and ditched, one in which selected or privileged elements of national and regional news became a matter of shared discussion much more quickly. These developments enhanced a degree of national integration already striking to many foreigners. Carl Philip Moritz remarked on the difference between German towns, which were often sovereign entities, and those of England:

There are no fortifications—town walls, gate, or the like; no exciseman on the lookout, no menacing sentry to beware of; you pass through town and village as freely and unhindered as through wide-open Nature.[4]

Population growth

If England was becoming smaller through faster travel, newspaper reportage, the tying-together of local markets into regional ones, and regional markets into national, by the late eighteenth century it was also becoming much larger in terms of population (see Fig. 4). Historically the population had been dwarfed by that of the nearest European neighbour and rival, France. In 1550 England and France had populations of 3 and 17 million respectively, in 1680 the figures were 4.9 and 21.9 million. The late seventeenth and early eighteenth century appears to have been a period in which the population of England and Wales declined from a higher level in the 1650s. Then in about 1760 the population growth rates of England and France diverged, the difference becoming marked by the 1780s. In 1801 England as a whole had 8.7 million, London 900,000. France's population was 29.1 million, Paris 550,000. By

1821 the French population was still much larger, but the proportions had changed greatly from the sixteenth century: England had grown to 11.5 million, France to about 31 million. And the great growth of London was one indication of England's domination in international trade and hence national strength.

The reasons for the much more rapid growth of the English population in this period are several, perhaps especially the long-term effects of the growth of rural industry over several centuries, and the low agricultural prices (and high real wages) of the late seventeenth and early eighteenth centuries.[5] A consequence of the rapid growth of population was that its age-structure also changed markedly. In the late seventeenth century there had been 630 dependants (mostly children under 15, but also adults over 60) for every 1,000 people between those ages. By 1821 the rapid growth of the previous half-century had created a population with a dependency ratio of almost 850, by far the greater part of it caused by unprecedented numbers of children and adolescents. Times of higher prices, lower real wages, caused far greater suffering in such a population, and a very strong incentive to put children to work at younger ages.

Greater Britain

The population of England and Wales, or of Britain as a whole, had not been an accurate indicator of the nation's importance for centuries. (Indeed, the size of the population could only be guessed at before the first census in 1801.) A seafaring people, the English looked far beyond Dover, and Land's End at the tip of Cornwall, and even John o' Groats at the furthest reaches of Scotland. The American colonies, the Caribbean sugar islands, Hudson Bay and Newfoundland, west African slaving posts, and Indian and Chinese ports had become part of the mental landscape of the nation. They were familiar places to thousands of sailors, soldiers, servants, planters, and traders in the seventeenth century, and the source of much wealth to investors at home, including the King, aristocracy, and great merchants. In the period of this book the other parts of the British Isles became much more clearly political fiefdoms of England, and the Empire grew enormously in extent.

Wales had been politically subordinated to England since the sixteenth century. It was something of a backwater, with a predominately pastoral economy that sustained perhaps 400,000 people

in 1700 and less than 600,000 in 1801. Politically it was dominated by 30–40 landed families who between them returned most
of the MPs to parliament and vied with one another for territorial
supremacy. Although some of these squires retained a sturdy independence from government and even dabbled in Jacobite politics,
Wales did not pose a threat to the English political establishment
as did Scotland and Ireland during the eighteenth century. Only
with the rapid expansion of its industrial frontier did this situation
change, generating a grass-roots Chartist movement that exploded
into rebellion during the 1830s.

Scotland became ever more a part of Great Britain in both political and economic terms. The thrones of Scotland and England had
been united in the person of James I in 1603, but the crucial changes
occurred with the Union in 1707, when Edinburgh lost its parliament, and after the defeat of Charles Edward Stuart, the Stuart
'Young Pretender' to the British Crown.[6] The invasion he led in
July 1745, first through Scotland and then south as far as Derby by
December, was the greatest threat to the rule of London and the
Hanoverian dynasty in the entire century. After the final defeat of
the Jacobites at Culloden in April 1746, Parliament passed legislation to criminalize Highland dress and bagpipes, erased the hereditary judicial rights of landlords, confiscated many rebel estates,
and built a network of military roads through Scotland that also
helped suppress endemic cattle-rustling. More important, Scottish
lowland improvers, indistinguishable from their English counterparts, set about transforming the Highlands with profitable cattle
farms, and then sheep; in the lowlands, industrial production and
export, with strong ties to England, accelerated after mid-century.

The changes that brought prosperity for some Scots with capital
ended the way of life of others, and by the early nineteenth century despair and starvation and emigration haunted the Highlands.
In Ireland, peasant despair came sooner. Ireland and the Irish Parliament had been made subordinate to that of England in 1494,
and Ireland had been a constitutional dependency of the British
Crown from the time of Henry VIII. Legislative prohibitions by
the English Parliament, which formally declared supremacy over
Ireland's in 1719, had already deprived Irish industry of virtually
all external markets. The Irish Parliament was in practice controlled by government patronage directed from London. The hatred

of England engendered by Cromwell's bloody victories in the seventeenth century and the Irish resentment of Scots and English planters who had taken Irish land, lay behind much of the legal and social condition of eighteenth-century Ireland. Catholics (the vast majority of the population) were forbidden by law to own land throughout most of the eighteenth century, and the extraction of high rents by the Protestant descendants of the planters helped generate increased agrarian violence by a desperate peasantry from the 1760s. An increasingly reform-minded Protestant gentry and yeomanry extorted a degree of constitutional independence from the British Parliament in the 1780s, and some civil rights for Catholics. That independence ended after attempted rebellion by the (largely Protestant) United Irishmen against English rule in 1798. The rebellion was suppressed by London with remarkable ferocity, including summary trials of civilians by courts martial of doubtful legality. The Act of Union of 1801 abolished the Irish Parliament, and made Ireland contitutionally part of the United Kingdom. To the 558 members of the House of Commons were now added 100 Irish MPs, a change with significant effects for nineteenth-century British politics. Meanwhile the Irish Secretary in London, through his agents in Dublin castle, centralized the control of prosecutions under the criminal law, in a largely vain attempt to subdue agrarian and political violence. Evicted and desperate Irish men and women were common sights on English roads in the worst years. Irishmen filled some of the most laborious English trades, including London coal-heaving, and competed and fought with English labourers.

Empire and patriotism

The poorer Welsh, Scots, and Irish who came to England were visibly foreigners, not least because they had their own languages. In Wales the mass of the population, below an Anglicizing gentry, was 90 per cent Welsh-speaking. At the end of the eighteenth century almost 20 per cent of the Scottish population, mostly in the western Highlands, still spoke only Gaelic, and probably 50 per cent of the Irish population spoke only their native tongue. These were significant numbers of people. Wales had a population at the end of the century of about 585,000, Scotland 1.6 million, Ireland about 4.5 million. Of the 14.9 million people of the British Isles, we can calculate that about one-fifth did not speak English as their first language, and a large proportion of that fifth did not speak English at all.

In both the Irish and Scots cases the hostility of the English state to traditional, uncommercial, and disloyal peasants, speaking barbarous tongues and with barbarous customs, was overt. The Highlands and the Irish *gaeltacht* were somewhat larger versions of that affront to improving landlords in England itself: the waste, the uncultivated common. And as the Empire widened immensely, more and more such populations came under English suzerainty. The West Indies and mainland American colonies founded in the seventeenth century accounted for half of British exports later in the eighteenth. Throughout the period war and naval dominance added possessions of other European powers, new discoveries, or colonies which formerly had been only posts for trade. The eighteenth century was the age of Cook and Botany Bay and Hawaii, Clive and Hastings and the extension of British control in India, Wolfe's conquest of Canada. Trade immensely increased both Britain's international presence and her commercial dominance over her European rivals, particularly France. The slave trade (on average 50,000 Africans a year were shipped to America in the half-century after 1700) was substantially in English hands, and black slavery replaced white indentured labour in British Caribbean possessions. War, for fully half the period, engaged Britain as a great power, an imperial power, and, by the end of the Napoleonic Wars, as the dictator of the terms of peace to Europe (see Ch. 10). By the end of this period, too, English exports and shipping dominated the seas.

The wealth and international importance of Great Britain would reach its apogee in the nineteenth century; the prolonged decline to her present international status began sometime after 1870. But the period covered by this book was, for England, that of accession to dominance. At the political summit, the sense of command, of conquest of wider realms, permeated economic experience and political debate. Many of the modern trappings of state such as Windsor costume (the court dress designed by George III), the uniforms of the Guards regiments, the coronation coach, date from the eighteenth century. They are symbolic of the power of the British state at its height. They also epitomized, for the radicals among the successful American rebels who split the Empire in 1776, and for democrats in England, the vices of privilege, inequality, aristocracy, and oppression.

For many, George III came to symbolize both state and nation by the end of his long reign (1760–1810). Aristocratic and bourgeois, he embodied late-eighteenth century English upper-class sensibility, a monarch who felt equally comfortable in the character of a gentleman farmer. But George also took his state duties with the utmost seriousness, and from the 1780s encouraged and often organized elaborate state ceremonial. The King took a direct hand in the Handel centenary of 1784, including a concert in Westminster Abbey given by no fewer than 500 musicians. The performance began, naturally, with Handel's Coronation Anthem, and celebrated the aristocratic order, monarchy, Church, and the greatness of Britain:

Le spectacle bien magnifique. The great aile of the Abbey was converted into a most superb theatre with very rich & elegant decorations; at the west end the orchestra in the gallery *vis-à-vis* the Throne or Royal box, in front of which seats for the Lords & Ladies of the Court, hung with white satin with festoons of gold fringe; behind these on each side the Throne seats for my Lords the Bishops & the clergy of the Abbey with purple; the two side galleries & the body of the aile which formed the pit hung with crimson damask & festoons of the same colour. The audience was splendid to a degree. It consisted chiefly of the first persons in the Kingdom of both sexes.[7]

In the aftermath of the humiliating defeat by the Americans, the regime increasingly made the King himself the object of national celebration. In this decade too the annual sermon by the most recently appointed bishop to the House of Lords began to refer (for the first time since the Revolution of 1688) to the 'sacred' person of the King.

George III's role as a symbol of State and national power made his mental breakdowns later in life (probably from porphyria) ironic, double-edged, and politically dangerous. His recovery from the first onset of madness in 1789 was marked by elaborately organized national rejoicing: again, the focus of attention was on the great State thanksgiving in Westminster Abbey. It was widely reported: provincial and London newspapers vied with one another in describing the illuminated transparencies which celebrated George the King. In the ensuing wars with Revolutionary France, the calculated celebration of monarchy by loyalists to the regime reached its highest point of the century, as an expression of nationalism, political order, and social hierarchy. But republicans and democrats, in England and abroad, saw in the King's complete mental incapacity from 1810, and the triviality of his son, who ruled as Prince Regent until 1820 and then as George IV, another message. Rule by those who inherited place and title was absurd. The monarchy itself epitomized the incapacity and redundancy of those at the pinnacle of the social hierarchy.

2 Hierarchy

Social structure

When two of the sons of George III, the Dukes of Kent and Sussex, saw a model of the social pyramid early in the nineteenth century, they were shocked. At the top of the pile of blocks representing different social classes was a tiny cube for the royal family and the peerage,

so strikingly insignificant, compared with all below, and especially when compared with the cubes representing the working and pauper classes, that the Duke of Sussex impulsively pushed the elbow of his royal brother, saying— 'Edward, do you see that?' And the whole party for the moment seemed confused, feeling and seeing the real weakness of their class as to numbers, compared with all the others.[1]

The pyramid of cubes, constructed by the manufacturer and reformer Robert Owen, embodied both old and new ways of thinking about English society. Viewed only from the side, it echoed some very old traditions of Western and Christian thought. The Great Chain of Being reached from God and the angels down to man, and then descended through all the orders of the animal and vegetable kingdom. Human society was held to mirror the Creation: the structures of State and Church were expressed as similar hierarchies, codified in rules of precedence on ceremonial occasions, embodied in titles, the order of funeral processions, the allocation of pews in church. When George I came to England as the first Hanoverian king, in 1714, it took three hours to sort out the order of precedence among peers, bishops, and other great men for his triumphal entry into London. By the eighteenth century England had very old state and church and legal structures, all of them unremittingly graded into a series of relations of inferiors to superiors. The monarchy and the peerage topped them all.

But such traditional diagrams of social hierarchy had been one- or two-dimensional. The sculptural mass of Owen's blocks vividly expressed a relatively new idea, the quantitative relationship between rulers and ruled, the weight of sheer numbers. The first detailed estimate of social structure in this sense was compiled by Gregory King in 1688; similar calculations were made by Joseph Massie in 1759 and by Patrick Colquhoun at the end of the century. Owen's model of status or income divisions was based on Colquhoun's estimate, which drew partly on the first census of 1801. 'Status or income': in fact, these early models of social structure implicitly recognized their interdependence by combining elements of both, in not very well-defined ways.

Many attempts have been made to refine these estimates and to draw more accurate conclusions about the size of different social groups, but it seems likely that in their overall shape the tables capture much of the reality of eighteenth-century society. First, they all show a much greater inequality in the distribution of income than is the case in the late twentieth century.[2] Secondly, they suggest that income inequality in England decreased from the late-seventeenth to the mid-eighteenth century (King to Massie), with most gains made by the poorest 60 per cent of the population (see Fig. 5). In the later eighteenth century, however (Massie to Colquhoun), income distribution became more unequal again; indeed, by the end of the century there was greater inequality than in 1688. These contemporary estimates agree with many other kinds of evidence showing higher real wages in the late seventeenth and early eighteenth centuries, followed by an increasingly rapid decline in the late eighteenth.

Aristocrats and gentlemen

The pyramid of income, and even more that of wealth, conformed fairly closely to a hierarchy of social roles. For the Dukes of Sussex and Kent, the monarchy and aristocracy (one-hundredth of 1 per cent of the population, fewer than 300 families) was the knowable social world. They were represented by the tiny top cube of Owen's model. Those with some share in national political power and position included the top 3 per cent or so of the adult male population, the men who were termed landed gentry and great merchants. They in turn might deign to recognize another 3 per cent of those below them in the social pyramid as 'ladies and gentlemen'— the recognizable political public. The line dividing gentlemen from all those below was of critical importance in public and private life. The line could be crossed by prospering merchants, less frequently

TABLE 2.1. *The distribution of income*

	GREGORY KING, 1688	
	Average annual family income (£)	Number of families
Temporal lords	6,060	200
Baronets	1,500	800
Bishops	1,300	26
Knights	800	600
Esquires	562.5	3,000
Merchants by sea, greater	400	2,000
Merchants on land, greater	400	3,264
Gentlemen	280	15,000
Persons in greater offices	240	5,000
1% of Population		
Merchants by sea, lesser	200	8,000
Merchants on land, lesser	200	13,057
Artisans and handicrafts	200	6,745
Law	154	8,062
Persons in lesser offices	120	5,000
Freeholders, greater	91	27,568
5% of Population		
Naval officers	80	5,000
Clergymen, greater	72	2,000
Military officers	60	4,000
Science, liberal arts	60	12,898
Freeholders, lesser	55	96,490
Clergymen, lesser	50	10,000
10% of Population		
Shopkeepers and tradesmen	45	101,704
20% of Population		
Farmers	42.5	103,382
Manufacturing trades	38	162,863
Building trades	25	73,018
Common seamen	20	50,000
Miners	15	14,240
40% of Population		
Labouring people and outservants	15	284,997
60% of Population		
Common soldiers	14	35,000
Cottagers and paupers	6.5	313,183
Vagrants	2	23,489

Notes: Percentages of population are cumulative, beginning with the highest income group.

[a] Where Massie gives more than one income group for an occupation they have been numbered consecutively and distributed throughout the table.

Sources: The figures presented here are the revised estimates of Peter H. Lindert and Jeffrey G. Williamson, 'Revising England's Social Tables 1688–1812', *Explorations in Economic History*, 19 (1982), 393, 396–7, 400–1. We have recast their tables so that the original categories, which were arranged by sector of the economy, are in descending order by annual income.

TABLE 2.1. (*cont.*)

| | JOSEPH MASSIE, 1759 | |
	Average annual family income (£)	Number of families
Titled, gentry 1[a]	26,940	10
Titled, gentry 2	13,470	20
Titled, gentry 3	10,776	40
Titled, gentry 4	8,082	80
Titled, gentry 5	5,388	160
Titled, gentry 6	2,694	320
Titled, gentry 7	1,347	640
Titled, gentry 8	1,078	800
Titled, gentry 9	808	1,600
Merchants 1	600	1,000
Titled, gentry 10	539	3,200
Titled, gentry 11	404	4,800
Merchants 2	400	2,000
Tradesmen 1	400	2,500
1% of Population		
Titled, gentry 12	269	6,400
Master manufacturers 1	200	2,500
Merchants 3	200	10,000
Law	200	12,000
Tradesmen 2	200	5,000
5% of Population		
Freeholders 1	152	20,124
Farmers 1	150	3,354
Clergy, superior	100	2,000
Military officers	100	2,000
Farmers 2	100	6,708
Master manufacturers 2	100	5,000
Tradesmen 3	100	10,000
Innkeepers 1	100	2,000
Naval officers	80	6,000
Freeholders 2	76	40,249
10% of Population		
Farmers 3	70	13,417
Master manufacturers 3	70	10,000
Tradesmen 4	70	20,000
Liberal arts	60	18,000
Civil officers	60	16,000
Clergy, inferior	50	9,000
Manufacturers wood, iron—London	41.25	9,854
Manufacturers wool, silk—London	41.25	9,853
Building—London	41.25	3,910
Farmers 4	40	80,498
Master manufacturers 4	40	62,500
Tradesmen 5	40	125,000
Cottagers, greater	40	20,000
20% of Population		
Freeholders 3	38	80,498
Labourers—London	27.5	20,000
Manufacturers wool, silk—country	25	70,384
Manufacturers wood, iron—country	25	70,384
Building, country	25	107,567
50% of Population		
Mining	23	14,300
Seamen, fishermen	20	60,000
Alesellers	20	20,000
Labourers—country	16.25	200,000
Husbandmen	16	134,160
Soldiers	14	18,000
Cottagers, paupers	7	178,892
Vagrants	3.2	13,418

TABLE 2.1. (*cont.*)

	PATRICK COLQUHOUN, 1801–1803	
	Average annual family income (£)	Number of families
Peers	8,000	287
Bishops	4,000	26
Baronets	3,000	540
Eminent merchants	2,600	2,000
Knights	1,500	350
Esquires	1,500	6,000
Higher civil offices	800	2,000
Lesser merchants	800	13,000
1% of Population		
Capital manufacturers	800	25,000
Warehousemen	800	500
Gentlemen	700	20,000
Capital ship repair	700	300
Teachers	600	500
Eminent clergy	500	1,000
Lunatic houses	500	40
Shipowners	500	5,000
Lawyers	350	11,000
Liberal arts	260	16,300
Lesser civil offices	200	10,500
5% of Population		
Better sort freehold	200	40,000
Professional skills	200	5,000
Theatre	200	1,000
Shopkeepers	150	74,500
10% of Population		
Educating youth	150	20,000
Tailors	150	25,000
Naval officers	149	7,000
Military officers	139	13,064
Lesser clergy	120	10,000
Farmers	120	160,000
20% of Population		
Dissenting clergy	120	2,500
Innkeepers	100	50,000
Lesser freeholders	90	120,000
Clerks, shopmen	75	60,000
Artisans	55	445,726
50% of Population		
Halfpay officers	45	4,015
Debtors	45	2,000
Seamen	40	49,393
Mine labourers	40	40,000
Hawkers, pedlars, etc.	40	800
Seamen	38	52,906
Labourers, husbandry	31	340,000
Lunatics	30	2,500
Soldiers	29	121,985
Pensioners	20	30,500
Paupers	10	260,179
Vagrants	10	175,218

by the sons of great manufacturers, but it was also heavily policed against the 'middling sort', those immediately below the line, with the weapons of snub, ridicule, and parental approval of marriages.

These social distinctions at the top of society were a matter of constant concern to the literate public. It was clear who was a peer: England, unlike many Continental aristocracies, restricted inherited titles, and hence seats in the House of Lords, to one male heir. Their families, wherever possible, used legal settlements to reinforce the common law's emphasis on primogeniture: the inheritance of the land, with the title, by the eldest son (see Ch. 3). This emphasis on dynastic power meant that a tiny group of families dominated both Houses of Parliament. In the Lords their heads sat as dukes, marquesses, earls, viscounts, and barons. In the Commons they arranged or bought seats for their sons, brothers, friends, and political spokesmen. Politics at this very highest level was an intimate business, similar to a family quarrel, in which everyone knew everyone else of any consequence, or could find someone who did.

Peers were of course also gentlemen, but below the peerage, it was clear who was a gentleman in some circumstances, but not in others. Courts of honour in the armed forces and particularly the army continued to enforce the supposed distinctions of a warrior élite. Accusations of 'ungentlemanly conduct' underlay most courts martial of officers, one of the most serious kinds of misconduct being familiarity with men in the ranks, or disrespect for a fellow officer. The duel was still more important in enforcing the code of honour; indeed, military courts virtually forced insulted officers to duel. To consent to duel with an opponent was to recognize his genteel status. Inferiors were whipped, and hierarchy and discipline in both the forces relied heavily on the cat-o'-nine-tails. In the navy, most midshipmen in their teens or early twenties would become officers and had already some of their status, so that it was not unusual for seamen, and even lesser inferior officers, old enough to be their fathers, to be court-martialled for striking a midshipman.

Outside the forces, the code of honour was also observed and assumptions about the proper role of the officer and gentleman continued to inform relations in genteel society for much of the century. In 1759 Sir Edward Littleton, an MP and country squire, was affronted by breach of a marriage contract for which he took responsibility. He had introduced the suitor to the woman's family, and to express his outrage and brand the man a cad, Sir Edward horsewhipped him handsomely. The cad sued. Both criminal and civil courts decided in his favour, but those who thought like Littleton knew who was the gentleman.

But who was really a gentleman? Visitations by heralds of the College of Arms (which in earlier generations had confirmed official gentry status by the right to a coat of arms) fell into disuse by the 1730s. Even in the sixteenth century there were self-styled gentlemen, and by the eighteenth the claim to gentlemanly status was based on opinion: on assessments of family, income, occupation, and connection. As in earlier centuries, considerable status-anxiety surrounded claims to gentility, as new wealth and people of unknown background had to be vetted for entry. Mistakes could be costly. Clothing was a clue, but could be misleading: conmen and impecunious suitors to heiresses were known to dress well. The 'Coventry Gang' of thieves were said to dress as gentlemen and servants, changing roles on different jobs. What mattered to real gentlemen, then, was an accurate estimate of real worth. That meant annual income, notably income from land.

At a period when a labourer earned perhaps £20 a year in wages, the squire with a good rental income in the many hundreds or thousands of pounds was undoubtedly a gentleman (see Table 2.1). How much mattered: £500 yes, £300 probably, £150 doubtful. But some men without income from land qualified too: officers, some clerics, some lawyers, some doctors. In fact, anyone with sufficient private means and the right tastes and social presence could qualify. If they were well-enough connected through family ties or patronage to those with real wealth and influence, they were indubitably gentlemen; if they were poor and 'lacked connexion' but were still in the ancient professions, or educated at the two universities, they were nominal gentlemen. However, the professional distinctions were many. Physicians were gentlemen. Surgeons were ambiguously so (being described as barber-surgeons before 1745). Apothecaries were also on the margin, although some gentlemen did apprentice their sons to the trade. Barristers were gentlemen, solicitors generally were not, 'low attorneys' and scriveners certainly were not. By 1730 the author of *Angliae Notitia* was conceding gentility to 'polite genteel traders' in overseas commerce. Anyone who lived by manual work was clearly not a gentleman, although some wealthy domestic tradesmen and wholesalers, mercers for example, were considered genteel, as indeed were a few great manufacturers. Dr Samuel Johnson, conservative in such matters, had no difficulty acknowledging the gentility of the rich Southwark brewer Ralph Thrale. Wealthy clothiers were admitted to the commission of the peace in the West Country, if not to the balls and *conversazione* of county society. Money could win acceptance if it was suitably decanted to upper-class taste, although as Defoe recognized, it could sometimes take a generation or two for the *nouveaux riches* to be accepted into 'polite' society (the connotation of social polish attached to the word in the eighteenth century).

Gentility privileged Anglicanism. There was still a social stigma attached to Dissent, or Nonconformity as it came to be called. The principal sects, with origins in the seventeenth century, were the Baptists, Presbyterians, and Congregationalists or Independents. Nonconformity with State Anglicanism, in theology and ritual, barred such Protestants from public office. But by taking the oaths abjuring popery, and occasionally taking the sacraments ('occasional conformity') many did so. Not until the 1780s was Methodism considered to be outside the Anglican Church.

Dissenters could vote; Catholics could not. Conscientious Dissenters and Catholics (barred from the universities) had to be richer and more cultivated than any nominally Anglican, nominally educated, graduate of Oxford or Cambridge, to be recognizable gentlemen. Indeed, Dissenters were most likely to be educated in a 'Dissenting academy', often with high standards, and in Continental or Scottish universities. So too were Catholics. Yet there was a small but undoubtedly respectable class of old Catholic English gentry and aristocrats, some of great wealth. And the taint of Dissent, even when allied with the greater taint of trade, could be left behind in a generation, especially in the professions. William Osgoode, who retired to England after being Chief Justice of Quebec, moved in the highest circles. But he was careful never to mention that before attending Oxford and Lincoln's Inn, he had been known as the son of a rich Dissenting hosier in Leeds. The Chief Justice was a gentleman. His father was not.

Images of the social order

Beneath the gentry and other gentlemen there was everyone else. Much of the literature (and indeed older historiography) of eighteenth-century England is surprisingly vague about who else there was. Certainly there were many acutely felt distinctions in the other 90 per cent of the population, but viewed from the summit, even if one was not a royal duke, it tended to look like a lump—or two lumps: 'the middling sort' and what Owen at the end of our period called the 'working and pauper classes'. Simplifying descriptions of the social structure were frequently the product of polemical debate. Versions that described England in terms of two classes of people tended to be espoused by the upper crust, or by those who wished to stress the contractual basis of society or, alternatively, to dramatize its power relations. In *Jonathan Wild*, for example, Henry Fielding aligned 'Mankind . . . under two great divisions, those that use their own hands, and those who employ the hands of others' as did Thomas Malthus, who denounced the utopian schemes of ameliorist philosophers by insisting that the 'inevitable laws of nature' would separate society 'into a class of proprietors, and a class of labourers . . . with self-love the mainspring of the great machine'. Adam Smith thought the laws of nature had some human assistance, but he expressed it in conventional terms as a duality:

Laws and government may be considered in this and in every case as a combination of the rich to oppress the poor, and preserve to themselves the inequality of the goods which would otherwise be soon destroyed by the attacks of the poor, who if not hindered by the government would soon reduce the others to an equality with themselves by open violence.[3]

Dyadic views of society gradually gave way over this period to more complex formulations. 'Class' as a descriptive term for a social stratum with a broadly similar experience of life, particularly material life, was used by Defoe in 1709; by Owen's time it was beginning to be associated more clearly with its proto-Marxist connotations (see Ch. 12). But for much of the period the social distinctions most often drawn were in origin either juridical (freeholder, copyholder, commoner, pauper), or descriptive of a way of earning a living (yeoman, husbandman, manufacturer, artisan, servant), or of earning not enough of a living (the labouring poor). Of course, an individual might well be described by a term in each of these categories. And then there was the social and political epithet that gentlemen used of those whose only political forum was the street: the mob. In the eighteenth century, a period in which the electorate declined from 24 per cent of the adult male population to 17 per cent, the mob could, on occasions of political excitement, embrace a great many people, including both some of the middling sort and many of the labouring poor.

Two kinds of distinctions used by historians or contemporaries of the ungentlemanly population at large are of particular importance. One is the social gradation of agricultural communities, and the ways in which conventional images of agrarian England were affected by industry. Another is the difference between the middling sort and those below them.

Images of agrarian society

Convictions about the primacy of 'landed society' continued to shape political and social beliefs in the eighteenth century. The term 'landed society' in its narrow sense meant the gentry and aristocracy who lived on their rents: the squire and lord of the manor who ruled a parish, the great territorial magnate like the Duke of Bedford with almost a whole county on his rent rolls. However, its wider connotations embraced all who continued to be employed primarily in agriculture. They might be large and prosperous tenant farmers; owner-occupiers of many or a few acres of land; skilled workers like shepherds and hedgers; young farm-servants who lived with the farmer's family; or the day-labourers of both sexes who hoed turnip fields, dug ditches, and helped constitute the large force of hands needed at harvest. For those who were not gentry, most of the tasks and many of the tools were ancient ones. They worked within cycles of planting and harvest, breeding and slaughtering, that were celebrated in Church ritual and the imagery of Scripture. The agricultural year was expressed in social institutions as old and as diverse as the market, the fair, lambing and shearing, the harvest, the gleaning of fields after harvest, the opening of the fallow field to commoning beasts, and the holding of manorial courts.

Tenant farmers might rent their lands for lives (defined in length by the life-spans of living, named persons), or, increasingly, for terms of years. They might be very wealthy, employing scores of labourers, and working many hundreds of acres. Men working the land on a much more modest scale were called husbandmen, and between them was a group of men of middling rank who often owned rather than rented, or who had good copyhold tenures (but who also might rent) called yeomen. This was an ancient term of changing sense, but still one with strong connotations of economic independence (see Ch. 6).

Servants in rural society, in the narrowest definition, were farm-servants, whose rights and obligations were largely prescribed by Elizabethan law for 'servants in husbandry'. (The term 'servant' also had a much wider sense in both ordinary and legal usage, as a person employed for a period of time. Not only domestic servants, but also many industrial and other workers, were included.) Unmarried young men and women, farm-servants lived as part of the farmer or yeoman's household, and were hired for a year. The status was most common (compared to that of labourer) when real wages were high and farm labour was scarce, because it was at such times that farmers were anxious to secure a certain supply of help. This was the case from the mid-seventeenth to the mid-eighteenth centuries. Labour was in a good bargaining position until about 1750 in part because of high agricultural production, low food prices, and little population growth. The great growth of rural industry provided an alternative, competing, source of employment. However, the rural economy changed markedly from mid-century: rising prices, population growth, increasing harvest failures, declining real wages, all benefited the owners of land rather than those who worked it. Landlords became much richer in the later decades of the century; farmers probably made few gains in most parts of the country; and most of the poor, labourers, and servants of all kinds, experienced a marked decline in living standards, for reasons dealt with in later chapters.

Agriculture was of critical economic importance, although recent estimates are revising it downward. In 1700 older statistics suggested it provided about 60 per cent of male employment, but the extent of dual occupations (combining farming with a rural industrial trade) suggests a lower figure. In 1800 the figure was perhaps 40 per cent, but of a population that was double that of a century before. Throughout the period, then, a large part of the population derived their livings directly from farming, or from supplying its needs.

Land also had great emotive significance in the minds of England's rulers. The traditional life of the shires was the pre-eminent image of England held by the gentry and aristocracy. Their sports were the rural ones of hunting, riding, shooting; their rents were their primary source of income; if they turned their hands to a practical vocation, it was most likely to be farming. Landscape-painting, and portraits of prize horses and cattle and pigs, celebrated the source of their wealth. Their primary residences were not in London, but in the Shires. Their literature and art echoed that of classical Greece and Rome in its celebration of the virtue, beauty, and antiquity of country life, of Arcadia. Shelves of good and bad poetry imitated Virgil's *Georgics*; most of it presented the drudgery of farm-labour as pleasant rustic recreation. Agricultural writers debated whether Virgil was as good a farmer as he was a poet. Yet at the same time a traditionalist country gentleman might know the local husbandmen and commoners, 'his peasants', in more realistic terms. In the first half of the century there was a recurrent argument on their behalf, stressing the virtues of independence, bravery, and patriotism to be found in an active, self-supporting class of small owners and occupiers of land, particularly those with access to commons. The classical argument that property, however small, meant independence, and that independence was a social good, was convincing to such paternalist landlords.[4]

The self-conscious construction of an idea of rural society was also enacted on ceremonial occasions, celebrating the ties and marking the degrees of deference. The great country house of the territorial magnate who owned thousands of acres could dominate the local agrarian economy. His annual dinners for hundreds of his tenants, the celebrations on the birth of his heir, were among many occasions that marked his place in the county and his prescribed social obligations, even if he lived in London much of the year. The country squire with some hundreds of acres, who lived in an ancient manor house, acted as the local JP, and named the rector (perhaps his younger brother) who preached in the village church, re-enacted a role dating back several centuries. In some villages this role had been in the family for generations. The squire's right to hunt (the prerogative of landed gentlemen alone) and to be elected to Parliament for the county, and to be named in the commission of the peace (and thus act as a JP), were all determined largely by whether he met stiff qualifications, in annual rental income from land, set by Parliament. To be a landed gentleman was to stand at the centre of a tradition, to hold a position with gratifying associations of permanence, authority, and antiquity, reaching back to classical times.

Yet the role might be acquired within a generation, with the purchase of land from wealth earned in harder or dirtier ways, for the English countryside had been fertilized by commerce and industry for hundreds of years. Much money made in overseas commerce or plunder, and in woollens or other industry, had always been invested in socially remunerative broad acres. In the eighteenth century nabobs with Indian fortunes and Liverpool merchants in the slave trade, to name only two groups of the newly rich, continued the tradition.

As we saw in Chapter 1, the unspoiled countryside that we see in Georgian art was in large measure a social construct, something of a theme park even in the eighteenth century. Instant ruins, quiet lakes with Greek temples and other follies, and extensive deer-parks were created by landed magnates at enormous expense in conscious pursuit of a style with classical connotations. But outside the park walls and model villages the countryside as a whole was permeated with domestic industry, structures of outputting in which nail-masters, clothiers, and other capitalists employed thousands of domestic workers in villages, in cottages on the waste, in large forest communities that abutted enclosed parishes. In villages and towns there were tradesmen and shopkeepers and land-agents and artisans such as blacksmiths and wheelwrights who directly served the agricultural sector, but there were also framework-knitters, cutlers, nailers, clothiers, mercers, and a host of other manufacturers and traders. The more prosperous were thought of as 'the middling' sort; the rest were 'the labouring poor'.

The middling sort

The language of 'sorts' first entered English parlance to espouse a dyadic view of society, to distinguish the gentlemen of authority, the 'better sort', from those 'inferior' to it. However, by the time of the Civil War, the term was being increasingly applied to those situated between the great and the small, to the independent small producers in agriculture and industry whose allegiance was critical to the outcome of that struggle, especially on the Parliamentarian side.

Over the course of the next century and a half, the middling

sort, so defined, actually declined as a proportion of the population. Many small producers became partially proletarian, losing out
to the large farmers and manufacturers who produced for the market and to the merchant-middlemen who controlled the distribution and indirectly the production of Britain's diverse products.
These people, who turned over capital for a profit, were the quintessential middling sort of the eighteenth century. Capitalist tenant
farmers, who paid rents to their landlords and hired day-labourers
and farm-servants, were important in village communities. They
were overseers, churchwardens; they knew the resident squire (if
there was one) on fairly familiar terms; and they were the principal
employers of agricultural labour. They were joined by a diverse
medley of tradesmen and professionals whose presence illustrated
the increasingly complex nature of Britain's market society and
the dramatic expansion of its state after 1688. Generally speaking, the term 'middling sort' in the eighteenth century increasingly
meant those in urban occupations: merchants, tradesmen, substantial shopkeepers, master manufacturers, as well as many in the emergent professions of medicine, teaching, the law, the civil and armed
services. Although the term occasionally included the lesser gentry,
on the grounds that it was equivalent to the Commons within the
orthodox trinity of political power of King, Lords, and Commons,
it normally denoted people who were not of gentlemanly origin,
however much they aspired to gentle status. It referred to men of
substance whose palpable economic and political contribution to
society, as employers, consumers, minor office-holders and property-
owners, entitled them to recognition and to at least a modicum
of respect. Even so, taking town and country together, they were
not as demographically important as their seventeenth-century
predecessors.

The middling sort were not a middle class in any proto-Marxist
sense of the term. They were seldom defined as a group whose
collective interests and identities pitted them against the landed
aristocracy. That sort of confrontation, driven by the tensions
between industrial and landed capital and by a grievous sense of
political exclusion, only emerged in a dramatic way in the second
quarter of the nineteenth century. Many of the middling sort were
clients of the rich; others were clearly beneficiaries of the state,
bound by the constraints of political patronage that determined

its favours. Many of the Georgian professions were themselves genteel and exclusive, too devoted to occupational élitism to propound wider identities. Lawyers, clergymen, officers in the armed forces, overseas merchants, bankers who provided mortgages for the gentry, seldom found much in common with shopkeepers, tradesmen, master weavers, and tenant farmers, even though all might be inscribed, in one context or another, as part of the middling sort.

This did not mean that the middling sort were unduly deferential or compliant to those above them. As the principal denominations of Protestant Dissent acquired a more affluent, urban, bourgeois complexion, so their second-class status within an Anglican hierarchy rankled. Middling electors in the more open urban and county constituencies prided themselves on their political independence and frequently resented the ossification of electoral politics at the hands of the landed grandees (see Ch. 4). Moreover, the sorts of values espoused by the middling sort within their own communities—industry, thrift, self-discipline, credit-worthiness, domesticity—often stood in stark contrast to those observed by the landed aristocracy and ultimately helped fuel the attack upon aristocratic vice at the end of the century. Indeed, the means by which middling values were upheld, the growth of voluntary associations and clubs within what were often precarious commercial environments, provided a critical base for the promotion of a wide range of public issues, from local improvement schemes to campaigns against the debt laws and slavery. The middling sort may have been politically and economically fragmented, but its resources and consumer power were very significant in the development of a new public sphere in which arguments about the wisdom or folly of public opinion, or what the eighteenth century termed 'the sense of the people', could be framed.

Patricians, plebeians, and publics

In many ways the view of the world taken by the middling sort dominates our own consciousness, in part because by the nineteenth century middling people had become a middle class. To a large extent, the late Victorian and twentieth-century polity has been that of professional, manufacturing, shopkeeping, middleclass people. Its public values of individual responsibility, family propriety, sexual modesty, the sanctity of markets, individuated property rights, heavy policing, a figurehead monarchy, and the pre-eminence of manufacturing and trade over agriculture, have profoundly shaped the world from which we look back to the eighteenth century. But the eighteenth century was different, and one of the chief sources of its distinctiveness in our eyes was the nature of public order and disorder, and the social roles—some historians call it theatre—that flourished in that arena.

Both petty landholding and industrial employment or by-employment conferred independence from farmers and great landlords, although it might lock workers in chains of debt to those who supplied the raw materials and bought the products of their industry. Those obligations were enforced by law, as we shall see. Certainly, increasingly, industrial work tied the labouring poor to markets: both the markets for their products, and markets for food and other essentials, as households increasingly came to rely on industrial income alone. Such ties to market conditions created other conditions of freedom, however: they weakened direct dependence on landlords and gentlemen, the rulers of the rural world. In most parts of England, the gentry thus stood outside the employment relationships of agricultural and industrial labour. As justices they thought of themselves as arbiters of those relationships, and as the rulers of rural society, custodians of its social peace.

Arbiters and custodians were needed. For industrial populations—colliers, weavers, tinners, metalworkers—were notoriously the leaders of the most threatening kinds of public disorder. Strikes, food riots, turnpike riots, militia riots—thousands of them throughout the century—were dominated by workers in rural industry. Workers in town-based industries, and in London, were similarly active in defence of their interests (see Chs. 7–10). In neighbourhoods where resident gentry were rare, too, agricultural smallholders and farm-servants could be equally active in pursuit of their interests, in enclosure riots, massive protests against landlords encroaching on common lands, or rough music against bailiffs and stewards who worked too hard to swell the rent rolls of their employers. Such breaches of the peace were a main concern of the gentry and the government, and profoundly shaped social relationships at all levels of the social order. Indeed, more than one historian has argued that the relationship of mob and gentry constituted the primary social relationship in eighteenth-century England.

The problem of public order was one of the two greatest concerns of early-modern governments; the other was dynastic attack from without, by war or succession. Widespread riot threatened not only local government: it could become part of a crisis that allowed the dynastic enemies of the monarch to topple the regime itself. Historians of Tudor and Stuart England have emphasized how much central government was involved in seeking to soften the impact of dearth (from harvest failure) and unemployment (from disruption of export and internal markets in the textile trades) on the labouring poor. Those concerns continued to be expressed in law and custom (see Chs. 4–6), not least because all participants in the early eighteenth century knew how fragile regimes could be. Charles I had been beheaded in 1649; his son James II had fled into exile in 1688. The attempt of the latter's son ('James III') to regain the throne by invasion in 1715–16 had been preceded by widespread riots with a Jacobite flavour, prompting the new Whig and Hanoverian government to make riot, hitherto a common-law misdemeanour, into a capital offence by statute.[5]

In the countryside and in town and cities, the gentry and magistrates of eighteenth-century England had to deal with the demands of the mob, in ways that contained disorder rather than inflamed it. How they did so will appear in more detail at many points in our account, but the framing context can be described in a few sentences. The rulers of eighteenth-century England lacked the legitimation conferred by a democratic franchise, and the contribution to consensus politics made in modern states by mass communications. Nor did they have much armed force. There was a standing army (in spite of rhetoric to the contrary) but it was for most of the period incapable of dealing with widespread riot, and quite unsuited to the resolution of small disturbances, where it could exacerbate the problem by killing people. The magistracy could call on a range of other traditional forces in times of riot (the posse, the parish constable, the militia) but none were very effective.

Instead, the gentry met the mob, or less organized popular discontent, with a range of carefully considered responses. One was direct negotiation, in which a broad range of agreed values was publicly rehearsed. A recognition of the justice of claims; promises to deal with grievances; an assertion of patriotic fellow-citizenship; and (usually) unfailing good manners. Standing outside direct employment relations, the JP could act as the disinterested mediator of industrial disputes. Living on rents, he could promise to deal with millers and farmers suspected of profiteering with food in times of dearth. And his claims to a paternal reputation were encoded in a repertoire of other acts: charitable subscriptions in times of want; introducing legislation on behalf of weavers in the House of Commons; his very willingness to meet the mob, unarmed, and (he made clear) unafraid.

Such conciliation did not always succeed: in such cases the Secretary at War sent troops, and the judges came down on assize or special commission to hang a few offenders. However, the limits of such legal terror (as contemporaries almost invariably referred to it) resembled the limits on coercion by troops. Englishmen abroad marvelled at, and were sickened by, the atrocious punishments and the multitude of executions in similar circumstances in Europe. In England, the need to conciliate the people generated ties of understanding and direct acquaintance, even on the part of peers, that were uncommon in Europe. (We should add that Englishmen in the West Indies, dealing with slave rebellions, easily matched any European despotism in the ingenuity and cruelty of the retribution they inflicted.)

The reciprocities of the English gentry and mob (or patricians and plebeians, the terms contemporaries sometimes borrowed from classical Rome) have been described as theatre. The metaphor captures the fact that the roles were so often replayed in so many localities, throughout the century. In urban contexts the mediations were more complex, but long-held expectations on both sides made treating with the mob a matter of practicable politics, at least until the Gordon Riots in London in 1780.[6] The metaphor is useful also, in that it reminds us that the participants were often deeply aware of earlier renditions, by their parents, and grandparents. In some villages, indeed, riots over local rights (rights of common, for example) recapitulated struggles from a century before, in which both the lord of the manor, and the villagers, still bore the same family names. And like all public acts in societies where tradition, custom, and ritual are still strong, the confrontations of rioters and gentlemen had understood limits. They could be, therefore, the vehicles of real negotiations, testings of mutual strength, and ultimately the means of resolutions of differences.

But a great gulf also separated those with the greatest political and social power, and the mass of the population, on a host of issues, great and small. Popular and state religion had diverged markedly in the upheavals of the mid-seventeenth century, when the bishops had been (briefly) abolished, and a host of radical, often millenarian, sects, had been the initiators of political demands. With the restoration of monarchy and Church in 1660, and the decline of theology as a root of political tension after the early decades of the eighteenth century, popular beliefs and educated ones were often very different. High culture and low culture may have become increasingly distinctive. We can see evidence of this gap in one of the most deep-rooted of early-modern beliefs, witchcraft, which first the judges and then Parliament (in 1736) declared, after centuries of penal sanctions, not to be a crime. Mobs continue to identify and punish witches into the 1750s and beyond. Another instance is the wife-sale, a form of divorce among the people which gentlemen tolerated early in the century, but came to condemn as barbarous and immoral (see Ch. 3). And a wide range of robust or cruel popular amusements, including naked foot-races and public bathing, cockfighting and bull-baiting, were increasingly attacked rather than indulged or supported, by gentlemen in country and town.

In part, such divergences of gentry and plebeian understandings of tolerated behaviour followed the increasing acceptance by the upper classes of the values of evangelical Anglicanism in the second half of the century (see Ch. 11). More broadly, we see that division growing as the upper classes, from mid-century, increasingly took a view of civil society that more and more resembled some of the important values of the middling sort. Aristocracy and gentry had always been deeply interested in profits from their estates; they knew very well that agrarian capitalism was the source of their revenues. However, other market-oriented behaviour, notably buying and reselling commodities to make a profit, had the taint of trade. Even the judges in the high courts took the view that for one party to a bargain to profit unduly at the expense of the other was ungentlemanly, and perhaps unlawful.

That attitude changed, first gradually and then rapidly, in the second half of the century. Gentlemen and peers increasingly repudiated a thick but patchwork inheritance of law and custom that had protected popular entitlements. A parliament of landlords and gentlemen came to believe, as hosiers and farmers and middling tradesmen always had, in the simplifying 'wisdom' of the market. That change widened the gap between rulers and ruled, and made the theatre of understandings, the reciprocities between patricians and plebeians, the gentry and the mob, a thing of the past. The social hierarchy remained much the same, but the skein of ties within it changed.

3 The Politics of Love and Marriage

Introduction: The Clandestine Marriage Act of 1753

'A Gentleman might have the satisfaction of hanging a Thief that stole an old Horse from him,' observed Daniel Defoe, 'but could have no Justice against a rogue for stealing his Daughter.'[1] Many would have agreed. Yet it was not until 1753, after almost a century of failure, that Parliament finally agreed to pass an Act to prevent clandestine marriages and to curtail youthful elopements. Under the terms of the Act, no minor was allowed to marry in England and Wales without parental consent, forcing those who wished to elope to hazard their chances of success by travelling to places like Guernsey or Gretna Green. At the same time, the only marriages that were deemed legal in England and Wales (although not in Scotland) were those performed by an ordained clergyman at an Anglican church or chapel after the publication of the banns, or alternatively by episcopal licence. All other forms of marriage, whether public betrothals or unlicensed marriages by clergymen within the 'peculiars' exempt from episcopal jurisdiction (even in private or public houses), were no longer considered to be legally binding, although hitherto they had been recognized as such under both canon and common law. The only exceptions to this rule were the marriages of Jews and Quakers, whose nuptial discipline (and strong endogamy) was felt to be within the spirit of the new law.

The 1753 Act was designed to regularize state control over marriage and in general terms, echoes a theme we intend to emphasize throughout this book; namely, the triumph of law over custom. The statute eliminated the popular practice of swift and inexpensive marriages, particularly for the craftsmen and unskilled classes of London who routinely married in their thousands within the rules of Fleet prison. It also diminished the significance of those community customs that had surrounded the big weddings of small farmers, of which the formal church ceremony had only been a part. More significantly, at least for the well-heeled, the Act made it more difficult for fortune-hunters to run off with young heiresses, or for aristocratic minors to compromise parental plans for consolidating the status and prosperity of their lineage. It also removed much of the legal uncertainty that surrounded clandestine marriages, uncertainty that had generated some well-publicized and litigious cases concerning serial bigamy and bogus contracts: most notoriously, the case of the *demi-mondaine* Constantia Phillips, who had eluded her creditors by marrying a bigamist and then fell out with her second husband, the young, rich merchant Henry Muilman, when under family pressure he attempted to annul their marriage in order to make a more respectable match.

Marriage and property

Marriage had conventionally been a critical means of consolidating wealth and status among the propertied classes, and remained so in the long eighteenth century despite the growing distaste for purely mercenary marriages. Opponents of the 1753 Bill claimed that it enshrined the claims of property over romantic love and concentrated wealth in fewer families. Both arguments were somewhat overdrawn but they did highlight the significance of marriage as a distributor of wealth, especially marriages involving members of the landed and commercial élite. From the Restoration onwards, when royal wardship no longer threatened the integrity of noble estates, the landed aristocracy had embarked upon new and successful strategies for consolidating their wealth and estates, the vast acres of which underpinned their political influence. The most important legal instrument in this consolidation was the strict settlement, normally drawn up upon the marriage of the eldest son, by which the main estate devolved by patrilineal descent and the claims of other near kin were formally accommodated, wherever possible from ancillary sources of wealth so that the estate would not be unduly encumbered with obligations to younger siblings. In order to preserve the family patrimony from reckless heirs, eldest sons were allowed no more than a life interest in their estates. They had to agree to leave them in trust to their 'contingent remainders'; that is, to their unborn heirs. In conformity with the principle of male primogeniture, this meant their unborn sons, and if they failed to sire any, to the unborn sons of their brothers, or even more distant male relatives. Barring demographic catastrophe, and it should be noted that in the early eighteenth century a significant number of aristocratic sons either never married (20 per cent) or remained childless (24 per cent), while roughly 30 per cent of all aristocratic children died before the age of 15, the family estate remained within the patrilineal family. Even if a family produced female rather than male heirs, the family estate often fell to a male relative rather than to a daughter and her husband, usually with the proviso that the relative assume the family name. Wherever possible, patrilineal inheritance took precedence over cognatic descent. The only rich group where this imperative was less evident was the mercantile élite, whose wealth was wrapped up in trade and mobile investments as much as in land, and whose quest for green-acred gentility was less pressing, especially among families of Dissenting or Huguenot origin.

Patrilineal inheritance inevitably created some tension among landed families. Younger sons and daughters sometimes had to forgo marriage in order to preserve the family patrimony. The number of aristocratic daughters who never married rose to 26 per cent in the early eighteenth century from a low of 13–15 per cent in the Jacobean era. The number of younger sons who remained bachelors was as high as 37 per cent, although for this sibling group there was a far greater tolerance of sexual licence and the prospect of a career in politics, the armed services, or the law. The pressures on all upper-class children (male heirs included) to marry well if they married at all was formidable, not simply in order to sustain their station in life but also to create intra-class alliances that would improve their standing in the county and give them greater access to the spoils of politics and the state. Among the sons of peers the quest for heiresses was fierce and competitive. At the beginning of the eighteenth century, when the tax on land was high and the political patronage of the aristocracy less formidable than it was to become in later decades, 44 per cent of all sons of peers married heiresses, three-quarters of them outside the nobility. Over time the search for heiresses became less intense, but the percentage did not fall below 20 until the last two decades of the century. The mercenary character of these matches was underscored by the willingness of newspapers to trumpet an heiress's worth in hard cash.

Yet during the course of the eighteenth century the wisdom of such alliances came under attack. Mercenary marriages were seen as disastrous to marital harmony. They were seen as a spur to adultery by both parties, breeding suspicions about the legitimacy of heirs and generating hatreds that could destroy a family fortune, as indeed happened in the case of *Dineley* v. *Dineley*.[2] In the late seventeenth and early eighteenth century, when the cynicism surrounding upper-class conjugality was at its height, mercenary marriages had helped to create a predicament where the aristocracy had failed to reproduce itself; that is, they produced less than two children per couple. To compound matters, such matches were viewed as incompatible with the spirit of the age. With the decline of patriarchalism as a political force after 1688 and the steady infusion of Enlightenment ideas, couples demanded greater emotional compatibility within marriage and cherished domesticity as an ideal that was fundamental to social order. Many were coming to agree with Addison that 'the married state, with and without the affection suitable to it, is the completest image of heaven and hell we are capable of receiving in this life'.[3] The pioneers of this new domesticity were the urban middling class, but its propagation through weeklies like the *Spectator*, and more melodramatically through Hogarth's *Marriage à la Mode*, which graphically depicted the rapid degeneration of a mercenary match between the aristocracy and the bourgeoisie, meant that it penetrated polite circles. Gradually such sentiments had an impact upon the marriage patterns of the landed gentry and aristocracy.

Evidence for this can be seen at various stages of the marriage process. Upper-class children continued to solicit and heed their parents' advice about marriage prospects. Given the financial power that their parents had over them, and their own predisposition to marry according to their social station, they would rarely do otherwise. However, they increasingly demanded the right to refuse prospective partners whom they found obnoxious, rejecting the divine right of parents in much the same way as their forebears had rejected the Divine Right of Kings in 1688. Authoritarian parents did not always respect this decision and one can certainly find examples of fathers bullying their children into blind marriages. Yet increasingly parents gave children the opportunity to find partners within a well-defined social sphere. The emergence of the 'season' in London and in various provincial pleasure towns, where young people could mingle at balls and assembly rooms, was designed precisely for this purpose. Foreign commentators, in particular, remarked on the greater freedom enjoyed by upper-class

English children as compared with those on the Continent with regard to getting to know one another before marriage. Such freedom, of course, could be flouted. There was a widespread fear that the masquerade was an inducement to sexual licence, and one purpose of the Marriage Act of 1753 was to rein in the impetuous passion of youth and subject it to parental advice and supervision. Indeed, an upper-class daughter was continually advised to approach courtship with due modesty and guard against 'the first impressions of love . . . till such time as she has received the most convincing proofs of the attachment of a man of such merit, as will justify a reciprocal regard'.[4] Such circumspection, it was hoped, would better reconcile personal choice with family interest.

In charting the rise of the companionate marriage among the landed classes in the eighteenth century, historians have emphasized a series of interrelated developments. They have noticed the greater frequency with which husbands and wives shared the same society at balls, at the races, the assembly rooms, the theatres. Even a few London clubs such as Almack's opened their doors to women. They have also noted the way in which marriage partners addressed each other in more affectionate, less formal terms, and how families become more child-centred than in previous centuries. Above all, they have stressed the changing status of wives within the household: their greater financial independence under equitable trusts; their better education at boarding-schools; their growing devotion to maternalism, especially their decision to breast-feed their own children rather than farm them out to wet-nurses, a decision that significantly reduced the incidence of infant mortality and according to one historian, represented 'one of the finest fruits of the Enlightenment'.[5]

Yet the progressive effect of these changes needs to be qualified and we should be very wary of talking, as the same historian has done, about the rise of the 'egalitarian family'.[6] Women's social and intellectual space was still limited. Clubs were predominantly a male domain. Female salons and debating-societies could be found in the metropolis, but rarely in the provinces. Upper-class women were schooled principally in politeness, in those social graces that made them a better catch. Only a few had the intellectual training or opportunity to dabble in science or the writing of novels and religious tracts. Women's overriding vocation was marriage and motherhood, and the imperatives of finding and pleasing husbands, as Mary Wollstonecraft and others well recognized, could lead to empty, frivolous lives. In fact, the cultural obsession with maternalism fundamentally altered perceptions of female gender in ways that paradoxically repressed women's active sexuality and rendered them dutiful, passive, benevolent, self-sacrificing mothers at the service of the family and the state. Prior to the eighteenth century conception was linked to sexual orgasm; thereafter this link was severed, turning women paradoxically into asexual reproductive bodies. Despite the fact that the Enlightenment encouraged a more expressive sexuality, and publicized, most dramatically in the periodic exposés of homosexuality, the notion of non-procreative sex, women's sexuality was displaced and colonized in the shape of the nurturing mother. As one historian has emphasized, the companionate family was 'a more thoroughgoing psychological appropriation of women to serve the emotional needs of men than ever was imagined in earlier divisions of labor by gender'.[7]

Moreover, the gendered role assigned to middle- and upper-class women within the family was radically circumscribed by the law. Wives may have achieved some financial independence through their separate estate, but the integrity of these estates was sometimes whittled away by judicial review and was in any case administered by male trustees. Where no trustees were specified or where they had died, the separate estate was managed by husbands. Furthermore, the terms in which marital breakdown was adjudicated by the courts were heavily weighted towards husbands. Wives could not sue in the civil courts for adultery; husbands could, by bringing an action of criminal conversation against male lovers for 'trespassing' their wives' bodies. Modern divorce was only attainable in the eighteenth century by a private Act of Parliament, a situation that made it the recourse of none but a few powerful men. A wife could bring an action in the ecclesiastical courts for a judicial separation on grounds of adultery or life-threatening cruelty, but it was very difficult for a woman (unlike a man) to get a judgement for adultery unless there were aggravating circumstances such as the transmission of venereal disease or sodomy, mainstream opinion having a horror of anal sex. A private act of separation was possible if enough familial pressure could be brought to bear on an estranged spouse, but even so, the only thing that prevented a husband from demanding a restitution of conjugal rights was the bond he signed promising not to do so. Without such an agreement and a separate estate, a woman was vulnerable to devastating interventions by her husband. She could be virtually defenceless under the common law: her personal property could be seized, her future legacies confiscated, her contracts voided, and her children taken from her. Although Mary Wollstonecraft believed that women had a 'natural right' to their children, the courts generally thought otherwise, even where the husband was the culpable partner in the dissolution of the marriage. For a wife, a unilateral separation was a very dangerous and desperate step to take. She was susceptible to recapture and confinement by her husband; she had no right to habeas corpus under the law.

There were thus very severe impediments to a propertied woman separating from her husband in the eighteenth century. Very few did so. Judicial separations and divorce amounted to only 0.1 per cent of all marriages around 1750, and 2.7 per cent of all aristocratic marriages. The proportion of women declined among those who so petitioned as the century progressed. The great majority of well-to-do women stuck to their marriages through thick and thin, and, in a society that still acknowledged the double standard, risked social disgrace by taking lovers. As the *London Evening Post* cynically observed in its issue of 15–17 August 1754, keeping a mistress was a '*sine qua non* of a fine gentlemen', but wives were 'reckoned sorry Jades, and fit only to keep the Name and Title of a Family'. Even in the more permissive sectors of the aristocracy, double standards often prevailed. The Duchess of Devonshire tolerated a *ménage à trois* in her household, and two illegitimate children by Lady Elizabeth Hervey, but when she became pregnant by Charles Grey, she was banished to the Continent for nearly two years for her indiscretion. All was eventually forgiven, but the point was made. Sexual licence was a male, not female, prerogative.

The fear of bastardy that was the conventional explanation for the double standard operated also at lower levels of society, but among the aristocracy dynastic interest sharpened it. For the same reason the upper-class family's strict settlement was usually constructed to prevent the disaster of female inheritance under the common law (where there were daughters but no sons) as part of the strategic need to foster primogeniture, the prerequisite of family political power. By the end of the century, the subordination of aristocratic marriage and family life to property and especially to dynastic interest had thus became an object of democratic criticism, both for political reasons and as an expression of the values of the middling sort. Here is Tom Paine, in *The Rights of Man* (1791), on primogeniture:

The nature and character of Aristocracy shows itself to us in this law. It is a law against every law of nature, and nature Herself call for its destruction. Establish family justice and Aristocracy falls. By the aristocratical law of primogenitureship, in a family of six children five are exposed. Aristocracy never has more than one child. The rest are begotten to be devoured. . . . To restore, therefore, parents to their children, and children to their parents—relations to each other, and man to society—and to exterminate the monster Aristocracy, root and branch—the [Revolutionary] French Constitution has destroyed the law of primogenitureship.[8]

Plebeian courtship and conjugality

The promoters of the 1753 Marriage Act were principally concerned with upper-class courtships and marriage, but the debate on the Bill inevitably brought plebeian conjugality into focus. Opponents of the Bill believed that it would seriously prejudice the migratory poor for whom 'Fleet weddings' had become a way of life. Supporters retorted that regular marriages were the necessary underpinnings of social and political order; it was time that the irregular marriages of the poor were brought under control and sexual nonconformity placed under greater scrutiny. Indeed, as clandestine marriages declined among the propertied class, so the discourse on sex and marriage turned increasingly upon the lower orders, whose habits were routinely thought to be improvident, dissolute, and in need of reformation.

To what degree the Marriage Act altered plebeian habits of conjugality and intensified their official vigilance are matters of dispute among historians. It seems fairly clear, none the less, that plebeian nuptiality did change during the course of the long eighteenth century (1660–1820) resulting in earlier and more frequent marriages, higher levels of bridal pregnancies, higher levels of consensual unions, and higher levels of illegitimacy. Whether this represented a dramatic departure in plebeian sexual behaviour, a fundamental rupture from the prudential and economically motivated marriage customs of the past towards a new, expressive sexuality is something we must discuss.

Since the development of historical demography some forty years ago, historians have become increasingly interested in the self-regulating features of demographic behaviour in the face of marginal resources and scarcity. Although it is clear that the involuntary checks upon population growth were a conspicuous feature of early modern societies, such 'positive' factors (as Malthus called them) as epidemics became less influential over the long term. The last outbreak of the plague in England was in 1665; the introduction of cotton clothing and better urban sanitation reduced the likelihood of typhus epidemics; and parish inoculations made smallpox a less lethal killer. Furthermore, as we shall suggest in Chapter 5, a series of good harvests in the first half of the eighteenth century raised nutritional standards and immunity to disease, even allowing for the skewed distribution of income and food.

Over time the 'mortality-dominated high-pressure' equilibrium between population and resources gave way to a 'fertility-dominated low-pressure' one.[9] What increasingly warded off demographic catastrophe were the preventive checks upon population growth. These included prudential marriage strategies and relatively late marriages. Few people married until they were in an economic position to set up independent households. In the seventeenth century this was normally when a couple had access to land of some sort; or when the putative husband had formally completed his apprenticeship and had saved enough money to set up in business; or, for the very poor, when they had saved enough money in service, whether domestic or in husbandry. The consequence was that the average age at first marriage in the period 1650–99 was 27.8 years for men and 26.2 years for women, London excepted. There a significant proportion of London-born women married before the age of majority, driving down the mean age to 21 as compared to 25 years for immigrant women. Yet outside the metropolis, the age of marriage for ordinary people was noticeably higher than for members of the landed aristocracy whose sons and daughters generally married before the age of 25. The exception to this rule within the aristocracy was younger sons, who often had to establish themselves before they entered the marriage market, frequently marrying in their thirties, although to brides who were ten years younger.

In this respect they were little different from the richest of London businessmen.

Over the course of the eighteenth century, the age of first marriage among the aristocracy and gentry rose slowly and then levelled off. That of the lower classes fell, to a mean of 26.4 years for men and 24.9 years for women by the late eighteenth century, and to 25.3 years for men and 23.4 years for women during the next fifty years. By this time many plebeian couples were marrying markedly earlier than their aristocratic or gentry cohorts. A two-to-three-year decline in the age of first marriage over two centuries might seem inconsequential, but in an age of imperfect forms of family limitation, even where they were exercised, a fall of this magnitude could lead to one or two more children per couple per generation and geometrically to a quite significant build-up of the population; especially if a higher percentage of the population actually married (see Fig. 4). Although infant and child mortality rates changed little for the mass of the population, the fall in the age of marriage also generated a more youthful society in the nineteenth century than that which had existed in the seventeenth. By the mid-1820s 58 per cent of the population was under 25 compared to 46 per cent in the mid-1670s.

Historians have sometimes interpreted this overall increase in fertility as a broad response to real wages, with people marrying earlier when their prospects seemed brighter. The correlation between these indices seems forced, and only works if one accepts a forty-year lag between real wage and fertility changes. Rather more convincing is the notion that the fall in the age of marriage was related to the changing nature of economic production, in particular, to the growth of full or partial proletarianization. Fewer craftsmen were able to set up in business for themselves as the eighteenth century progressed. There were therefore fewer incentives to delaying marriage, especially if wages were reasonably high. The same was true of industrial workers in the countryside, and of cottagers who made a living out of the forests and wastes and very often supplemented their existence with seasonal waged work. To judge from the demographic record of Terling in Essex, early marriages could also be found among wage labourers whose livelihood was linked to commercial food markets and whose prospects of inheriting land were remote. Late marriages, on the other hand, still prevailed among servants-in-husbandry who hoped to save enough money to stock a small farm. They were also found among those who had access to common-right privileges in an open village, and among labourers in those closed villages where access to work, cottages, and welfare was tightly controlled by local landlords. It was only with the advent of enclosure, the decline of farm service, and the introduction of Speenhamland systems of poor relief in 1795, by which welfare benefits were determined by family size and the needs of subsistence, that the fall in the age of marriage became general in agricultural areas.

The timing of plebeian marriages in the long eighteenth century was therefore temporally and geographically uneven. The trend towards earlier marriages were first evident in industrial or proletarian settings, becoming more general as access to land and customary rights diminished and as incentives to save for a conventional niche in society declined. Marriage increasingly depended upon the early mobilization of hands and wages, and after Speenhamland, upon a predictable, if paltry, subsistence. This inevitably had some impact upon traditional courtship practices and upon the permanence and kinds of unions that were forged.

Plebeian marriages were less bound by material considerations than those of the landed aristocracy and middling classes. There was usually little or no property to transact, and the power of parents to influence the choice of spouses, even where they were still alive, was correspondingly slighter. In closely knit villages, however, plebeian courtships were subject to community sanctions. Men and women of the lower classes belonged to homo-social worlds before marriage. They met members of the opposite sex in the highly public contexts of fairs, wakes, harvest festivals, and officially sanctioned holidays, whose dances and merrymaking were important preliminaries to courtship. Once courtship began, young couples began to see each other on a more regular basis, leading to an exchange of love-tokens and to night-visiting or 'bundling'; that is, to premarital forms of sex-play that normally stopped short of intercourse. Such visits were not undertaken lightly. They were publicly sanctioned rituals that could draw peer resentment if their boundaries were violated. Once a couple was publicly betrothed (even before they were churched) full sexual relations could commence. Many brides went to the altar pregnant; as many as 20 per cent in the early eighteenth century, rising to 30 per cent and sometimes 40 per cent a century later.

The traditional courtship and betrothal rituals worked best in stable societies where access to land or a trade was a reasonable expectation. They tended to break down in the more mobile, wage-earning world of the eighteenth century, especially in the towns and expanding industrial areas where in-migration was substantial, or in villages undergoing enclosure, where the turnover in population could be dramatic. One index of this disruption was the rise of illegitimacy, which in the largest sample we have to date appears to have risen from 1.5 per cent of all recorded baptisms in 1660 to around 5 per cent at the end of the Napoleonic Wars. Of course, these figures should be read with care. Parishes may well have underregistered illegitimate births, especially in large towns where there were workhouse infirmaries, lying-in or foundling hospitals; unwed mothers or wives whose husbands were abroad may well have concealed them. Moreover, the relatively small number of illegitimate births can be seriously skewed by the prevalence of repeaters, by what one historian has described as a 'bastard prone sub-society'[10] in which a cluster of families had illegitimate children over several generations. Even so, the evidence of parish examinations concerning the paternity of illegitimate offspring provides some compelling, if inferential, evidence that illegitimacy was often the product of frustrated courtships, of promises to marry that went awry. In London, Nantwich, and in the various villages that have been closely scrutinized by the historical demographers, there was a remarkable concordance between the age of women at first marriage and the ages of the mothers when they had their first illegitimate child, with the majority in each case falling within the 20–24 year cohort, and a significant minority in the subsequent one (25–29 years). Moreover, while bastardy sometimes cut across social and economic boundaries, it was usually the product of symmetrical unions, and of unions of more than a few casual encounters. In other words, bastard-bearers were seldom sexually precocious teenagers; nor, save for a noteworthy minority in London's West End, were they women who had been sexually exploited by their masters, their masters' servants, or by gentlemanly rakes. Normally they were young working women in their twenties who, after five to ten years of employment, were thinking about getting married to men of their own social class. For one reason or another, perhaps war, or job insecurities, or male opportunism, their hopes for marriage never materialized.

The long-term rise in illegitimacy and prenuptial pregnancies provides little evidence for those who argue for a new sexual hedonism at the end of the eighteenth century. It does suggest, none the less, when every allowance is made for underregistration, that in some early nineteenth-century parishes half of all the first-born children were conceived out of wedlock. This was disconcerting enough to moralists and Malthusians who believed that plebeian sexual profligacy was out of control. It was amplified by the knowledge that many plebeian couples were not legally married at all but were cohabiting in what were often termed common-law unions. The London magistrate Patrick Colquhoun remarked on the 'prodigious number among the lower classes who cohabit together without marriage'[11] and such conventions were not simply confined to soldiers, sailors, and costermongers for whom sexual nonconformity was a way of life but included workers in the populous trades such as tailoring and shoemaking. Cohabitation was also quite common in the industrializing areas of the north, where those who entered into some sort of common rite were said to be 'married on the carpet and the banns up the chimney'.[12] Among the handloom weavers of Culcheth in Lancashire, for example, where illegitimacy was not stigmatized, women entered into common-law unions as often as they were married in church. Where they were securely employed in textile industries, women may well have found it more advantageous to remain unmarried in order to retain control of their earnings. Cohabitation was also to be found in mining and slate-quarrying villages, in the hosiery district of the East Midlands, and in the Kentish village of Ash-next-Sandwich, an arable and market-gardening region with little industrial employment. Here at least 15 per cent of the couples living in the village in the early nineteenth century were not legally married.

One can only conclude from all this that the attempt to regularize plebeian marriages in 1753 was a failure. Although there is some evidence that the parish authorities cracked down on sexual nonconformity in the immediate aftermath of the Marriage Act it proved impossible to police plebeian marriages in a routine way. Indeed, it is quite likely that after the prohibition of clandestine marriages, common-law marriages increased. In response to state interdicts, the banns of marriage were proverbially put up the chimney! In this instance, at least, there was a triumph of custom over law.

Gender relations in plebeian households

In reviewing the courtship practices of eighteenth-century society in 1779, William Alexander claimed that 'the poor' were 'the only class who still retain the liberty of acting from inclination and from choice'.[13] Alexander arguably exaggerated the degree to which the propertied classes had to 'sacrifice their love at the shrine of interest or ambition', and he overlooked the fact that peasants could be quite circumspect in choosing their partners where the transmission of property was involved. But he was essentially correct in assuming that the plebeians were less troubled than the propertied classes by etiquette, money, and social advancement in the selection of their partners and indubitably less concerned than their bourgeois counterparts with female chastity as the touchstone of a woman's moral standing. As Place recalled of his youth in London in the 1780s, 'want of chastity in girls' was not considered disreputable, and 'did not necessarily imply that the girl was an abandoned person'.[14] The same was true elsewhere. At Portland, for example, it was reported that young women were not stigmatized for losing their virginity during courtships, even if the courtship was subsequently broken off.

Plebeian men and women were less bound by social convention and parental approval in the choice of their partners, but this did not mean they necessarily had more harmonious marriages. Once united, poor working couples had to face the hard realities of making ends meet. A wife's contribution was critical to the family economy, but in terms of waged work, at least, it was seldom as substantial as a husband's. In textile environments, such work was often cooperative and appears to have given rise to more harmonious gender relations than say, in London, where women's waged work was ghettoized into low-paid jobs such as needlework as early as the seventeenth century, and where wives had to contend with a stronger tradition of male libertinism and an artisan drinking culture that could whittle away family incomes. Yet everywhere plebeian couples had to confront the potential loss of earnings brought on by having children, at least until such time as they could make a small contribution themselves. The fact that much work was seasonal and intermittent, punctuated by periods of un- or under-employment, could also put a strain on familial relations. In tough times men might simply up and leave. Fifteen per cent of all marriages in eighteenth-century Colyton ended in desertion. Twelve per cent of all applications for relief in London were made by wives whose husbands had left them, twice as many as came before the parish overseers in the countryside. Most of the deserted wives were in their mid-thirties, having been married for five years or more. They often had dependent children; in the south-eastern counties typically two or more.

Marital discord was common to all classes. In the case of the propertied, it is principally registered in the Church courts; in the case of the non-propertied, in the poor-law examinations and the popular literature concerning the 'struggle for the breeches'. The labouring classes were less likely to take their marital troubles to court than those who were richer, partly because they often lacked the financial resources to do so, but also because their lives were more public and more immediately mediated by non-kin. Living cheek by jowl with their neighbours and sometimes taking in boarders, their private lives were subject to greater public scrutiny and to informal intervention than those of the propertied classes. As the principal sources of neighbourhood gossip and in some sense its moral guardians, women were critical in this regard. They were likely to be the first to learn of marital tensions and irregularities and probably the first line of resort when domestic breakdown ensued.

The record of the Church courts with respect to sexual defamation would suggest that wives were subjected to greater moral vigilance than husbands, and that a double standard of sexual morality prevailed amongst all classes. The evidence is far from watertight, for the Church courts declined in importance over the course of the century and were increasingly the province of the middling rather than the plebeian classes. Whether the evidence of the petty and quarter sessions would modify the picture is unclear. It seems likely, however, that female adultery was universally viewed more seriously than male, not only because of the double standard, but because female adultery was a blight on male authority within the household. In fact, judges reinforced this bias by agreeing to the confinement of wives who brought the honour or credit of the husband into disrepute. Predictably, husbands were allowed some latitude in disciplining their wives; in fact, the law was quite ambivalent about whether wife-beating constituted legitimate correction or criminal assault. Habitual or excessive wife-beating none the less drew social opprobrium. Neighbours might intervene, crowds might gather to decry the aggressor, and if such mediation failed, a recognizance might be taken against the husband to keep the peace, either by neighbours or the wife herself. In late eighteenth-century London, at least one woman a week appeared before the magistrates to complain of conjugal abuse. Occasionally husbands were ritually hazed or roughed up for their actions. Such community-endorsed sanctions, known in the West Country as skimmingtons, had conventionally been directed at scolds, complaisant cuckolds, or marital mismatches. But from the eighteenth century they were also directed at wife-abuse and were sometimes initiated by women. In Billinghurst, Sussex, for example, a gentleman was hazed by local women in 1748 for mistreating his wife, the daughter of a local shopkeeper, by starving her on bread and water for three days. Assisted by some men, the women 'went before his House, where they rung what they call Rough Musick in order to get him out'.[15] They then carried him in a blanket to the local pond and ducked him before a large crowd of spectators until he promised to mend his ways.

Rough music belonged to a customary repertoire of community action that sought to regulate gender relations in the eighteenth century. It coexisted with the wife-sale, the public auction of a spouse at open market. At first sight the rituals of the sale appear aggressively, humiliatingly patriarchal. A wife was led to market in a halter like an animal; she was auctioned off before a crowd for a nominal price; and the bargain was sealed over a pot of beer in the local pub. Yet from the 300 or so cases that have come to light, principally in a period when popular culture was increasingly under attack, it appears that wives were consenting parties to the sale, and that they were often sold to their lovers, and frequently to lovers of higher social standing. In other words, while the symbolism of women as chattels is inescapable, wife-sales were a form of popular divorce in an age when legal divorce or judicial separation was beyond the reach of the labouring poor. To underscore this point, it is worth emphasizing that many plebeian men and women regarded the sale as legal and were prepared to argue its legality before a court of law. In 1795, for example, a woman appeared before the Westminster magistrates to lodge a complaint against Joseph Chipman for assaulting her. He pleaded in his defence that he was married to the woman, but that she now cohabited with another man and 'that he could not bear such an affront'. She replied she was no longer his wife and produced a stamped receipt which said 'July 5, 1795—received of James Clark, one pound one shilling, for Joseph Chipman's wife; both parties being willing to part.'[16] It was signed by the two parties and attested by two witnesses, and was clearly felt to be a binding contract by the ex-wife. Much of the ritual of the wife-sale was in fact dictated by the fact that the sale of animals, in open market, was one of the most binding contracts that could be made, under the terms of Elizabethan statutes.

After 1815 wife-sales met with a mixed response in plebeian circles, just as they had lost the easygoing tolerance of the gentry several decades before. In 1824 a female crowd at Shudehill market in Manchester showered the parties with mud, regarding the transaction as indecent and degrading. Such hostilities probably represent the growing fissure within plebeian society between the rough and respectable, generated by the growth of popular evangelism and the respiritualization of the family. Yet before 1815 wife-sales appear to have commanded widespread support and there are examples of crowds protecting the parties from official intervention. Although many estranged couples in the eighteenth century likely parted with less publicity, wife-sales did give the parties a measure of legitimacy within their own communities in much the same way as public betrothals. While the sales were far less egalitarian in their rituals than public troths, allowing the husband a patriarchal saving-of-face, they illustrated once again the force of custom in the making and breaking of plebeian marriages. That was something that neither the Marriage Act nor evangelical homily was able to expel.

4 Political Order

The legacy of 1688

On 4 and 5 November 1788, in towns and country houses across the nation, Britons celebrated the centenary of 1688 with a good deal of pomp and conviviality. The 4 and 5 November were remembered as the days when William, Prince of Orange, landed in England upon the 'Protestant tide' to deliver the nation from the rule of James II.[1] They were commemorated as a founding event of the eighteenth-century polity, an event that distinguished Britain from much of continental Europe in grounding the nation's governing institutions upon a stable frame and instituting a rule of law that preserved the liberty of the subject. Although the toasts, orations, and sermons of the festival offered different and competing interpretations of the so-called Glorious Revolution, especially with respect to the finality of the settlement and the degree to which it enshrined a doctrine of popular sovereignty, Britons were largely in agreement that it was a pivotal event. Without it, remarked one newspaper, 'Bigotry and superstition, despotism and tyranny, would long ere this, have defaced this fair and flourishing isle.'[2]

The 1688 *coup d'état* was not a social revolution. It did not institute changes that fundamentally altered the social and economic structures of society. Nor did it abolish monarchy or facilitate the entry of hitherto unrepresented groups to formal political power. In this sense the Glorious Revolution was far less radical than the American or French. The change of dynasty in 1688 could only be termed revolutionary in the extremely limited sense that it removed a Catholic king from the apex of power and placed constitutional impediments upon the royal prerogative; in effect, making the monarch *primus inter pares*, the first among the politicians, capable of ruling only through Parliament. Even the notion that the 1688 coup represented an implicit contract between Crown and people in which rights of resistance were in extraordinary circumstances permissible—a notion much touted by radical groups a century later—was hedged by the fiction that James II had abdic-

ated by fleeing from England. Thus the narrative of freedom constructed at the centenary, whereby 1688 stood as a milestone in the
development of British constitutional liberties, was really a progressive Whig myth. The settlement of 1688 (including the constitutional
Acts which followed in its wake) was pre-eminently anti-absolutist
and pro-Protestant, designed to shore up the alliance of the Anglican
Church and State, to provide the judiciary with a significant measure of independence from the Crown, and to prevent abitrary and
pro-Catholic policies by the monarch. It was a conservative act carried out by reluctant revolutionaries of the political élite.

The settlement of 1688–9 created a constitutional monarchy in
which Parliament was a central feature of political life, but so too
were the courts. The judges of the three common-law benches
(King's Bench, Common Pleas, and Exchequer) sat in Westminster
Hall, adjoining Parliament, for much of the year. Between the law
terms they went on circuit throughout the Kingdom, frequently
acting as spokesmen for government policy, sometimes conveyed
to them by the Lord Chancellor before their circuits. These twelve
men were simultaneously the oracles of the common law, the guarantors of liberty against executive tyranny, and often also statesmen in their own right. The Chief Justices of King's Bench and
Common Pleas were often given peerages, sat in the House of Lords
and engaged actively in debate. In their courtrooms, particularly
when hearing 'state trials' of constitutional issues, they also helped
shape politics. Some, like Charles Pratt (later Lord Camden) in the
Wilkes cases of the 1760s, rendered judgements that gave comfort
and assistance to the political enemies of the administration. Charles
II had swept his benches of the judges who gave him trouble; no
Hanoverian monarch or government could do that.

In Parliament, although the Crown could create its own ministries, formulate its own policy, and choose its own unpaid JPs to
administer at the local level, the Commons and Lords controlled
the size of the armed forces and the vital matter of supply. From
1689 onwards Parliament met annually and its lower House, the
Commons, was elected frequently; every three years from 1694–
1716, every seven thereafter. It therefore became imperative that
monarchs actively seek parliamentary majorities to facilitate the
work of the executive. Over time it became patently clear that the
Crown could not sustain first ministers who did not command

a majority in the Commons, the House that had pre-eminent control over the raising of taxes. George II was forced to recognize this pressing reality in 1742, when he reluctantly agreed to Sir Robert Walpole's resignation after seven successive defeats in the Commons. Similarly, George III had to come to terms with the parliamentary suspicion of his early favourite Lord Bute, and in 1782 had to agree to a ministry headed by Lord Rockingham who had persistently opposed his coercive policy towards America. Certainly no ministry could long survive without the full support of the crown, but the King needed parliament-backed ministries as much as they needed him.

Party politics

In the later years of Queen Anne, if not before, the monarch was often the prisoner of party. Broad party affiliations linking the localities to Westminster had first emerged during the Exclusion crisis of 1679–81, when the Shaftesbury Whigs had attempted to exclude James, Duke of York, from the throne on the grounds that he was a Catholic and a pawn of France. Although party configurations had an unsettled life in the aftermath of 1688, they re-emerged with a vengeance in the early eighteenth century when the issues of war, religion, and the succession deeply divided the nation. In the final years of the War of Spanish Succession, when the economic consequences of long Continental campaigns reverberated through the Shires and when it was clear that a distantly related German dynasty would replace the last Stuart queen if the terms of the Act of Settlement of 1701 were observed, party conflict reached fever pitch, with volatile but partisan electorates returning in effect party governments to power.

This rather unique situation did not last. The Tory party, the champion of hereditary monarchy, was too closely identified with the exiled House of Stuart to serve as a viable government after the Jacobite Rebellion of 1715, even though the majority of its leading politicians were not in favour of a Stuart restoration. With the advent of a Hanoverian dynasty, the Tories were proscribed from office, at least as a collective group, and proscription took its toll on party morale and reproduction. Although party affiliations still retained some vitality in the first four decades of Hanoverian rule, particularly over the status of the Anglican Church within the political order, the number of Tories in the Commons shrank from 178 in 1722 to little more than 100 by the mid-century in a house of 558 Members. Lord Dupplin could still configure the Members elected in 1754 according to party affiliation, but by this time such distinctions were of little political relevance. Other factors seemed more important in a world that had become pre-eminently and blandly Whiggish.

Political patronage and oligarchy

Eighteenth-century parties were institutionally less salient than their modern counterparts. Although historians have discovered the existence of party clubs and whips, there were no nationally co-ordinated party offices, agents, or conventions. Eighteenth-century parties were built up from a weft of local and regional allegiances, controlled and mediated by the great men of property. In the counties the principal players were the landed aristocracy, although the distribution of property could influence the degree to which such magnates had to heed the inclinations of the lesser gentry and freeholders. In the smaller boroughs, landed magnates held greater sway. If their patronage was substantial enough and the electoral structure suitably pliable, and this was frequently the case, they could determinedly influence the choice of representatives to Parliament, if not actually nominate them. Some rotten boroughs were in reality family heirlooms, handed down from generation to generation or sold to the highest bidder. Larger boroughs, with more diversified economic structures and more representative political structures, were more difficult to control. They were more likely to return local men of commerce or respected country gentlemen than clients of the aristocracy, although in some big boroughs all candidates had to chart the muddy waters of electoral venality if they wanted to get elected. In mid-century Hull, for example, poor voters routinely expected 2 guineas for their vote, an expectation that was regarded 'as a sort of birthright'. The same was largely true of Bristol: with its 4,500 voters and strong tradition of electoral bribery, few candidates after 1750 stood a chance of winning without an outlay of L.10,000, a very formidable sum by eighteenth-century standards.

As party strife slowly ebbed during the Hanoverian era, so the intrinsically oligarchical infrastructure of British politics became more pronounced. Two factors helped transform this structure into something of a system. First, the Septennial Act of 1716 had the effect of driving up the price of seats in the Commons, to a point that electoral expenditures averaged £5,000 at the end of the century, five times the cost in 1700. This predicament helped consolidate the power of the territorial grandees, who were better able to bear the cost than many country gentlemen. It also encouraged electoral compromise among local rival factions. The result was that the number of contested elections fell dramatically, reaching its nadir in 1761 when only 17 per cent of all seats in the Commons were contested, including 10 per cent of the English counties (4 out of 40) and 20 per cent of the English boroughs (41 out of 203). At the same time that an increasing number of voters were deprived of the opportunity of going to the polls, the number of borough seats controlled by private patronage (either by nomination or influence) grew from roughly a third in 1690, to half by 1761, to nearly two-thirds by 1790.[3] In 1793 the Friends of the People calculated that 60 per cent of all MPs for England and Wales were 'returned by patronage', a figure that some historians have considered too conservative. John Cannon, for example, has calculated that the figure should be nearer 66 per cent, with approximately 40 per cent of MPs returned by the aristocracy, a clear indication of the informal power of the Lords over the Commons, by reputation the more important House. Indeed, the political patronage of the peerage more than doubled during the course of the century.[4]

If the electoral power of the territorial grandees increased over time, so, too, did the means by which the government could turn its own resources to political advantage. In the seventeenth century the ability of the Crown to reward its servants was not inconsiderable. After 1688 it grew dramatically. As England became increasingly embroiled in European wars and in the expansion and defence of its commercial empire, so resources had to be developed to fund, supply, to fight and administer them. All this meant new jobs: in the army, the navy, the fiscal bureaucracy, especially in the Customs and Excise, and even in the central administrative departments.

How far this expanding state was ridden with political jobbery and corruption has become a contentious issue among historians. It has recently been argued that Britain's success in waging war in the eighteenth century was predicated upon an administrative efficiency that does not square with its old image as a corrupt regime whose *raison d'être* was 'to provide outdoor relief for the political classes'.[5] The cost of public office and pensions was not high by European standards, and the increasingly bureaucratic ethos of government in Britain made it strikingly different from France, where the venality of office and the existence of a permanent, hereditary officer class made it impervious to change. Yet this argument about 'Old Corruption', as the Radicals later dubbed the spoils system, can be overplayed. The exigencies of war and the political pressures for public accountability inevitably generated some efficiency and internal audit, especially in the fiscal departments; but the overall system of office-holding was not overhauled. The new was grafted on to the old; indeed, probably helped to sustain it; and without any clear distinction between political and civil service, the fruits of office were there for the taking. Archaic departments were ransacked for sinecures; pluralism was rife; and even positions in more efficient departments such as the Stamp Office were given over to political aspirants who fulfilled their obligations by deputy. In practice, few offices were open to those without some political introduction, without some token of actual or potential advantage to those in power. As the papers of the Duke of Newcastle attest, politicians regularly clamoured for even the meanest of positions, for themselves, their families, or their clients. Office-holding rarely generated vast fortunes outside the law and plum positions such as the Paymaster-General of the Forces, where the balances derived from office could be lent over the short-term to the holder's personal profit. Yet it certainly greased the wheels of patronage and enabled the pre-eminent to cut public figures commensurate with their political standing and social rank. The salary of the 2nd Viscount Townshend as Secretary of State in the 1720s, for example, was £1,950 per annum, not a large sum given the importance of the position. The actual gross income that he derived from office, however, allowing for working expenses, fees, and secret service money, was about £8,000 per annum, significantly more than the rental he derived from his Norfolk estates. Much of this money was whittled away by expenses in London and Hanover, personal and official, but it enabled the peer to shine in metropolitan society in a way his father had never done, and without encumbering his profitable landed estate and endangering his patrimony.

The fruits of office, then, were important to the social reproduction of the peerage and the gentry as the political élite of the nation, just as the contracts for government loans and victualling the armed forces could be lucrative sources of income for merchant-financiers. This state of affairs was marshalled by the government to shore up their support in the Commons. In 1754 when Lord Dupplin classified the returning Members by party affiliation, he also arranged them by function. On the ministerial side he calculated that there were forty-five placemen who held their offices at the pleasure of the Crown, ten who held them for life, and eight who might be termed lawyer-placemen. There were also thirty-two army or navy officers who were well disposed to the government (out of a possible seventy-two), and twenty who were merchant-contractors or financiers, many of them affiliated to the Bank of England or the East India Company. This group constituted the hard core of the Court-Treasury faction in Parliament, 115 in total. This was insufficient to secure a majority on important political business, but it was a start. Together with various aristocratic factions—the Prince of Wales's coterie, the Fox-Cumberland faction, the fifteen Scotsmen under the leadership of the Duke of Argyle, the regional packs of Lord Powis and Lord Rockingham, and so on—plus some eighty-odd country gentlemen who generally offered support—it was anticipated that the ministry was assured of a substantial majority in the House.

Dupplin's list offers some important insights into the structure of parliamentary politics at mid-century. It illustrates what we have already suggested, that the bipolarity of party was giving way to a tripartite grouping in the Commons, one that reflected the infrastructure of political practice. Through the disposition of direct favours, the government in power was able to build up its own phalanx of supporters within the Court and Treasury. Yet it had to come to terms with two other broad groupings: the country gentlemen, hitherto loosely connected to party but proud of their political independence and local standing; and the aristocratic factions, whose control over the smaller boroughs in particular made their support critical to the ministry. Country critics of eighteenth-century politics had long railed at the way in which successive governments had shored up majorities through political jobbery and subverted the independence of the Commons with executive influence. Place bills to remove office-holders from the Commons had long been a rallying cry. But in practice no government could insulate itself from parliamentary censure by the distribution of favours alone. To this extent the Country critique was misplaced. It was on firmer ground in highlighting the fact that the mix of aristocratic and Court patronage insulated the House from electoral pressure. As newspapers such as the *Craftsman* pointed out in the aftermath of the 1734 and 1741 elections, had the 'sense of the people' been taken from the larger and truly open constituencies, then the Opposition coalition of Tories and Whigs would have won both contests hands down. Indeed, in the terms of the total votes cast, the Tories or Country coalitions gained a majority in three of the first four Hanoverian elections, in 1722, 1734, and 1741. The sclerotic structure of electoral politics, brought on by patronage, was there for all to see.

Politics beyond Parliament

In 1754 the Duke of Newcastle thought himself politically unassailable: writing to Horatio Walpole, he described the new Parliament as 'beyond my expectations', with 'more Whigs in it, and generally well-disposed Whigs, than any Parliament since the Revolution.'[6] Yet within little more than two years, as a result of the loss of Minorca to the French and the ensuing scandal, Newcastle's reputation was seriously tarnished and his majority in peril. Indeed, despite his seemingly impregnable support in the Commons, he was forced to give way to a more popular ministry under the leadership of Pitt the Elder.

The Duke of Newcastle lost popularity over the Mediterranean island of Minorca because he deviously attempted to shift the responsibility for its capture exclusively on to Admiral Byng, whose life was cynically sacrificed to a nationalist sentiment that demanded a more bellicose, blue-water policy to protect Britain's burgeoning empire. The crisis of 1756/7, in fact, revealed one of the paradoxes of eighteenth-century politics: the importance of public opinion in an increasingly oligarchical age. Although the electoral structure of the country was increasingly dominated by patronage and jobbery, it was never invulnerable to wider political forces. From early on in the century Londoners had the benefit of a daily press and by the 1750s there were four dailies and five tri-weekly newspapers, some of which had quite wide provincial circulations. In addition, the provincial towns had thirty-two papers in 1753, bringing the total circulation of the press (as calculated from the stamp-duty returns of 1756) to about 29,500 newspapers a day. This was an unprecedented number by European standards, most of whose countries still had only official gazettes whose news coverage was very perfunctory and whose circulation was limited. Just how many people read these papers is rather more difficult to calculate, for we know they were passed around and readily available in inns, public houses, assembly rooms, and coffee-houses. Even so, it has been estimated that one in seven adults read the provincial press on a weekly basis, with the number considerably higher in the capital where foreign observers were astounded to find labourers perusing newspapers. This speaks to a wide political readership, and judging from the content of the newspapers themselves, which followed the Minorca crisis keenly in ballads, acrostics, and sustained commentaries, a sophisticated one.

All politicians had to develop thick skins if they were to tolerate the barbed commentaries of the press, which showed little deference to rank or party. Sir Robert Walpole was so aggrieved by his ratings that he subsidized his own partisans and habitually tried to bribe or bully his critics into submission. Press criticism did not necessarily translate into effective political opposition outside Parliament, but there were institutions and conventions that did make this possible. Voters in the more open boroughs, especially in big cites like London, Norwich, or Newcastle, regularly voiced their opinions about the central issues of the day, and it was perhaps no accident that the electoral record of the cities, with their large middling electorates, ran counter to the national trend, with more elections being contested in the Hanoverian era than in the Augustan. Corporations and grand juries were also able to state their concerns through addresses to the Crown or instructions to their members. Instructions, in particular, were used with effect during the Excise crisis of 1733 and in opposition to the Spanish Convention of 1739. Apart from the specific content of their message, they underscored the belief, still firmly adhered to in an age of deferential politics, that MPs were delegates of their constituents to whom they were ultimately responsible. It was one of the Radical Whig legacies that survived the stultifying effects of political oligarchy.

Addresses and instructions were both used to mobilize public opinion during the Minorca crisis. Once the press had exposed the chicanery of the government in doctoring the dispatches of Admiral Byng so as to exculpate itself of any responsibility for the loss of Minorca, opposition opinion in the City of London and in the counties mounted a campaign for a public inquiry. Some thirty-six constituencies, nearly half of them counties, addressed or instructed their members in this manner, linking their concern over Minorca with demands for a change of ministry and a national militia to defend Britain's shores and to revivify a public spirit that appeared to have been corroded by political preferment and opportunism. In some cases, instructions called for parliamentary reform. Newcastle and his cohorts proved powerless to stop them, and sensing the weight of the county communities against him, the Duke resigned rather than face a divided House without an experienced and reliable debater to defend him. Newcastle survived the crisis, unlike the hapless Byng, who was court-martialled and shot to stiffen naval morale and vindicate national pride. But the episode did illustrate how a carefully coordinated campaign which mobilized important segments of the political nation, especially city merchants and country gentlemen, could sever the seemingly durable sinews of patronage which, under normal circumstances, insulated the Whig grandees from popular political pressure. The long campaign to dismiss Walpole that culminated in his resignation some fifteen years earlier told much the same story.

Crowds in politics

The freemen and freeholders who, as part of the formal political nation, instructed their MPs in 1756, were not the only players in the Minorca crisis. There were also the crowds who burned Admiral Byng in effigy in the ports and inland towns of England for his refusal to engage the enemy in a determined and courageous manner, and who, as the focus of attention switched to the ministry, pelted Newcastle's coach with mud as he was passing through Greenwich. Interventions of this kind, often ritualized as mock-executions or forms of rough music, were not untypical of political crises in the eighteenth century. They raise important questions about the political involvement and maturity of ordinary people, and their relationship to those who held formal political power.

Crowds were an unwelcome intrusion into the lives and

calculations of the political élite and, when seemingly hostile, were quickly classified as riotous mobs who might be hanged under the terms of the 1715 Riot Act if they did not disperse within one hour of the Act's public reading. Yet at the same time crowds were necessary to the political regime. The common people had traditionally been invited to enter public space to see justice done at the gallows, the pillory, and the cart's tail, from which malefactors were whipped around the market-place. Indeed, the whole purpose of exemplary punishment, which was designed to deter the public as much as to inflict pain on the bodies of the victims, was meaningless without an audience. Within the political arena, crowds attended political trials, and after one of the dramatic appearances of Wilkes in King's Bench the crowd was so thick that the judges had difficulty getting to the bench. (Lord Chief Justice Mansfield dramatically declared that he would do justice should the heavens fall, or even should his own life be forfeit to the mob. He released Wilkes on a technicality.)

At elections the mob was fully in evidence. Although some journeymen and labourers were able to vote in the more open constituencies—one male adult in three voted in mid-century Norwich elections, for example—many were excluded from an electorate that enfranchised 24 per cent of all adult males in 1715 and 17 per cent by the end of the century. Even so, the unenfranchised could play an incidental role in the electoral process: parading the candidates' colours; distributing handbills; joining in the electoral treats; hissing or huzzaing their favoured candidates; and sometimes even serving as bruisers at the hustings, where rival factions routinely sought to intimidate their opponents' supporters. The right to jeer and heckle candidates became a customary feature of the Englishman's birthright, and was sometimes used quite devastatingly. In 1784 when the unpopular Lord North was returned by the eleven eligible voters of Banbury quite against the public tide, the inhabitants of the town refused to let anyone wear his colours and staged a counter-chairing at the end of the election. 'A weaver, decorated with a blue ribband, attended by thousands of approving spectators, was carried round in a chair covered with scarlet shag . . . preceded with music, flags &c', one newspaper reported, while North himself was 'chaired unattended, save by the electors themselves . . . whose feeble huzzas was not sufficient to drown the groans and hisses, and the incessant cry of "No North!" as they passed.'[7]

Elections were not the only occasions when the plebeian presence could be felt. There was also the annual calendar of royal and national anniversaries, including Restoration Day (29 May) and 5 November, the day that commemorated the discovery of the Gunpowder Plot (1605) and the Revolution of 1688. On these days bells would be rung, cannons fired, and corporate bodies would process to the church or cathedral to hear a celebratory sermon before repairing to town halls, taverns, and assembly rooms for dinners and balls. In a regime whose legitimacy rested in some measure on popular consent, the common people were necessarily included to pay tribute to Britain's political heritage, and their participation was rewarded with bonfires, beer, ox-roasts, and various forms of revels. Public anniversaries were occasions for the distribution of ruling-class largesse and the symbolic enhancement of the regime. They were also potential flashpoints for political contention.

In the opening decade of the Hanoverian accession this was very much the case. The advent of the German Elector to the throne provided no immediate respite to the torrid party conflict of the previous reign. As Whig and Tory battled for advantage, the dynastic struggle that had bedevilled British politics in Anne's last years spilled over on to the streets. Over twenty riots were reported on Coronation Day, 1714, with Tory mobs attacking Whig partisans and in one instance insolently parading a mock-monarch with a turnip-topped wand before a procession of Whig clothiers to the cry of 'Here's our George, where's yours?' This kind of confrontation continued into the following year, transforming political festivals into a veritable calendar of riot and symbolic assault, with Whigs taunting Tories with the Pretender's purported illegitimacy by parading warming-pans, and Tories in turn deriding Whig heroes and George I's rumoured cuckoldry at the hands of a Swedish count. By the time that the Whig-dominated Parliament had moved to impeach two of the leading Tory Lords, the situation was at fever pitch. The Pretender was actually proclaimed at Manchester and in one village in Somerset. In Lancashire and the West Midlands thirty Dissenting meeting-houses were pulled down in a display of Tory fury by nailers, buckle-makers, and textile-workers that surpassed the Sacheverell riots of 1710. The Whig response was to pass and read the Riot Act; and to billet troops in the most disaffected towns.

It is difficult to determine the exact dimensions of popular Jacobitism south of the Scottish border. Relatively few Englishmen actually joined the rebels in 1715 and 1745, even though the Jacobite army reached Derby in the last uprising, so we are heavily dependent upon newspaper reports, court records, and the State Papers Domestic to calculate its reach. Part of the problem is that some accusations of Jacobitism were malicious and designed to discredit political opponents. Another problem is that demonstrators often went in for rhetorical or symbolic overkill, caricaturing party rivalries in dynastic terms, thus blurring the boundaries between Toryism and genuine Jacobitism. Still another is that Jacobitism was a malleable script that could be used for a variety of purposes: to deflate the pomposities of a Whig corporation; to demarcate Tory territory; to reassert plebeian licence in the face of official disapprobation; to serve as a language of social protest. Southwark minters, Hampshire Blacks, Devonshire weavers, Newcastle keelmen, Staffordshire poachers, south-coast smugglers all used Jacobitism as an idiom of defiance. So, too, did Midland miners in the 1756 bread riots, who, having ransacked the houses of two substantial dealers at Nuneaton, warned that 'the Pretender would come and head them' if they were opposed by force.[8]

If we follow the notable commemorations of Tory-Jacobite anniversaries, especially the 29 May (Restoration Day) and 10 June (the Pretender's birthday) then we can suggest that there was a considerable undercurrent of Jacobitism until the early 1720s, becoming thereafter regionally specific. The chronology of seditious words in select counties reveals much the same pattern. Toasts to the Pretender and denunciations of King George by lower-to-middling people are quite voluminous until about 1724, petering out thereafter, save in the West Midlands and Lancashire, the heartland of Toryism, where sympathy for Jacobitism survived the Forty-Five. In other former hot spots of Jacobitism, however, sympathy for the Stuarts had ebbed. In Bristol, where Jacobite bonfires had blazed on Brandon Hill in the aftermath of the 1715 Rebellion, Stuart sympathies declined markedly after a Tory mob disrupted Whig festivities on the King's birthday in 1735. What little disaffection surfaced in the 1745 Rebellion was not taken very seriously. This was not true of London, where there was a resurgence of Jacobite oath-taking and cursing the King in 1745/6. Yet much of it came from a beleaguered Irish minority rather than the population as a whole. By that time popular opposition to the Whig regime in the capital had begun to take different forms.

Jacobitism appears to have survived most persistently in areas where Anglican–Dissenting rivalries remained a continuing bone of contention. Despite the fact that the Protestant Dissenters were second-class citizens in the Hanoverian regime, unable to participate in local government unless they took the oaths of conformity, they were riveted to the Whig cause because they feared prosecution at the hands of the Tories. Where Dissenters were socially visible and politically powerful, they were often resented, and this resentment often took the form of Tory-Jacobitism. Where Anglican–Dissenting rivalries were muted by the emergence of Country coalitions of Whigs and Tories in the mid-century, Jacobitism generally lost ground.

By 1740 the political sympathies of the common people were changing. One barometer of this change was the career of Admiral Vernon. A staunch Whig but vociferous critic of Walpole, Vernon was dispatched with an ill-equipped fleet to the Caribbean to satiate the mercantile demand for a more aggressive commercial and imperial policy in transatlantic waters. His capture of Porto Bello from Spain with only six men-of-war made him a popular hero at home, and his birthday in November 1740 was wildly celebrated throughout the Kingdom. In the ensuing general election, Vernon was nominated to no less than six constituences, probably an all-time record in British parliamentary history. At one level Vernon was the intrepid admiral in the tradition of Drake and Raleigh, a defender of liberty and Protestantism against the Catholic foe. At another, he was the quintessential patriot, a counterpoint to Walpole, a man of political integrity who never played politics for preferment even though this inevitably hampered his career, and whose naval paternalism and opposition to regressive taxation gave him broad appeal. Vernon's popularity was a commentary on the parasitism of the political élite, upon the self-interest and sycophancy of politicians, upon the enervating consequences of foppish, metropolitan manners. It signalled not only a new push for empire but a populist disenchantment with time-serving politicians.

We might conclude this section by comparing the pro-Vernon agitation with the Minorca crisis of 1756–7. Both epitomized a new public mood of bellicose mercantilism, an intoxicating mix of Protestantism, patriotism, and empire that not only buoyed up Vernon and destroyed Byng, but worked to the discredit of the ministry in power. That mood was in part created by a vibrant political culture that stood in stark contrast to the oligarchical structures of formal political power. Through the agency of the press, the official forums of the more open constituencies, and the politics of celebration, campaigns could be launched against ministerial power, although the success of such campaigns necessarily depended upon the way they were played out in the factious politics of Parliament and the Court. No popular movement could of itself wrest power from the incumbent grandees; it could only create the context and discourse for such as assault.

Crowds were an integral feature of the politics of celebration, helping to dramatize issues and to open up public space. It was in this context that the politics of the common people was most palpably felt. Yet the concordance between popular belief and the public sphere of middling-to-upper opinion was sometimes fragile. In the years 1739–41 there was a singular convergence of public opinion against Walpole. In the years 1756–7 there was not. The bitter demonstrations against Byng had the effect of deflecting attention away from ministerial responsibility for Minorca. At some point they proved counter-productive to the patriot project of Pitt and his allies.

Moreover, the common people were to view parts of that patriot project with singular distaste. When steps were taken in 1757 to activate the militia, a key part of the patriot programme of reform, there was widespread rioting throughout the country. Gentlemen were threatened; country houses were attacked; enrolment lists were forcibly taken from magistrates and constables. The lower ranks saw the Militia Act as an underhand form of conscription; they disliked the fact that there was no provision for pay; they feared, after two years of serious bread-rioting, that the militia might be used against their own kind. 'If you would have men raised', ran one letter to two Lincolnshire gentlemen, 'you may raise them by the assistance of your long green purse and be damn'd if you will . . . if a Ticket be drawn and fall to a poor man's lot to go that has a large family, which of you Buntin ass'd fellows will maintain his family till its capable of taking care of itself.' The letter went on to criticize the 'just-asses and the other start-up officers' that bought 'a commission for a trifle' and sold 'his nation to make his fortune when he comes abroad and throws Thousands of Poor mens lives about it'.[9] The gentry wanted a pledge of personal service from the plebs in the nation's hour of need, but ordinary people saw the Militia Act as an upper-class trick to recruit them for war at minimal cost. 'They had better be hanged in England than scalped in America,' claimed protesters from Chesterfield. 'They have no confidence in Government.'[10] No amount of patriotic rhetoric was going to dispel the common people's deep distrust of the Establishment's intentions on this most publicly touted of measures.

Conclusion

During the first half of the eighteenth century there was a discernable tension between the closed and increasingly oligarchical world of patronage politics and the broadening terrain of extraparliamentary politics. The tension was to some extent held in check by the ideological appeal of Whiggery, which justified its conservative practices by posing as the only reliable bulwark to a Jacobite and Catholic repossession of Britain. But once the Jacobite threat had ebbed, the bloodless pursuit of preferment among the élite stood in marked contrast to a robust political culture that could mobilize dissident forces against the government and compromise the seemingly predictable certainties of electoral politics. After 1760 the balance between the worlds of patronage and extraparliamentary politics tipped irrevocably in favour of the latter. As we shall see in Chapter 11, the issues surrounding Wilkes and the American and French Revolutions raised aspirations that could not be contained within the formal structures of parliamentary politics. New modes of mass petitioning and association and the growing development of the public sphere transformed the dynamics of national politics. Even conservatives recognized the imperative of appealing to broad sections of public opinion in new ways, despite their constant misgivings about politicizing men of little or no property; hence the increasing resort to loyalist addresses to the Crown and to loyalist associations in the final quarter of the century.

Until the final decade of the eighteenth century there was a rough consensus among the propertied classes that the political settlement of 1688 and its aftermath had served Britain reasonably well. Even those who demanded change were prepared to do so from the referent of 1688, as the centenary celebrations themselves revealed. With the French Revolution and the birth of democratic societies the wisdom of this constitutionalism was vigorously questioned. There was a new impatience with the old order, a deepening critique of its leadership, and pressing challenges for those who wished to preserve it. In the vortex of war and revolution, Britain's political landscape would be transformed, giving rise to new polarities and new movements for reform.

5 Harvests and Dearth

Food riots preceded the Minorca crisis, and helped shape its outcome, including the militia riots of 1757. We shall return to the food riot in Chapter 9, but its significance to both governors and governed will be better appreciated once we have considered some concerns of all European governments in the eighteenth century: harvest failure, dearth, poverty, and their consequence hunger.

In May 1800 Henry Legge, a son of Lord Dartmouth, wrote to the Home Office from Birmingham in alarm, 'Many thousands especially Children, are all but starved, & unless some better support both in Quantity and Quality of provisions can be procured before very hot Weather commences, some putrid epidemic disease must be the Consequence'.[1] For the first time in almost two hundred years, the mass of the English poor appeared to be facing starvation. The staggering increase of food prices in 1795–6 and again in 1800–1 dwarfed the earlier dearths of 1709–10, 1728–9, 1740, 1756–7, 1766–7, 1772, and 1782–3 (see Fig. 7). In most of those years there had been food riots, sometimes in many counties, an outpouring of pamphlet literature about possible causes and solutions, the deployment of troops, and the invocation (although less application) of the Tudor and Stuart laws to regulate markets in foodstuffs (see Ch. 6). But England until the 1790s appeared largely to have escaped, probably by the mid-seventeenth century, the dangers of the classic subsistence crisis. Famine still struck the Highlands of Scotland during the eighteenth century, and Ireland was badly hit at times of high prices and trade depression. On the Continent, starvation of the ancient kind still afflicted France and most other polities. In England, in spite of periodic dearth and high prices, not only was famine avoided, but nutritional levels were better than those on the Continent. Perhaps the variety of grains sown in England in different seasons helped to prevent dearth; government policy, described below, may also have been important. The resulting escape from the classic subsistence crisis had profound implications for population health and population growth in England. It also affected economic productivity as well as social relations, including the place of coercion and consent in the maintenance of public order. England differed from France in many ways, but the escape from the manifold dangers of dearth, for most of the century, was one of the most important.

Plenty and want on the eve of industrialization

In most years up to the 1750s harvests were good, food prices were low, and England was a substantial net exporter of grain. Government bounties encouraged such exports, but the abundant supplies and low prices meant that real wages rarely dropped, and a customary standard of living was sustained for most people year after year. Before mid-century there were only three significant years of harvest failure, dearth, and high prices, in 1709–10, 1728–9, and in 1740. In the second half of the century a sustained rise in average food prices which probably outstripped that of wage rates appears to have placed a greater proportion of the working population closer to the fear of want; it was after about the 1770s that there was a sustained rise in the cost of poor relief, peaking in 1818 (we discuss the poor law below). A greater cause of alarm to both the poor and the government was the much-increased incidence of harvest failures and short-term price-rises, which plunged large numbers of families into fear and want, multiplied the problems of public order when food riots became widespread, and caused a great deal of hard thinking about the role of markets and market regulation.

The seasonality of prices meant that the crisis in a year of dearth usually began in the late winter and spring, before the new harvest caused a drop in prices. But there were also longer-term economic effects of bad years. Poor harvests reduced employment in agriculture, and the pressure on family budgets reduced demand also for manufactures. Where harvest failures and high prices (which sometimes occurred in successive years, as effects carried over) coincided with other cyclical downturns, the pressure on the poor was exacerbated. Severe winters caused a decline in economic activity; other causes of unemployment, such as the interruption of particular trades by warfare, also played a significant role at particular times. Thus the Birmingham toy trade and Midland nail-making (to take one regional example among many) were greatly disrupted by the American Revolution. However, such effects were local, and differed markedly according to trade and locale. The toy trade and nail-makers' crisis was the armament manufacturer's opportunity, and Birmingham and Midland entrepreneurs and wage-earners in those trades benefited greatly from wars; so too did the West Yorkshire woollen industry. Demobilization, on the other hand, was usually a disaster for many of the poor. The return of thousands of men glutted unskilled trades, and even some of the more skilled ones, since legislation specifically exempted returning soldiers and sailors from the apprenticeship requirements, where they were still being enforced. A combination of dearth and demobilization coincided in the early and mid-1780s, and the combination was a disaster for a large part of the labour force in manufacturing areas.

The effect of high food prices, like that of war, varied greatly by occupation. One reason that food riots so often happened in industrial areas was that workers there were far more likely to be directly dependent on the market. In more agrarian regions, farmers and landlords supplied their labourers and living-in servants directly with food, outside the markets in which prices were rapidly rising. The degree of sensitivity to price-changes also depended on whether the family of a labourer or nail-maker or weaver also had access to other resources of its own. Where common rights still existed and were open to the majority of inhabitants; where gleaning (which could supply a poor family with three months' bread) was permitted; where poaching and nutting and berrying could supplement wages, either agricultural or industrial, the impact of dearth was mitigated by substitutions. Some arguably were nutritious additions to the diet, rather than diminutions.

Household economies with access to such resources (often the province of women) were insulated to a degree from both trade cycles (which on the downturn eroded monetary wages), and harvest failures (which in their extremities decimated real wages). Where rights over land continued for workers in a growing rural industrial sector, early marriage and the advantages of child labour further sustained household economies. In particular regions and trades, however, there were particular dangers. Famine in earlier centuries had been a greater danger in upland pastoral areas in England, and such communities, particularly if they had few communication links with the outside, could suddenly be struck destitute in the eighteenth century also. If a local trade was in decline (such as cloth-making throughout much of southern and western

England) the impact of large inflows of unskilled labour, or technical change, or changing markets could leave so many close to subsistence that a sudden doubling of food prices in times of dearth struck particularly hard. Migration, often to London, seems to have been one common resort. Enlistment in the army (leaving the family destitute) was another. Those who remained behind were crucially dependent on private charity and poor relief.

Crisis years caused by harvest failures were once thought to be the most important determinants of mortality; we now know that was not the case. The issues of disease, general mortality levels, and the extent of poverty are best considered in light of what is known of the distribution of income.

The distribution of income and of want

The variety of circumstances, the many different ways of piecing together a living in London or in different parts of the countryside, makes it very difficult to generalize about the changing contours of want. For example, it is clear from the extent of the poor's access to land, at least until mid-century, that figures for the distribution of income between different sections of the population must be approximations only. Certainly reliance on standard wage rates and price series alone must give a misleading sense of the social structure in many parts of the country. But the estimates of contemporaries probably took at least some of the hidden earnings of the poor into account. The three best all suggest strongly that the inequality of the distribution of income was much greater than that of England in the mid-twentieth century (see Fig. 5). Such figures can be used to make gross estimates of the proportion of the population that would be plunged into dire want by changes in food prices, if for the purposes of the argument we make a number of convenient assumptions, including the clearly unwarranted one that everyone bought in the market, at the recorded market price. However, the exercise does show how remarkably volatile market prices were in the later part of the century, and why those changes aroused anxiety. Relatively small shortfalls in harvests could have highly disproportionate effects on prices, and those dependent on markets watched the weather and the harvest with anxiety each year. If we assume that all families were buying in the market-place, a population with the structure described by Massie and Colquhoun would suffer destitution, through price-changes alone, to a great extent. In the period 1772–1802, using annual average wheat prices for the industrializing county of Stafford, 10 per cent of the population could not, unaided, have bought sufficient bread in a year of low prices, even if they had been able to eliminate all other expenditures. In a hard year, the proportion rose to 20 per cent, and in a very hard year, such as 1800–1, 45 per cent of the entire population would be thrown into such destitution: all their expenditures would have gone on bread, and even then many would not have been able to buy enough to keep up health and strength.

The wide range of ways in which people avoided the market and found other sources of food and income means that these estimates can only be used to show the comparative pressure of different years, and to emphasize the importance of those other ways of getting a living. We should, however, note one other estimate of the differential social effects of changing grain prices. Landlords and farmers, the wealthier sections of landed society, were either not affected by price-rises, or benefited from them, in sales and rents. A recent estimate suggests that even in the worst dearths of the early-modern period, of the kind that came only once a century, aristocratic and gentry landlords, and farmers, and those in their households would have felt little or no effect on their consumption levels. However, shopkeepers, minor professionals, and artisans would have suffered an 11 per cent decline as a result of the price-rise; labourers and the workless poor would have suffered a 32 per cent loss of consumption of foodgrains if they were buying at market prices. Lesser deficits in supply would still have had devastating effects on the diet and health of the poor.

Cycles in family poverty

There is one important characteristic of want and poverty that such gross statistics (even if far more accurate than they are likely to be) fail to capture: that is the social and individual effects of cycles in the experience of families. In addition to the well-known impoverishment that would result from having a large number of young children (followed by relative prosperity if there were industrial or other employment opportunities for them as they got older), the relationship of labouring families to the land also had a significant effect on their experience of want. Not only was it a matter of whether they had common rights; it also was a matter of whether, through inheritance, they were likely to escape from an acute dependence on wage labour sometime in the future. The importance of this possibility should not be exaggerated, but it appears that a far greater proportion of the labouring poor of the Midlands had at least some access to land, with common rights, than was formerly believed. An assessment of Northamptonshire suggests that in many of the most populous parishes still unenclosed, more than half the population had significant income from land, either as occupiers or landlords. In such circumstances some young men who worked as weavers or wool-combers would find themselves, in the course of years, following their fathers as smallholders or cottagers. Of course, if inheritance was likely, so too was assistance from members of the family better placed to escape some of the impact of sharp market fluctuations.

The evidence of families who had earlier in their lives relied on day-labour and rural industrial employment (weaving, nailmaking), and then moved on to smallholding and farming with access to commons, has important implications. It shows that numbers of people from the class most exposed to dearth and unemployment eventually could hope to escape some of its effects. On the other hand, it shows that a proportion of that population of the more fortunate working poor, with some land, knew what it meant to have suffered real want, and probably carried with them the attitudes (suspicion of profiteers in food markets, a view of the poor laws) characteristic of their origins. Finally, it suggests that when enclosure of common lands took place, and many smallholders lost their land, a far greater proportion of the population found themselves exposed directly to the impact of market prices for food (see Ch. 7).

Malnutrition and disease: Long range and international comparisons

As well as specific cases of hardship and cycles of impoverishment caused by harvests or family formation, larger changes over the course of the century probably also had significant effects on the health and wellbeing of the poorest half of the population. In the second half of the eighteenth century many of the working poor looked back to the early decades of the century as a golden age. In addition to the significant rise in the trend of food prices after mid-century, commons were enclosed in increasing numbers, and harvest failures increasingly developed in the same years. And in the second part of our period (1765–1815) the disruptions of war became more common: thirty-one years of war compared to fifteen before 1765, and greater numbers of men enlisted than before, in both absolute and proportional terms.

Recently historians of nutrition have attempted to measure the longer-term effects of food prices (not just those in dearth) throughout the century in more direct ways. Nutrition in youth determines adult stature, and stature is closely related to life expectancy (the tall being favoured). One approach has been through analysis of records of the heights of large groups of men, usually soldiers, to assess the changing incidence of want, and to make international comparisons. The findings to date suggest that England in the eighteenth century was indeed distinctive in the adequacy of its nutrition, compared both to earlier and later centuries, and to France. That fact had significant implications for population growth, for health, and for economic productivity.

We have mentioned that England had escaped the classic subsistence crisis: with the possible exception of the late 1720s, famine-related mortality disappeared by the second quarter of the seventeenth century.[2] In any case, it appears that in early-modern times such crises probably accounted for no more than 10 per cent of normal mortality, and price fluctuations in general for no more than 16 per cent of deaths (although they had much greater impact on marriage and fertility rates). Price-shifts and dearth created very significant problems for the authorities, in terms of public order, and probably much suffering in specific localities. But the general impact of all price fluctuations on the death rate in England was minimal after 1640, and apparently nil after the mid-eighteenth century; famine mortality ended even earlier, as we have seen. However, it has also been suggested that the real significance of high food prices was that they exacerbated the chronic malnutrition of the poor.

The current best estimates suggest that toward the end of the eighteenth century the top fifth of the English population, landlords and wealthy farmers and professionals and merchants, enjoyed on average twice the caloric intake in food that was obtained by the bottom fifth of the population. The diet of the rich was not always a healthy

Harvests and Dearth

one (they often consumed too much meat and alcohol, not enough fruit and vegetables), but their poorest fellow-citizens had one much worse. That poorest 20 per cent had an average food intake of less than 2,000 calories a day, providing enough energy for only six hours of light work, or one hour of heavy labour. Early death was an inevitable result. Endemic disease not only caused malnutrition (disease makes large claims on diets), but was itself caused by the fact that diet was poor. And susceptibility to disease was the trigger for high mortality rates among the poor.

The causal relationships, however, are very difficult to disentangle in practice, particularly in trying to explain patterns of mortality. The impact of crisis years on mortality in early-modern England was largely due to the increase of infectious disease, and it may be the case that most of the effect arose from migration in search of work and bread. Introducing disease into populations without developed immunities increased the death rate, often in places distant from the dearth which drove the original migration. Thus London had high death rates in the late seventeenth and early eighteenth century among people aged 20–39, among whom would be found many migrants from rural areas without immunological protection. Such a mechanism may also explain why death rates often lag price-rises by a year or so. If migration played such a large role in disease, the control of internal migration in years of dearth through enforcement of the laws of settlement (described below), as well as poor relief itself, must have kept death rates from disease lower than they would otherwise have been.

Comparisons with France help us to see the distinctiveness of English experience. There the national average caloric intake was less than in England, and in the bottom 50 per cent of the population, especially in the bottom 20 per cent, much lower. Similar deprivation, it has been suggested, would have existed in England also if the authorities there had not been as responsive to food riots and other disorder as they were, regulating internal and export markets in times of dearth. Poor relief also was sufficiently sustained in the last quarter of the eighteenth century, the period of greatest price-rises, that malnutrition was much rarer in England than in France, where state poor relief was exiguous. (The relative contribution of each of these state policies is unclear, in part because regulation of markets and the provision of poor relief was so local a matter in the eighteenth century.) It has also been suggested that the high degree of market integration and urbanization in England led to greater mobility, and over time, a higher degree of auto-immunization from disease at an early age. To these differences is attributed the fact that French mortality rates were about 40 per cent higher than the English at the end of the eighteenth century.

Policy and practice of the poor law

If the greater generosity of English poor relief helps in part to explain the apparently better nutrition of England compared to France, it is none the less clear that the amount and kind of relief in England changed significantly, both over the century as a whole and in individual years. It also had a great range of variation in practice, although administered under a common body of law. This was because the statutory regulations governing the poor law were often framed in very general terms, allowing parish officers a good deal of discretion over the implementation of welfare policies in their own neighbourhoods; subject, of course, to the disposition of the ratepayers who financed them and to appeals to the bench concerning entitlements. Only after 1795, when the propertied classes became increasingly concerned about rural order, pauperism, and the cost of welfare, did the magistracy assume a strikingly interventionist role in the administration of relief, monitoring the rates, approving the overseers, and prescribing by standing order the modes of relief to be followed in the parishes under their jurisdiction.

Poor-law provision was not universal in the eighteenth century. It only applied to those who could establish a legal settlement in an English or Welsh parish. Throughout much of the seventeenth century such an entitlement could be established by birth or residence but after 1691 such entitlements were severely restricted in favour of those derived by merit, whether paying the rates, serving a parish office, or making some definable contribution to the local economy. In recognition of the increasing mobility of English society, workers were encouraged to establish their own as opposed to their 'native' settlement by serving an apprenticeship or a full year's service in husbandry or domestic service. If they did not gain a settlement in this manner, they held the settlement of their parents, grandparents, or (if they were married females) their husbands. After 1691 only illegitimate children could gain a settlement by birthright, a state of affairs that placed their fragile lives in jeopardy, since parish officers were often vigilant in removing unwed pregnant women from their jurisdictions, imperilling illegitimate births in the process.

Whether the Settlement Acts discouraged large numbers of poor people from seeking relief is an issue much debated among historians. Local studies for the later eighteenth century suggest that perhaps a quarter of all household heads had settlements elsewhere. In view of the localized nature of many labour-markets, this may not have been a serious inhibition; but where removal would have seriously uprooted a family, it almost certainly was. Families sometimes safeguarded themselves against such a removal by obtaining certificates from their home parishes testifying to their willingness to provide relief elsewhere. Such certificates can be found in some London parish records for the mid-century decades, and in Norwich later still. It is far from clear how extensive such practices were, and the ubiquity of begging in many urban areas suggests that many long-distance migrants resorted to casual charity when their meagre resources had been depleted. In these circumstances poor people were extremely vulnerable to the charge of vagrancy, the laws against which could expedite their removal with more facility than those of the poor law. In London, where perhaps 8,000–10,000 migrants flocked each year, as many as 800–1,000 were shipped out again in the wagons of hired contractors.

The Settlement Acts did have an inhibiting effect on poor-law applications. So, too, could the stigmas and disciplinary codes of pauperism. Recipients of relief were sometimes 'badged'; that is, forced to wear signs of their dependent status upon their clothing. Under the Workhouse Act of 1723, the parish authorities were enjoined to deny relief to any applicant who refused to submit to the regimen of workhouse discipline. By the 1770s nearly 2,000 workhouses were institutionally available for this 'test', and although it was neither universally nor persistently enforced, it probably did deter some applicants from applying for relief. Despite the adequate provisions that existed in many workhouses, inmates were 'tasked' and idlers were refused food or subjected to a diet of bread and water. More serious offences could even lead to a day's solitary confinement, while at the Romford workhouse in Essex, those found guilty of profanity were ordered to stand on a stool all day, wearing a statement of their crime. 'Pride, though it ill become poor folk, won't suffer some to wear the badge,' observed one commentator; 'others cannot brook confinement; and the third sort deem the workhouse a mere state of slavery.'³

Parish officials were also empowered under the founding Elizabethan statutes to set the able-bodied poor to work, whether in workhouses or in the neighbourhood, where they might be employed in farm service, local manufacture, or in mending roads. To what extent such practices were implemented is difficult to determine. Unemployed labourers in the rural south were certainly given rate-assisted employment akin to the 'roundsman system' of the nineteenth century; the unemployed in Norwich repaired roads; while in Essex, the majority of workhouses were situated in the textile areas where inmates could earn money spinning. Parishes were often quite assiduous in apprenticing young paupers, whether to local employers or, in the case of some London parishes, to factory masters in the north; often, as the Chelsea workhouse records reveal, until they reached the age of 21. Nineteenth-century reformers often argued that the injunction to set the poor to work was bypassed in the eighteenth century, but they underestimated the extent to which it was attempted, not simply for profit, but to inculcate industrious habits among the poor.

Even so, parish officials encountered difficulties in finding work for the able-bodied, not only because their numbers tended to swell in periods of substantial unemployment, but because the changing location and concentration of industry over time tended to undercut employment opportunities in many areas. This was true in Essex, where the decline in the textile industry and in other industrial by-employments had by the end of the century reduced the workhouses to refuges of the old, the chronically ill, and the helpless. In these situations parish overseers had increasing resort to direct outdoor relief. Such relief was traditionally of two kinds. In the first instance money was disbursed for the provision of regular 'pensions' to select inhabitants, particularly to the aged as a form of income supplement. Second, occasional payments were made to a wider range of poor people to pay their rent, to supply them with fuel or clothing, or to help them over a period of sickness or unemployment. Precisely how many people availed themselves of these benefits is difficult to determine with any precision, at least before the early nineteenth century, but local studies suggest that the regular pensioners probably encompassed 2–10 per cent of their respective parish populations, the median range being 4–6 per cent. Occasional relief took in a wider segment of the population, including many able-bodied adults. In the rural hundred of Carhampton roughly a quarter of all adult males received some relief in 1771. In the Somersetshire town of Bridgwater 16 per cent of the adult population were on the parish payroll in the mid-1780s. By the turn of the century a similar proportion of the total population was provided with some form of poor-law assistance, rising to 20 per cent in the aftermath of the Napoleonic Wars.

Poor-law relief was not, then, an insubstantial feature of the lives of the poor. It could tide families over a difficult period, aid the recovery of principal breadwinners, ward off total destitution in cases of family breakdown, and provide a rudimentary health service for those without other resources. Because it was useful in emergencies, poor-law relief was often defended as a birthright of English men and women despite the niggardly and discretionary manner in which it was often administered. However, it is also important to recognize first that this entitlement was part of a regulatory code that was designed to inculcate habits of industry and prudence in the poor, to teach and exhort them to labour, and second that the exercise of this entitlement was in practice hedged by conditions that facilitated the organization of the labour supply in the interests of local industry. Occasional relief was sometimes seemingly generous because it was necessary to retain labour for highly seasonal tasks. Such appears to have been the case in the arable areas of East Anglia. Settlement laws were sometimes used to monitor the flow of labour to specific areas. In 1789 Matthew Boulton recommended that in Birmingham

every person Male or Female of bad or doubtful Character should be examined and sent to their own Parish which ought to be done even if they are Manufacturing Workmen as I am persuaded the trade of this Town during the approaching Winter will not be Sufficient to employ all the Legal and orderly inhabitants & consequently can't be injured by the expulsion of abandoned, idle & disorderly persons to their own Legal Settlements.[4]

This policy was put into effect in Handsworth in 1794, when trade was depressed and many hands were unemployed. To many workmen of the area, whose right to residence had not been questioned in a time of high employment, this was a flagrant abrogation of the paternalist obligations of a leading Midlands employer. As one broadsheet scornfully declared: 'there is too much truth in the assertion . . . that it is often more difficult for a poor man to pass the artificial boundary of a parish than an arm of the sea, or a ridge of high mountains.'[5]

Conclusion

However important poor relief was in preventing starvation or immiseration, the standard of living of the English poor rested to a far greater extent on the economic policies and social practices that regulated markets in foodstuffs and labour, and access to land. Hunger and malnutrition were biological issues that in fact were socially constructed, not only through the poor law, but by all the institutions, laws, and interests that created and sustained structured inequality in English society.

The eighteenth-century English working and indigent poor had not escaped the effects of malnutrition on their stature and health, although they were better off than the French, but until the very end of the century periodic dearths did not appear to threaten the security of the political and social regime. The great hunger of 1800–1 was perceived as such a threat. Why that should be the case has as much to do with government policy as it has to do with harvests, hunger, and disease. It has been argued that in the entire period since 1500 there was never an absolute shortage of food in England that made famine inevitable. Famine then, as now, arose from unequal distribution of entitlements to food and other necessary goods. The poor law was undoubtedly important to many people. Poor relief was crucial because relief was not likely to come from kin. The nuclear household had been characteristic of England for centuries, and low densities of kin nearby meant that relief had to be sought largely from the local community, or from the state.

However, famine came to stalk wartime England at the end of the century in part because of the consequences of a massive restructuring of other entitlements of a large part of the population: to land, to work, and to regulated markets. The effects went far beyond the issues of dearth, poverty, and nutrition. We must first examine the extent and importance of those entitlements, embedded in custom, before we can assess the effects of their erosion, and ultimate destruction.

6 Custom

Custom and customary law

'Custom' was a protean word in early-modern England. It had always had one of its modern connotations, that of the mores of a people, but its derivative older meanings still had far greater resonance. For lawyers, ancient popular custom was the origin of the common law. It had been refined by the judges into the custom of the whole country that was recognized in the courts, but both lawyers and gentlemen believed that its origin, and legitimacy, rested on the practice of the people.

There were a few large local exceptions to the common law, such as inheritance customs in Kent and in certain towns, where the common-law rule of inheritance by the eldest son might be displaced by equal partition among sons (gavelkind in Kent) or inheritance by the youngest son (borough English). Those two exceptions were in fact important instances of a plethora of local customs with the force of law. They were arguably more significant to more people than much of the common law, and defined rights and duties for a great many people. In thousands of manors, the practice of common-field agriculture and the inheritance of copy-hold land was largely determined by custom. In dozens of trades it helped sustain apprenticeship, payment obligations, and other practices around which men and women organized their lives and their livelihoods. Custom also maintained the existence and tolls of many urban and county markets; it determined who could elect Members of Parliament in many boroughs throughout the country; it defined participation in local government in thousands of parish vestries. Custom, in all these instances, had the force of law, or at least it did if (when it was questioned in a court) the judges decided that it did. They asked whether the particular or local custom in question could be accommodated within the larger principles of the common law although it differed from it, and whether it could be shown to have existed for a very long time. In this chapter we give more detailed examples of custom as both law and social practice, but we should also consider the ways in which custom informed general understanding. For the stability of the social order, whether one was a gentleman or a labourer or the widow of a copyholder, seemed in large measure to depend upon its observance.

In the first half of the eighteenth century the legal definitions of custom still coexisted with popular practice in a rich and complicated symbiosis. The fact that law recognized custom helped extend a more generalized legitimacy to any practice that could be convincingly presented as customary. Customary law also helped sustain the idea that relative social status, influence, or power, and even the standard of living enjoyed by those in a particular trade, was sanctioned by time and by usage. What had been claimed or practised in the past was what should be recognized and enforced in the present and future. Such claims of right had political as well as legal and social roots. In short, custom had many of the resonances that came at the end of the century to be struck by the word 'rights'. The early-modern political élite was to be very suspicious of the demotic use of rights speech when it spread widely in the 1790s. In contrast, they were comfortable with the idiom of custom, at least until the mid-eighteenth century.

The aristocracy and gentry had a particular interest in social stability in the widest sense. The taste came from the recurrent fear of any élite that its privileges and status are in danger, and the eighteenth-century aristocracy could never forget that the House of Lords had been abolished, and their cousin the King beheaded, a few generations before (see Ch. 4). Moreover, the gentry, however much they benefited from the parliamentary settlement of the late seventeenth century and the rising land values of the later eighteenth century, were constantly suspicious of financial capital, particularly that of London, and its possible alignment with administration. This was not only an important argument about civic virtue; it was also a moral critique of moneylending, market practices, and finance. Those attitudes were sharply reinforced by the experience of the South Sea Bubble in the 1720s, when a speculative boom in stocks (the first in English history) was followed inevitably by a crash which affected parliamentary opinion for a century. In contrast, landed wealth was held to be, by its very nature, stable, responsible, independent: on a higher moral plane.

That taste for social stability, the constant invocation among the gentry in particular of a better England where the values of county society would prevail, was inseparable from the lessons learned daily by the experience of government, of rule. Both the political élite, in cabinet and in the House of Lords, and the gentry, whether in Parliament or sitting as JPs, were acutely aware of the potential for social and political disaster should religion, want, or disaffection lead to popular disorder. Both the security of the regime and that of the existing social order demanded stability—of expectations, of standards of living, of relative social standing; that is, of customary practice, in a social, rather than a legal, sense.

The result was a dense network of legislation, as well as social practice and common law, that used the sanction of past practice as either legitimation or example. The first two instances mentioned above, manorial custom and the custom of trades, are good examples of this interpenetration of practice, belief, government, and law.

Manorial custom

The manorial custom of each group of parishes was unique. In a common-field village in the Midlands, or an upland manor in the north of England, and in a thousand other places, manorial custom defined both common rights and copyhold privileges for landholders of all social classes. The most important common right, common of pasture, was of critical importance to common-field agriculture, defining which animals, how many, and where, could take 'bite of mouth' on the open fields after harvest (see Fig. 9). The ownership of commonable freehold or copyhold land conferred such rights, but so too did occupation of ancient cottages. A number of other property rights, of less central significance to agriculture but often of great importance in household economies, usually lay over the same lands. The right to take turves or wood from the wasteland; rights to fish, gather acorns, and mast for pigs; or to take sand or gravel from the common, might all be matters defined by local custom. Who could take what, when, and where, were inscribed in immemorial practice. Sometimes that practice was written down in a custumal (the product of real or collusive litigation in the past); often it could be evidenced only by the testimony of aged men. The maintenance of such collective memory was a serious matter, for if custom was to be recognized as law, if it should be challenged, it was critical that accurate and convincing oral testimony be given in court. Children were taken on the annual perambulations of the parish, and sometimes doused in streams or sat bare-bottomed on boundary stones to help fix their memories of the limits within which local custom was observed, should it be called in question decades hence.

But customary law was not remembered only on the rare occasions when commoners, or a manorial lord, engaged in litigation. It was constantly enforced by the decisions of the homage, or jury, of freeholders and copyholders in the local manorial court. They settled disputes, made bylaws about the maintenance of the fields and common pastures, protected them from overstocking, fined transgressors, and supervised a small bureaucracy of pinders, fieldsmen, even mole-catchers. In short, the particular common rights that particular local custom defined were also subject to continuous enforcement, in all their differing specificity, in thousands of parishes, every day.

Beyond common of pasture and the other common rights already mentioned, most of which were found in almost all common-field villages, were a variety of claims recognized in only some places. Customs existed allowing the burning of furze for ashes, or even (some commoners claimed) the taking of game. In many more, the right to glean the harvested fields for fallen grain was maintained for the women and children of the labourers and the poor. Gleaning was often closely regulated: the parish church-bells were rung in many places when the fields were opened, ensuring that none of those qualified by local custom had an unfair advantage over others equally qualified. The sanction of religious precept was perhaps particularly strong with respect to gleaning customs: 'And when ye reap the harvest of your land, thou shalt not make clean riddance of the corners of thy field when thou reapest, neither shalt thou gather any gleaning of thy harvest; thou shalt leave them unto the poor, and to the stranger: I am the Lord your God' (Leviticus 23: 22). In other respects too, Church ritual still surrounded local custom and further sanctioned it. On Rogation Sunday (the fifth Sunday after Easter Day), the parish priest led the entire parish, in many places, on a beating of bounds, delineating the limits of the community and its customary law.

Local manorial custom also defined the inheritance and other rights of that large number of customary tenants who held copyhold land, a tenure which in some places was almost as secure as freehold, but which varied widely. Whether and how the widow or children of a copyholder could retain a dead man's holding; how much the lord of the manor had to be paid to enter a tenancy; whether a widow who remarried continued to have rights over the holding; how many lives a tenancy might endure: these and other important aspects of copyhold varied from manor to manor. All were defined by the local manorial custom. Copyhold land was held by large proprietors and by small, and like freehold land it had, in common-field villages, coincident common rights upon it.

The law of the manor thus had vivid meaning and substantial implications for the value of property. Where the village remained unenclosed, it was a law given daily expression in the activities of the fieldsmen, the practice of farming, as well as in the periodic meetings of the manorial court and the decisions of its homage. Moreover it had been unequivocally recognized in both high court decisions and government initiatives in earlier centuries. A large mass of case law dealt with particular customs in particular manors: whether commoners had the right to self-help in ending a nuisance created by the lord, such as extensive rabbit warrens; how the right of a widow of a copyholder, her right of 'free bench', was to be construed in this manor or that; whether the lord could enclose coppices and hence take land from commoners. There were a host of such issues. In the past, in the late sixteenth and early seventeenth centuries, for example, it had been clear government policy to defend the interests of commoners against aggressive lords of manors. The purpose had been to oppose enclosure, believed to lead to depopulation. Judgements sympathetic to that aim had set the stamp of the common law on local customs that agreed with the policy of the Tudor and Stuart state. The belief that the state and the courts would uphold the claims of commoners in a specific place might rest undisturbed for generations. Sometimes it was not justified. *Gatewards Case* (1607), for example, called into question all common rights claimed simply in the name of 'inhabitants', which were found in many manors. But often such distinctions were immaterial to local practice, until finally tested in the courts or abrogated by Parliament, as we shall see, in the eighteenth century.

The custom of trades

Within a great many trades there was a similar nexus of practice, government policy, and law, sustaining a popular view of customary right. Artisans and servants in husbandry alike found their contractual relations with employers defined largely by a body of venerable legislation, common law, and custom. Again a Tudor and Stuart inheritance provided a framework that was designed to ensure stability, obviate disorder, maintain local ties of dependency and loyalty. Wage-setting by justices, common after the Black Death, declined once the labour shortage of the fourteenth century had eased; by the fifteenth century it was in disuse, and a statute of Henry VIII exempted employers from compliance with JPs' assessments. But after 1540 inflation seemed to require, once again, state control over the demand for higher wages, by setting maximum rates. By the time of Elizabeth's reign, the government began with instructions to the JPs, but soon enacted comprehensive statutes. In the first few years of her reign her ministers and her Parliaments passed a framework of economic legislation that would last in many respects for hundreds of years. The Parliament of 1563 passed more such legislation than had ever been enacted in any session, including anti-enclosure legislation, reform of poor relief, licensing of middlemen in foodstuffs. Above all there was the Statute of Artificers, 5 Eliz. c. 4, the basic labour statute on which the English law of master and servant was henceforth to be elaborated.

The Statute of Artificers, in forty-four clauses, provided for the terms of contracts, the control of wages, the compulsory recruitment of labour where that was felt to be necessary, and the extension of the apprenticeship regulations found in many guilds to, nominally, the entire nation. It created three principal offences: giving excessive wages, receiving them, and refusing to work, and enacted the presumption of a yearly, renewable contract. Although some clauses had fallen into desuetude by the eighteenth century, the great statute still provided the wide framework within which most employment law in most trades was created. Apprenticeship requirements, wage-fixing, penalties against combination by men or masters, summary proceedings by servants for unpaid wages, summary imprisonment for servants who abandoned masters or neglected work, were all inscribed in supplemental legislation and by common law, and carried out on a regular basis by JPs throughout the country.

The Tudor and Stuart legislation had often been concerned to contain wages in periods of labour scarcity, and in labour's 'golden age' of high wages in the late seventeenth and early eighteenth centuries it is likely that much of the thrust of enforcement was in that direction. But there was also the ancient state and local government interest in preventing and controlling disorder (and the poor rates). Thus Parliament and high court judges were prepared to recognize and enforce the notion of a customary minimum wage in times of decaying trade, or even a higher minimum in times of dearth: legislation of 1603/4 provided for such *minima* in the textile trades. The law often sanctioned the claims of particular trades that the number of apprentices should be limited, a claim of crucial importance to skilled workers anxious to prevent an influx of the unskilled. High court judges sometimes stated that combinations among masters were as nefarious or more so than conspiracies among workmen, although they did not imprison the former as often as the latter. And as late as 1773, Parliament enacted legislation giving justices in quarter sessions power to set prices for silk-weaving in Spitalfields, and forbidding weavers to have more than two apprentices at one time. Much ancient legislation forbidding the use of machinery was still extant. Thus cloth-dressers in the textile industry claimed that 5 & 6 Edward VI, c. 22, 'An Act for the Putting Down of Gig Mills' made the eighteenth-century gig mill illegal. (The clothiers disagreed.)

At the lowest judicial level, JPs in many counties still made orders for wage rates in some years in the first half of the eighteenth century, including minimum rates in times of dearth. They also apparently enforced wage orders against masters much more often than they punished errant workers by imprisonment. Country gentlemen justices, living on their rents, still played an important mediating role in the eighteenth century. They maintained an appropriate social distance from farmers and ironmasters and other direct employers of most labour. They judged and enforced the claims of workers as well as employers, often seeing themselves

as disinterested enforcers of wider social peace, and as vigilant overseers of labour and other markets whose eructations could disorder
the body politic. Parliament held that mediating role to be important, and much legislation for trades required that the adjudicating
justice not be in the trade himself. Labour, particularly artisanal
labour, thus found powerful legitimation for some of its demands
that customary expectations of a secure standard of living, in a
constant relation to that of other trades and occupations, should
be maintained.

Thus the custom of the trade—with respect to wage levels, numbers of apprentices, hours of work, perquisites, and holidays—was
embedded in a set of expectations recognized, at least in many
instances, by Parliament and the courts. The central common law
courts in Westminster Hall often heard cases in which testimony
about the custom of the trade was crucial to the outcome. And Parliament, still occasionally enacting legislation that enshrined claims
of a particular trade in statute, also apparently approved much
older claims. It did so through inanition, by not touching the
scores of Tudor and Stuart Acts that defined the prerogatives and
claims of particular trades. Among woolcombers, shearmen, hatters,
leatherworkers, weavers, and in many other trades, the archaic
language of unrepealed Tudor and Stuart legislation conferred
protections sanctioned by both law and the custom of the trade.
In the words of West Country weavers, fighting an attempt in
1718 to lengthen the cloth-piece by half a yard, the old measure was
sanctioned by 'law, usage and custom from time immemorial'.[1]

Many aspects of what the trades called 'custom' were of course
claims, encroachments, negotiating positions, between employers
and workers, masters and servants, or members of different trades.
An illustration is one issue of significance throughout the eighteenth century: that of perquisites. The appropriation of some part
of raw materials, or of the finished goods, was common, widespread, and often denominated 'customary'. Braziers took 'filings',
textile workers took 'fents and thrums', shipwrights took 'chips'.
(The latter could be so large, and valuable, that for a long time
Deptford shipwrights refused to relinquish them for wage-increases.)
What was considered a perquisite could be considered theft by an
employer, and repeated legislation in the eighteenth century changed
the penalty structure for successful prosecutions from restitution

with gaol as an option, to simple gaol. The existence of extensive opportunities for resale in manufacturing areas meant that it was easy to realize the value of appropriated raw materials, and often hard to prosecute. In the Yorkshire textile industry, a government subsidy supported a private policing system designed to curb such embezzlement (the employers' term) (see also Ch. 8).

However, the claim that such takings were in fact part of custom often had much weight. Masters and servants might disagree about what constituted a proper taking, but employers often tolerated, or even openly condoned, the practice. It was an economy short of coin, where payment in kind ramified through domestic service and some trades, particularly in times of trade depression. And in periods of economic growth, particularly in skilled trades, employers bound with others in wage-fixing agreements could attempt to attract others' employees, and retain their own, by allowing takings to supplement the fixed wage rate. The fact that formalized money wage rates persisted in trades for many decades tended also to confirm the belief among workers that appropriations became entitlements after a particular period of time. The fact that in some occupations there was an undoubted right to fixed quantities (colliers taking coal, for example), tended to generate similar claims about less certain practices in other trades. Custom was the validating idea called in defence when employers tried to cut back on appropriation in times of bad trade, just as it was called on when attacks were made on customary rates of wages.

The custom of trades was different from manorial custom in that much of it rested, at one point or another, on legislation, as well as upon recognition in the common-law courts and in daily practice. This combination probably gave particular force to the claims of artisans, at least in their own minds. In this respect, and in some other important ways, trade custom strongly resembled a third great inheritance from the medieval and Tudor and Stuart state: the marketing laws.

The custom of markets

The medieval and early-modern state had good reason to fear dearths, as we have seen. They generated vagrancy, rebellions, and disorder, and the fear always existed that such social disasters might coincide with external threats to the stability of the regime.

The consequence was a highly visible body of legislation and administrative activity for the overseeing of markets, imbedded in local practice. Much of it was designed to ensure that the poor, the ordinary consumer, had first access to food markets, particularly in times of dearth, before large buyers swept them clean. Bells might be rung to do this; but laws could also be invoked. The fear of profiteering middlemen who raised prices to their own advantage, starving the poor, had deep roots in medieval law and practice. In the eighteenth century the most important statute was still 5 & 6 Edward VI, c. 14, which defined the offences which were also held to be criminal at common law. Forestalling (buying foodstuffs before they came to open market), regrating (buying and selling again for a profit in the same market or one nearby), and engrossing (buying large quantities for resale) were all misdemeanours, punishable by fine and imprisonment. A great number of other statutes, enacted over the course of five centuries, regulated particular markets. Thus an Act of 15 Charles II punished the regrating of cattle, and another of 31 George II forbade forestalling them on the road to London. All such practices were believed, until about the middle of the eighteenth century, to enhance prices, particularly in times of dearth. In the words of a statute of Edward I, repeated by Sir Edward Coke in the seventeenth century, and cited often in the eighteenth century, a forestaller was '*Pauperum Depressor & totius Communitatis & Patriae publicus inimicus* . . . a Depressor of the Poor, and a publick Enemy of the whole Community and to his Country'.[2]

These specifically criminal offences existed within a wider body of legislation that governed badgers and hawkers, allowed the government to halt exports of grain during dearth (and provide bounties for exports otherwise), regulated weights and measures, set the price of the standard loaf of bread and regulated bakers in other ways, and later in the century generated weekly reports of the prices of the principal grains in all the markets throughout the country. An administrative structure to survey markets and detect market criminals reached its apogee in the first forty years of the seventeenth century, when the government codified such matters in the Book of Orders, and the Privy Council spurred local justices into action. They were enjoined to search out hoarded supplies, prosecute the criminal farmers or bakers or factors, and bring the supplies to open market for the ordinary consumer. By the early eighteenth century that kind of national direction from London lay almost a century in the past, like so many other aspects of the centralized state. But prosecutions continued in local markets in years of high prices and dearth. Sometimes they were by informers, who took part of the penalty; sometimes they were on indictment at the instance of magistrates or private prosecutors. Such criminal charges were not numerous, but like most of the criminal law they were intended to be exemplary.

The connections this body of law had with custom, and beliefs about custom, were broadly twofold. In the first place, the laws for the protection of consumers, including the criminal penalties against profiteering middlemen, were held by the judges to exist at common law as well as by statute. Thus profiting by dealing in foodstuffs in ways that exploited the consumer was held to be an offence, or rather a variety of offences, by the custom of all England, recognized in the royal courts. Secondly, the laws were enforced in the eighteenth century with a strong element of popular participation, in which local expectations of what should be done came to have almost customary status. We now know a great deal about the eighteenth-century food riot, and it appears most often to be a more-or-less orderly demand by consumers (often groups of miners or other industrial workers, often women and boys) that local magistrates enforce the law (see Ch. 9). The ritualistic aspects of these demands, the clear sense of right that informed rioters, and the capitulation, acquiesence, or active support of JPs, conferred on the food riot something of the status of a legitimate statement of grievances. It was not custom in the sense of manorial custom and it was less specific than the custom of a trade, but it shared with both a set of expectations that informed custom in the broadest sense. It was rooted in law; it constrained market forces when they threatened the poor; it was often inscribed in ritual; it defined the entitlements and the expected behaviour of people at all social levels, from the poorest labourer to the richest local landowner.

It has been suggested, too, that the marketing laws were effective. Certainly that was the belief of contemporaries, at least before mid-century. It was also the belief of governments, that at least invoking the marketing laws in times of dearth could do no harm,

if only to placate the mob. As late as the riots of 1766, royal proclamations denounced profiteering middlemen, and encouraged
prosecutions. The ancient belief that the criminal law could be so
used to control the worst effects of dearth, the artificial rise of
prices that was held to be the consequence of speculative dealing,
may have had a grounding in fact. One recent assessment of the
price variability in English grain-markets from the sixteenth to the
nineteenth centuries shows that the period between 1600 and
1640, when the marketing laws were most rigorously enforced, was
also the period when price fluctuations were least pronounced. As
the early Stuart administrative apparatus collapsed, price-variability
increased, but was still held in check by the local activities of magistrates, encouraged by the mob. The suggestion is that perhaps
England escaped the recurrent danger of famine sometime in the
early seventeenth century precisely because of government surveillance of markets (see Ch. 5). Certainly that was the belief of the
eighteenth-century poor, of many country gentlemen, of some
judges, and perhaps of the King. Indeed, the established meaning
of 'police' until late in the eighteenth century was the effective
governance of towns, and especially the policies that ensured food
supplies and good order.

Custom: The foundation of property and order

Custom, then, seemed both part of a natural social order, and a
guarantee of collective wellbeing. Those beliefs were perhaps reinforced to an unusual extent by the relative demographic stagnation, good harvests, and political instability of the early decades
of the century. Governments had a strong interest in meeting economic discontent in a period of sharp political conflict; a relatively
stable economic environment and high wages made the notion of
customary standards and wage controls in trades appealing, and
the relative absence of harvest crises meant that the possibly contradictory demands on markets in foodstuffs (the need for middlemen to supply London, for example) were muted. At the same time,
the vast range of rights based on custom, or what was claimed to
be custom, elsewhere in the society—to be an elector, to be a member of a vestry, to inherit land in Kent, to hold a market or fair,
to take fees as an official—sustained the notion that a customary right was in some sense a property right, particularly where it

had received some recognition, in legislation or in the courts, as ancient. Thus the porters of London who claimed customary rights to spillage could point to the customs officers who made similar claims in their own work. In the central common-law courts, the rights of clerks and other officials to take fees were notionally fixed, but often slowly escalated over decades; they were none the less jealously preserved as property rights (and bought out in the nineteenth century). The notion of immemorial or ancient property rights, whether invoked by cottagers or shearmen, copyholders or weavers, was also resonant with constitutional claims: the ancient constitution, resting on rights and custom and usage. A political élite whose entire political philosophy was cast in such currency found it entirely natural to accept the claims of peasants and artisans couched in similar terms, at least as late as the 1750s.

But between the middle of the eighteenth century and the end of the French wars a massive delegitimation of the claims of popular custom, and an élite accommodation with a quite different set of legitimating notions, took place. In the process manorial custom was in large measure obliterated; skilled trades' claims to the protection of the law were laughed out of court; the notion that the state had a censorial and supervisory role in markets for labour and commodities was almost entirely set aside. The result, in the economic and demographic circumstances characteristic of these decades, was a great alteration in social relations, in relative inequality, and in the tropes of social legitimation.

7 The Disruption of Custom, the Triumph of Law

Introduction

I am extremely sorry that any one in the House of Commons should be found so ignorant and unadvised, as to wish to revive the senseless, barbarous and, in fact, wicked regulations made against the free trade in matter of provision, which the good sense of late Parliaments had removed. . . . But however I console myself on this point by considering that it is not the only breach by which barbarism is entering upon us.[1]

Edmund Burke need not have worried: Parliament did not repudiate free markets in food in 1797, nor even in the great dearth at the turn of the century. Burke's view had become the view of Parliament: that food rioters and paternalist country magistrates were misguided, foolish, ignorant, and dangerous. Indeed his language is characteristic. The legitimacy of many popular customs and claims, most of them rooted in ancient law and practice, came to be redefined in élite discourse as usurpation, archaic ignorance, immorality, even criminality. The process took a long time, but from the 1760s it becomes evident, accelerating through the next two decades (with some hesitations). By the critical period of the wars with Revolutionary and Napoleonic France (1793 to 1815), political power, economic change, and new ideas were rapidly reshaping much of the law, the temper of social relations, and the way in which the English viewed their society and the world. Practices and institutions long sanctioned by custom and law yielded to theories of political economists and to majorities in Parliament. At the same time a number of technological innovations transformed crucial industries; population expansion favoured capital rather than labour. Finally, there grew the conviction at the heart of central government that heavy policing (in the widest sense) could contain the public disorder that the Tudors and Stuarts had believed required state intervention in the markets for food and labour and land.

To choose precise terminal dates for such large changes is misleading, but some benchmarks in the processes described in this chapter show how wide-reaching was the shift of law, social practice, and ideology in half a century. In each of the following cases, popular belief and custom was supported early in the century by élite law and political practice; by the end of the century the relationship was broken.

1. Prosecutions for profiteering in food were last encouraged by the government in the great food riots of 1766; in 1772 Parliament repealed most of the legislation (led by Burke), and in spite of some doubts by the judges, by 1802 the threat of such prosecutions was over: food markets were to be largely unregulated.

2. Among rural masters and servants early in the century, the custom of living-in was still common, a social relationship that mirrored the ancient expectations of mutuality enshrined in the law and practice of the annual hiring. By mid-century living-in service was beginning to decline, as farmers increasingly hired men for short periods that limited their obligations under the old laws, and by the end of our period the courts emphasized the master's authority rather than mutuality.

3. Wage-fixing (of maximum, and sometimes minimum, rates) by magistrates, a power under the Statute of Artificers, fell into desuetude by mid-century, when labour began to be in oversupply; wage-fixing was re-established in the woollen trade in 1756, only to be repealed the following year, and when working people tried to invoke the Statute of Artificers in 1814 to help set minimum wages, the judges declared the justices' power discretionary. In 1815 Parliament repealed that part of the statute.

4. Apprenticeship regulations, the charter of rights for many skilled trades, provoked criticism from the Chief Justice in 1756 (continuing a century-old development in the law), because they were still enforced in both law and custom, and he believed they offended the higher laws of political economy. They endured, however, until 1803, when Parliament suspended the requirements in the woollen trades. By 1814 the ancient apprenticeship requirements were abolished for all trades.

5. Common-field customs at mid-century were still extremely important. In some of the most populous counties of England over half the population still lived in parishes and towns with common fields, regulated by manorial custom recognized in the royal courts of justice. But by 1815 only a small minority followed the

ancient ways, Parliament having enacted 3,400 separate enclosure Acts in the previous sixty-five years, all of which eradicated common fields or manorial wastes, and the customs that defined and sustained them.

Let us consider some of these changes in the social significance of markets, labour, and land in more detail, starting with the last: land.

Lost commons and customs

Arguably the most important attack on the claims of custom as law was the passage of so many enclosure Acts in the last four decades of the eighteenth century. Such statutes set in train a legal process that led to the resurveying and reallocation of the land of a parish or group of parishes in a manor, substituting compact modern holdings for the pattern of medieval strips scattered through the common fields (see Fig. 9). But its most important legal and social consequence was the obliteration of the customary common rights of the manor. What had been law for over 500 years ceased to be so; the history of struggles, over generations, of commoners and lords to define their respective property rights in the common lands and wastelands of the parish passed from the realm of lived custom, lived law, lived tradition and struggle, to total irrelevance. That this transformation happened in thousands of parishes (usually the most populous) in the lifetime of a generation meant that the familiar modes of a regulation of life that was communal (although not democratic) were breached in a striking way.

Although many ancient common lands had already been enclosed by 1750 through purchase or local agreement by the owners, between that date and 1820 a great deal more was dealt with by Parliament. Some 30 per cent of agricultural land, representing perhaps half the arable, was the subject of enclosure Acts. Until then very large areas of highly productive counties, especially in the Midlands, but also in East Anglia, East and West Yorkshire, Derbyshire, Gloucestershire, and other areas still lay in common fields. The manors and parishes that were open tended to be populous ones, and they were many: at mid-century about three-quarters of the cultivable land in Northamptonshire or Oxfordshire was still farmed in common fields. Local resistance to enclosure ranged from petitioning sympathetic local gentry (more rarely Parliament, which supported enclosure overwhelmingly), through stubborn non-compliance and foot-dragging, to mob action. Riot and sabotage was more widespread than historians formerly believed. In Northampton-shire, one of the most heavily enclosed counties, the players in a feigned village football match at West Haddon abruptly turned to the new fences, tearing down and burning £2,000 worth. In Wel-lingborough unknown persons stole and destroyed the surveyor's books.

There was resistance in many places to enclosure of wastes also, where common rights over them had attracted settlement and their communal exploitation. In Wilbarston, once rioters were sub-dued, they were forced to unload the waggons of fencing that completed the enclosure, as cavalrymen watched over them. The planned enclosure of the large waste near Burton-on-Trent (Staf-fordshire) was abandoned in 1766 because nearby food riots alerted the enclosers to how many poor people were 'ripe for any sort of mischief'. In 1771 Bills to enclose the parishes were proceeding in Parliament; 'some of the lesser people murmur which is a com-mon case,' wrote the steward to the lord, 'but can be of no con-sequence here'. He was mistaken. By May some of the first rails and posts (erected before the Act had been passed) were pulled down, and in a second attack sixty women pulled down more fences on 24 May. They were committed to Burton gaol, only to be rescued by a mob of 300. The magistrates began to proceed with prosecu-tions under a recent statute making the offence punishable by transportation for seven years, but could find no informers. When more fencing was erected the following year, it too was pulled down and burned.[2]

But in the face of a parliament of landlords, and a government speaking through the Board of Agriculture, resistance was easily seen to be futile. At enclosure all common rights ceased to exist. The larger commoners were compensated in the allocation of land and made the transition to the new agricultural practices of prop-erty in severalty; the smaller ones were compensated but sold out in large numbers as the costs of the process of enclosure accen-tuated the economic losses caused by loss of access to commons and waste. The household economies of the smallest commoners, those with marginal rights perhaps recognized in local customary

practice but ignored by the enclosure commissioners, were dev-
astated. Indeed, it has been persuasively argued that because commons were exploited primarily by women, enclosure Acts were an
important cause of the proletarianization of female labour during
this period. For women and men, the experience helped fuel the
fires of rural class grievances well into the nineteenth century.

But the huge wave of parliamentary enclosure Acts after the
1760s had a very significant impact on parliamentary and legal
opinion as well, and here too the effect was the denigration of
custom. In the narrowly legal sense, as customary rights disappeared there was a severe pruning of the law that was recognized
in English courts. Copyhold land still existed, unaffected by enclosure, and the incidents of copyhold were similarly unaffected. But
the destruction of the customs of thousands of manors with respect to common land meant that a vast simplification had been
effected in the English legal system. Common right survived in a
few places, but almost as a legal curiosity. And Parliament, although
it did it in a piecemeal process that occupied a generation, had
none the less used legislation to impose an enormous social and
economic and legal and indeed geographic change on the face of
England.

It did so in the name of improvement, in the name of economic
efficiency. This was an immensely significant change of perspective. Lawyers and judges had always scorned much legislation as
intemperate interference with the common law, and Parliament
itself had shown little interest in general schemes of legislative
improvement, thinking more in terms of Private Members' Bills.
Public general Acts were mostly matters of taxation, the armed
forces, criminal law, and poor law. But the experience of passing
thousands of enclosure Acts generated both a parliamentary claim
that such statutes were justified as general social policy, and a parliamentary process, culminating in the attempt in 1800 to pass a
general enclosure Act, and, ultimately the vesting of supervision
of the process in the Board of Trade and then (in 1845) in a Board
of Enclosure Commissioners. In short, Parliament learned both to
repudiate custom and to embrace purposive legislation in dealing
with the oldest property rights in the country, and it did so in
the name of a putative economic efficiency.

The wave of parliamentary enclosure could not have taken place without a preceding shift in the gentry's attitude to land and labour, and that shift was important in preparing the way for changes in other realms of law and social practice. At the beginning of the eighteenth century, decades before the main body of enclosure Acts began to stream through Parliament, genteel opponents of enclosure had argued that commoning communities nurtured independent smallholders, men who made excellent soldiers and sailors as well as husbandmen. Enclosure, they argued, would reduce that population to people who were only wage labourers or paupers. The promoters of enclosure did not disagree. But they argued that wage labourers without land were precisely what was needed for both capitalist agriculture and capitalist industry.

Apprenticeship, masters and servants, and machinery

As we have seen in Chapter 6, the 'custom of the trade' was an amalgam of old statutes, usages, and social customs built around them that were mutually reinforcing; in some well-organized trades new regulations imposed by bargaining power also became part of 'customary' claims. Journeymen and smaller masters cherished the apprenticeship requirements above all: they were seen as their partial guarantee against an influx of unskilled men and women, or the crushing competitive advantage of new men with great capital. Both of course continually entered the trades, but 'illegal' men could be discouraged from the more skilled or better organized parts of many trades, and the fact that they could be prosecuted successfully under clauses of the Statute of Artificers added great moral weight to the other pressures that union and trade associations could bring. Thus the linen- and cotton-weavers of Oldham in Lancashire advertised against the 'vile' practice of 'introducing a number of unfair and illegal hands' into the trade in 1781, warning that those not following the requirements of the Statute of Artificers would not be considered 'legal' members of that trade.[3] The Act and the custom were the central focus of early trade-unionism, what contemporaries called 'combinations'.

In all this there was of course an ambivalence, a divided interest. For those not within a skilled trade, apprenticeship regulations, where enforced, were a hardship. For some radical democrats, they could also be seen as a mark of privilege. One remarked in 1794 that a widening of the franchise would ensure (among other enumerated benefits) that

a poor and industrious man might no longer be prevented from getting his living by the various inclusive Franchises, Privileges and Charters of different trades and corporations, shutting him out from exercising perhaps the only trade he is capable of, and perhaps from the only spot where he might hope for success.[4]

This division of interest was marked by language: there were (in the eyes of those claiming ancient legal privilege), 'honourable' and 'dishonourable' trades.

If a flood of poorer workers was a threat to skilled workers, so too were innovating master manufacturers, especially those with large capital. They were likely to try (as in the woollen trade) to take on large numbers of apprentices, or unapprenticed men: 'loom shops', with dozens or hundreds of looms, were feared and hated. Such capitalists were also increasingly likely to want to introduce machinery. The destruction of traditional livelihoods by machinery was of course an issue. The Tudor and Stuart state enacted some legislation that prohibited the use of new machinery. Thus skilled workers who dressed the nap of new cloth relied in some parts of the country on a statute of 1551: 'An Act for the Putting Down of Gig Mills' (5 & 6 Edward VI, c. 22), and gig mills were little used, and then only for coarse cloth. Weavers invoked a 1555 statute (2 & 3 Philip and Mary, c. 11) which limited the number of looms that one person could keep. The textile industries were, however, the locus of some of the most productive technical innovations in the late eighteenth century. Most marked in cotton, the new inventions also affected wool: scribbling-, carding-, spinning-, and shearing-machines were all elaborated or introduced. The shearing-frame developed in the 1780s and 1790s threatened the very existence of the shearmen, the most skilled and best-organized workers in the trade. In such circumstances demands centred on apprenticeship, wage rates, and other traditional claims, became even more important.

The whole detail of Tudor and Stuart legislation was never observed to the letter, even within the trades, but it was understood (and indeed most law is like this) as a set of guideposts to acceptable behaviour, enforced by occasional prosecutions when particular individuals seemed to threaten the security of other members of the trades. In short, it was unlikely to be enforced when trade was good, more likely to be called on when trade was poor. However, at all times it reinforced notions of stability: the expectation that those recognized in a calling should not be undercut by outsiders, whether they were poor unskilled labourers or Irish immigrants, on the one hand, or men with very large capitals who had new ideas about how to organize production and profit from it. There was not of course stability in fact in industrial production in the early eighteenth century: there were a great many strikes, riots arising out of industrial disputes, and interventions by Parliament in the form of legislation (see Chs. 8 and 9). However, in general the last reinforced the older assumptions: that there were legitimate claims of right, that public order had to be maintained, that the best way to do so was to balance the interests of skilled labour and capital. Hence Parliament continued to enact apprenticeship requirements for scattered trades into the eighteenth century, usually embedded in omnibus statutes that regulated the rights of masters, journeymen, and apprentices alike.

But it did so more and more rarely. For those who sat in Parliament were increasingly thinking in other terms: technical innovation, free markets, large-scale production. As with enclosure, economic efficiency was the usual justification for the cumulative attack on the Tudor and Stuart legal inheritance that affected, and protected, the working poor. Classical political economy from about mid-century became increasingly insistent that the Statute of Artificers and much of the legislation that invoked, supplemented, or explicated it (perhaps particularly the provisions of the settlement laws), was an unwarranted hindrance on the market in men and women's labour. Smith summarized the argument in *The Wealth of Nations* (1776), but here, as on so many other issues, he restated an increasingly widespread conviction. A parliamentary committee recommended wholesale repeal of the apprenticeship laws in 1751. Strikes in Lancashire and other areas in the crisis years of the late 1750s drew from Sir Michael Foster, who tried indictments for conspiracy against the strikers, the following observations:

If no man must either employ or be employed in any branch of trade but who have served a limited number of years to that branch, the particular trades will be lodged in few hands, to the damage of the public, and that

liberty of setting up trades, (the foundation of the present flourishing condition of Manchester) destroyed.

  In the infancy of trade the Acts of Queen Elizabeth might be well calculated for the public weal; but now, when it is grown to that perfction
we see it, it might perhaps be of utility to have those laws repealed, as
tending to cramp and tie down that knowledge it was at first necessary to
obtain by rule.[5]

The judges had indeed been cutting back the extent of apprenticeship requirements, in the interest of fighting wage demands
and other trade-union activity, since the mid-1600s. Parliament in
the eighteenth century was still prepared to enact some legislation
requiring apprenticeship and limiting numbers of apprentices (both
crucial demands of skilled trades), or governing wages, until the
1770s, although it was increasingly of two minds.

  In 1725 and 1726, for example, the Gloucestershire weavers
had obtained Acts providing for wage-fixing, and a statute of 1756,
providing further for wage-fixing, was Parliament's response to a
countywide weaver's union in Gloucestershire. But the clothiers
organized in turn, and got the Act repealed in 1757, making their
case very much in terms of free markets and political economy.
The Spitalfields Act of 1773, which gave the London silk-weavers
wage-fixing, regulation of the trade by magistrates and limitations
on the numbers of apprentices, among other protective clauses,
lasted much longer. It was coerced out of Parliament by widespread
riot and sabotage by the London silk-weavers (the largest group of
manufacturing workers in London, 14,000 in number) in the 1760s
and 1770s, and its enactment helped guarantee peace in the industry for half a century (see Ch. 9). But the Spitalfields Act was an
exception to the trend, an exception that perhaps only survived
as long as it did because of the danger of disorders in London.
(We shall see a similar sensitivity with respect to the London food
supply.) The real trend was shown as apprenticeship requirements
that dated from the seventeenth century in a number of trades
disappeared: the Dyers' Statute of 1662 and the Hatters' of 1603
were repealed in 1777; the framework-knitters were unsuccessful
in seeking new apprenticeship regulations in 1778–9; and the final
parliamentary triumph of political economy over apprenticeship
took place between 1803 and 1814, when the demands of the
woollen workers and then all workers were repudiated.

The circumstances of that event reveal much about why this break with past tradition was such a decisive one. Part of the context was economic crisis in a number of trades, as skilled workers became anxious to protect their standard of living from an influx of unskilled labour, seemingly inexhaustible in supply, from Ireland, from disbanded soldiers, and from dispossessed cottagers from the agricultural sector. The great dearths at the end of the century increased such determination. On the other side, Parliament came to the conclusion that legal inhibitions on free movement of labour should be ended. The final parliamentary assault on the old law, as we have seen, occurred during and immediately after the war with Napoleonic France. The regulations on the woollen trade were suspended from 1803 to 1808, and repealed in 1809. So too were the anti-machinery provisions in the ancient statute book: for example, the 1551 Act against gig mills, also suspended in 1803 and then repealed by the Woollen Act of 1809. The apprenticeship clauses of the Statute of Artificers were repealed for all trades in 1814.

The origins of Parliament's change of attitude can be seen in the industrial struggles in woollens and worsteds, the most important of the textile industries throughout the century. The cloth-dressers, both in Yorkshire and the West Country, the two main centres of the woollen trade, tried to use the law, but also used strikes and machine-breaking, as gig mills were extended in use and the new shearing-frames appeared in the second half of the eighteenth century. Riots and other protest against machinery in the textile trades had always been part of industrial relations, and as a wide range of new machines were introduced they became more common. There were major riots and destruction of machinery in different parts of the country in at least eleven of the thirty-five years between 1767 and 1801, with different degrees of militancy in different communities, depending on the nature of the machinery and the impact it had, which depended largely on the way in which local production was organized. Sometimes such protest effectively delayed the introduction of new machinery for many years. For the shearmen, a well-organized labour élite, strike action, and widespread (but highly selective) machine-breaking and arson in Wiltshire in 1802, were followed by the organization of an appeal to Parliament.

In trying to use the law the cloth-workers were less successful. The Gloucestershire shearmen petitioned Parliament unsuccessfully in 1794 to extend and modify the Tudor legislation against gig mills, but by 1803, with trade in decline, a sophisticated committee structure in the trade throughout the textile regions was organized to oppose machinery on a national rather than local basis. The previous year West Country weavers had organized and hired a solicitor to prosecute employers for infringing the apprenticeship laws. But the clothiers now retaliated with a parliamentary campaign to repeal the old legislation on grounds that it was archaic, damaging to trade, and useless. The manufacturers knew Parliament better than did the weavers: legislation to suspend the old Acts was immediately passed, in spite of petitions of protest, followed by final repeal, as we have noted, in 1809.

The suspension took place, but final repeal was delayed for six years, in part because the new machinery divided the trade at many different levels. There were traditionalist clothiers and innovating clothiers, depending on the structure of the industry in different regions. Small master clothiers generally supported the old order and the weavers; new men, with large capital and promising technical innovations, wanted change, notably the freedom to exploit factory production. For all workers in the domestic and outputting systems, that meant loss of control of the workplace, the threat of lower wages and unemployment, and the intrusion of what was widely regarded as a seat of immoral and demoralized social relations. That too was an argument mounted against the repeal; it was ignored.

The general issue of apprenticeship was brought to the attention of Parliament in 1814 by an attempt to enforce the old laws by a number of trades. These included framework-knitters encouraged by the fact that they had mounted successful prosecutions under the charter of their company, which also set out apprenticeship clauses (although they got a very small penalty from a very reluctant Chief Justice). The London trades petitioned Parliament to tighten up the apprenticeship laws, as the most likely means to protect their standings. From 1809 a wide variety of trades used a solicitor to prepare cases against those breaking the statutes. It was evident that by the terms of the laws relating to informers such prosecutions, even when successful in the face of judicial hostility, yielded light penalties. Well-organized campaigning, and ultimately a petition of 300,000 names for the extension of the statute and better penalties, encouraged the trades to believe that their claims would be met. Their appeal was founded in large part on the fact that an artisan's apprenticeship, in the rights it conferred on him, was a species of property interest:

The apprenticed artisans have, collectively and individually, an unquestionable right to expect the most extended protection from the Legislature, in the quiet and exclusive enjoyment of their several and respective arts and trades, which the law has already conferred upon them as a property, as much as it has secured the property of the stockholder in the public funds: and it is clearly unjust to take away the whole of the ancient established property and rights of any one class of the community, unless, at the same time, the rights and property of the whole commonwealth should be dissolved, and parcelled out anew for the public good.[6]

It was the worst of times to make such an appeal to Parliament. England was at war with Napoleonic France. We can characterize the main bodies of opinion in the Commons and Lords by this date as a minority of Radicals and Whigs, on the one hand, and the Tory crusade against Republican, atheistic, Revolutionary France on the other. Among the Radicals and Whigs, Smith's view of the apprenticeship laws, as an affront to the free market, were held by most; those who might be expected to be more susceptible to arguments based on ancient usage and the paternal state, the Tory majority, were dissuaded from this view by the temper of the times. They were convinced that a great deal of trades activity, particularly combinations to raise wages or enforce the traditional claims of a trade, were, in these polarized and desperate years, the work of republican sympathizers. Combinations of workmen (that is, bodies of them who were agreed on common action to further a policy) were, in their eyes, very apt to be seditious Painite conspiracies, quite apart from their impact on the public peace and employers' interests. (They had acted on this view in passing the general laws against workmen's combinations in 1799 and 1800.) And this view prevailed. Retaining the apprenticeship clauses, such opponents argued, would only encourage combinations dangerous to both employers and the state. Parliament acted, without debate and without a division. The propertied were in unison. The apprenticeship clauses, like the wage clauses the previous year, were struck from the books.

Fears about machinery, fears that the repeal of the old laws would transform the trades, were ridiculed by large employers at the time this great legal change took place. It is true that growth of demand in many textile trades until the end of the war cushioned the impact initially, but by the late 1820s, to take the example of the élite cloth-dressers, work that had taken twenty-seven cloth-finishers to do in the 1790s was done by three men with two boy helpers and a machine.

Parliament was convinced of the arguments in favour of machinery, and against 'artifical' restraints on labour, by 1814. Why did the prudential, public-order argument—the traditionalist view that custom, stability, and social order were real social goods—an argument previously espoused by Parliament, no longer hold sway there? There had been criticism of the Statute of Artificers in the courts for a century, in Parliament for at least fifty years, yet, faced with militant and often violent demands by the trades, and countervailing demands by some employers (usually the largest), Parliament had continued to balance interests of capital and labour for much of the eighteenth century. As late as the Spitalfields Act of 1773, it had restated some of the older tradition of law. As we have seen, it had been Parliament's response to unusually violent and effective organization by the London silk-weavers. That Act appeared to guarantee not only industrial peace but some prosperity: provincial weavers and masters wished that it could be extended to the provinces, its provisions were extended to women workers in 1811, and as late as 1818 a Parliamentary Select Committee endorsed that view. The Spitalfields legislation was cited by other workers and small masters as the model for preservation and restoration of the old regulative structure in other trades; for the same reason, proponents of political economy, and the wealthiest employers, were determined to repeal it. Finally in 1824, at the behest of the richest silk-mercers and manufacturers, the Spitalfields Acts (including Amendments to the original statute) were repealed as an affront to the laws of free markets. Why Parliament no longer thought in terms of dangers to public order, their concern when the original statute was enacted, is illustrated particularly well in the related case of changes in the marketing of food.

Bread and markets

The marketing laws against forestallers, regraters, and engrossers were the charter of the food rioter, as the Statute of Artificers was the charter of the skilled worker (see Ch. 6). Very often the same men and women were both. The custom of markets, and the combination of gentlemanly and mobbish support of the old legislation that had grown up around it, was under attack from the 1750s. The food riots of 1766 were the last occasion on which government called attention to the medieval and early-modern legislation against forestallers, regraters, and engrossers. But in Parliament, in the London Common Council, and throughout the shires, many gentlemen continued to believe that middlemen enhanced the prices of wheat, bread, cheese, meat, and other provisions by intercepting food on the way to markets, by buying and reselling for a profit, and by hoarding. On the other hand, partisans of the new theories of political economy, in Parliament, the courts, and the universities (including Adam Smith of Glasgow), ridiculed the old laws. They argued that prosecuting middlemen destroyed the delicate balance of the price mechanism, which alone could ration supply, rationally and effortlessly. To interfere increased the risk of famine. Thus proposals by the traditionalists to stiffen the old laws in 1772 prompted followers of the new theory of free markets to action. Led by Edmund Burke, they managed to get parliamentary majorities for legislation which embodied Smith's analysis of the corn trade.[7]

The most important judge in England, Lord Mansfield, Chief Justice of the Court of King's Bench, apparently agreed. All the law books said that the old marketing offences were not only criminal by statute, but under the common law. However, exactly what consituted such an offence was a matter of judicial opinion, and Mansfield appears to have shared the views of Smith and Burke that the ancient law was based on ignorance. The law in fact became uncertain, because no cases apparently came before the high courts from 1772 until the end of the century. Yet all the guidebooks for magistrates continued to print the advice that the marketing offences were still criminal at common law, punishable by fine and imprisonment. Some highly respected legal treatises agreed.

So too did a minority in Parliament, where the repeal of 1772 never commanded total assent. Attempts were made in 1786–7, again in 1795–6 when food prices were extremely high, and in 1797 to enact new legislation to punish profiteering middlemen, and to erect public granaries. Burke was appalled: 'it is not in breaking the laws of commerce, which are the laws of nature, and consequently the laws of God, that we are to place our hopes of softening the Divine displeasure to remove any calamity under which we suffer, or which hangs over us.' He was gratified that all the legislation failed, horrified that it had been attempted.[8]

Had he lived, Burke would have been even more horrified that Mansfield's successor Lord Kenyon, who became Chief Justice in 1788, believed that the old laws had been valuable and regretted that they had been repealed. The crusty judge thought Adam Smith was no more than a windbag professor at the University of Glasgow, so blinded by abstract theory that he could not see the sufferings of the poor when prices were high and profiteers abroad in the land. While markets were clearing, wondered Kenyon, were the poor to abstain from eating? He therefore praised the common-law offences of forestalling, regrating, and engrossing, and promised severe punishment to anyone convicted under them. Traditionalist country gentlemen were delighted. They were even more delighted when Kenyon and the other judges on King's Bench proceeded in 1800–1 to craft the prosecutions of a Jacobin hop-dealer and a London corn-factor into new precedents that re-emphasized the old marketing offences.

The government, notably the Prime Minister, Pitt, and the Duke of Portland, who as Home Secretary was responsible for public order, were horrified. Both were devout followers of Adam Smith. Confronted with the extremely widespread food riots of 1800 and 1801, the worst in the century, they believed that only completely free markets could save England from starvation (see Ch. 5). They were particularly concerned that legal meddling with the grain market would interrupt supplies to London, supplies which had always been considered essential to national security. However, there was also another fundamental difference of opinion between Kenyon and the government: they drew opposite conclusions about the effect on the mob of prosecutions of middlemen.

The traditional view, shared by many country gentlemen, was

Kenyon's: confronted with a mob, one of the easiest ways to re-store public order was to promise, and carry out, a few exemplary prosecutions of profiteering middlemen. In the eyes of Portland, the great defect of this premiss was that it legitimized the actions of the mob. That was indeed the case: the food riot, and gentry responses to it for much of the century, rested on a shared hos-tility to middlemen by both rioters and gentlemen justices, and an attachment to the old law. But for Portland and most other min-isters, the great danger at the end of the century, in a Revolution-ary context, was that Kenyon's blind traditionalism would provoke more rioting, not less (see Chs. 9 to 12). They were delighted when Kenyon died in 1802. His successor was a fully committed partisan of classical political economy. Henceforth food rioters were given no promises of prosecutions of middlemen. Instead, they were them-selves prosecuted for riot, and were met with troops.[9] This repudiation of the oldest body of law protecting small consumers announced the willingness of Parliament and the courts to believe that free markets, prices 'finding their own level', was the answer to almost all issues of public economic policy that had, in earlier centuries, been considered a responsibility of the state and the guarantors of public order.

Conclusion

The title of this chapter contains a paradox: custom, after all, was a source of law (see Ch. 6). The common custom of the king-dom, at least that part recognized by the judges, became the com-mon law, and local manorial custom, trade custom, customary franchises—all specific, local instances—could be enforced also in courts. But the changes described in this chapter all had the effect of changing the meaning of custom, creating its modern connota-tions. Custom came more often to mean social practice without the force of law, for vast areas of custom-as-law were uprooted by the legislation and judicial rulings we have described. The common law endured, parliamentary legislation proliferated, but custom-as-law, that circle within which ancient practice, Tudor and Stuart statutes, community structures, and popular understanding met, withered.

More exactly, it was killed. For the salient fact about most of the changes we have described is that they were enacted by a

Parliament stupendously overrepresentative of the very wealthiest Englishmen. Less than 17 per cent of the adult male population had the right to elect members of the House of Commons, the lowest figure in a century. The House of Lords, the dominant part of Parliament well into the nineteenth century, consisted almost entirely of the richest landlords in England. The Lords, it is true, sometimes showed more attachment to the traditional inheritance than did the House of Commons, just as some judges, as we have seen, were less convinced of Adam Smith's truths than were others. But it was a matter of minor differences. By the end of the wars Parliament was unequivocally committed to *laissez-faire* (apart from tariffs on corn), perhaps most strongly in matters affecting labour. It enacted the legislation we have considered in this chapter in the face, often, of massive popular opposition, overt or concealed. Resistance to enclosure we now know was more widespread, deep, and persistent, even in defeat, than historians used to argue. The petition against the 1814 repeal of the apprenticeship laws contained 300,000 names. The number of food rioters in 1800–1 required the attentions of an army, barracked in manufacturing districts, that was larger than the one fighting Britain's enemies on the Continent, and resulted in capital prosecutions throughout England.

By the end of the wars in 1815, English society was very different from what it had been when the Georges came to rule. So too were the instruments of power, and the nature of social legitimation.

8 New Populations

Defoe's England

In the years 1724–6, a decade after the Hanoverian accession, Daniel Defoe published his *Tour through the Whole Island Of Great Britain*. Part travelogue, part social commentary, Defoe drew on his own experiences over several decades to introduce his contemporaries to the diversity of social life and landscape in Britain. Although as a Dissenter and former hose-factor Defoe looked at Britain with a predominantly mercantile eye, expressing wonderment at the range of articles from far afield that were bought and sold at Stourbridge fair, he did not neglect manufacture (see Fig. 10). Defoe remarked on 'the wonderful extent of the Norwich manufacture, or stuff-weaving trade, by which so many thousands of families are maintained'; he detailed the distinctive woollens of the West Country, its serges, druggets, and cantaloons. He noted the iron-foundries of the Weald, the Stroud-water cloths of Gloucestershire, the ironworks and glassworks of the west Midlands, the hosiery industry of the east, the burgeoning woollen industry of Halifax, a mere vicarage whose manufacture of shalloons and kerseys challenged the pre-eminence of better-known West Riding clothing towns. And as he (fictionally) approached Newcastle-upon-Tyne from the Durham side, he stared at 'the prodigious heaps, I might say mountains of coals, which are dug up at every pit, and how many of those pits there are'.[1]

Defoe pin-pointed many of the distinctive manufacturing regions of the country; before, in fact, the classic Industrial Revolution had taken place. Perspectives on the Industrial Revolution are, of course, as old as that revolution itself. They can often be read as a commentary on the present, replicating quite explicitly the social and economic preoccupations of contemporary society. Thus the emphasis of the mid-nineteenth century centred upon the 'Condition of England' question; that of the early twentieth century, a time of dramatic industrial unrest, upon the cataclysmic sundering of the old order. Correspondingly, the focus of the Depression years was upon economic cycles; that of the post-war boom, upon growth. Even so, until quite recently there was a broad agreement that the British Industrial Revolution, however defined (and different research approaches shaped the definition), occurred during the century 1750–1850, most probably during the years 1760–1830. It was principally associated with the coming of the factory and qualitative changes in industrial relations, with technological innovation, and with the very rapid pace of change in leading sectors of the economy such as cotton and iron. From this perspective Defoe's comments seemed largely prescient, a portent of things to come from a man who habitually accented change and improvement.

The long Industrial Revolution

That chronology, and the set of assumptions that accompanied it, have now been questioned. The current emphasis is upon the long build-up of industrialization, the close and historic association of industry and agriculture, the symbiotic and sometimes contradictory relationship of labour and capital-intensive enterprise, and upon fairly unremarkable rates of growth, with industrial output growing slowly until about 1770 and even then remaining under 3 per cent per annum before 1830. The current preoccupation with British economic decline is one reason for this change in emphasis. Another is the recognition that the conventional benchmarks of social structure at the end of the seventeenth century, such as Gregory King's table of 1688 (p. 19), seriously overlooked the extent of manufacture in the country. Local censuses and burial records suggest that King may have underestimated the numbers engaged in industry and the building trades by as much as 400 per cent, and these revised figures ignore the participation of women and children in the manufacturing economy. Britain at the dawn of the eighteenth century was already an industrial nation, but one whose industries were often technologically simple and predominantly located in the countryside. Allowing for changes in the gender division of labour and the introduction of compulsory schooling after 1880, which removed children from the workforce, it is even conceivable that proportionately more people were engaged in industry in 1700 than they were two centuries later. Most of them, we must add, were engaged part time in dual economies.

Industrial advance depended crucially upon two factors: the

ability to feed an expanding population engaged in non-agricultural work, and the availability of cheap labour. The agricultural revolution of the seventeenth and early eighteenth centuries accomplished the first. Improved animal husbandry, the introduction of root crops and clover, the floating of water meadows, all had the effect of raising agricultural productivity and keeping pace with population growth. Throughout the eighteenth century Britain was even a net exporter of grain and was able to sustain a very significant growth in the urban population that reached 27.5 per cent of the total in 1801, twice what it had been in 1670 and five times larger than in the early sixteenth century.[2] A minority of this population was engaged in industrial pursuits as opposed to transport and service. It is difficult to know how many; but as a crude measure it is worth noting that manufacturing towns constituted 37.3 per cent of the total urban population in 1750 and nearly 50 per cent by 1801. By that time Manchester and Liverpool, the centre of the burgeoning cotton industry and its port, ranked second and third in the urban hierarchy, while Birmingham, the nucleus of the metalware industry, ranked fourth.

Yet from the long-term perspective what was critical to British industrial advance was the availability of labour in the countryside. The growth of agrarian capitalism and the slow, but inexorable, engrossing of small farms into larger holdings made living off the land more difficult for many rural people. At the end of the seventeenth century labourers, cottagers, and paupers comprised 47 per cent of the entire population, and they frequently had to supplement their income with industrial by-employments (see Table 2.1). The probate inventories of seventeenth-century labourers (and many labourers engaged in spinning and weaving were too poor to leave inventories) suggest that as many as 60 per cent were engaged in by-employments, the percentage rising in the forest areas and in counties where woollen manufacture was well established. Rural industry was more related to the economic circumstances of the workers than to entrepreneurship or the availability of raw materials. Merchant-capitalists looked to areas where labour was cheap and underemployed and where poor wages could be supplemented by agriculture or rights to grazing, fuel, and materials from common land. It was in these circumstances that 'putting-out' capitalists provided men and women with raw materials (and sometimes looms and frames) to work up in their cottages. Generally speaking, this kind of family-based rural industry, or what is sometimes called proto-industry, was situated in areas of woodland-pasture, where manorialism was weak, partible inheritance pervasive, and labour supply plentiful. There were exceptions to this pattern. In 1700 about 16 per cent of the inhabitants of Wigston Magna, an open-field, peasant, arable village, were framework-knitters, the numbers increasing dramatically once the parish was enclosed. A different pattern was found in West Yorkshire, where manorialism was stronger and independent artisans combined farming with woollen manufacture in what was a profitable dual economy.

Regional specialization

The seventeenth century was the era of industrial by-employment; the eighteenth of regional specialization. To emphasize the difference risks making a contrast that is crude and overdramatic because many of the distinctive areas of regional specialization already existed in embryonic form before 1700. The coal industry of the north-west, the metalware industries of the Midlands, and the export-driven textile industries of the West Country, Essex, and East Anglia, to name but five, were already well established by the late seventeenth century, if not before, with rural workers often fully employed in industry. Even so, the period after 1660 saw a definite trend towards industrial intensification and specialization, a trend that Defoe noticed in his *Tour*. In the increasingly competitive climate of the eighteenth century, some old centres of industry faded. The Weald of Kent and Surrey, the major producer of iron and glass in 1600, declined in the face of the Midland advance. Its charcoal-based industries were no match for the coal-driven enterprises further north. Similarly, the woollen industries of the West Country were displaced in significance by the worsted industry of East Anglia, where collective bargaining was weaker and wages were 40 per cent lower by 1760. That industry, which at the beginning of the eighteenth century provided work for 72,000 weavers in Norwich and the surrounding countryside, held sway until 1770, when the cheaper cloths of Yorkshire began to edge it out of the domestic and foreign market.

The changing industrial vista can be mapped in the following

way. In the seventeenth century the conspicuous industries were
largely concentrated along a fault line that ran from Norwich to
London to the south-west, with pockets of intensive industry in
the Midlands, the north, and the Sussex Weald. During the course
of the eighteenth century the centres of industrial concentration
shifted to the Midlands, to the West Riding of Yorkshire, to Lancashire, South Wales, and the north-west. London remained the
largest city and industrial centre of Britain, and the naval dockyards
of the south at Portsmouth and Plymouth were among the largest
industrial enterprises, but on balance southern England deindus-
trialized. In part this pattern was shaped by the changing geography
of the agrarian regions, for those areas that specialized in commercial, labour-intensive arable crops were likely to deindustrialize.
Certainly there were exceptions to this rule, for the decline in
female agricultural work in the south and east encouraged the
growth of lace and straw-plaiting in counties like Buckinghamshire,
Bedfordshire, and Essex. At the same time, the growth of commercial agriculture eliminated the production of woollens in areas
such as Essex and Suffolk, and over time made even Norfolk, whose
light soils and proximity to London were a boon to arable farming, less industrial.

The changing industrial landscape of the eighteenth century was
predictably influenced by the availability of raw materials: wool,
wood, minerals, and increasingly supplies of coal. It was also determined by the ability of a town or region to adapt to new fash-
ions and circumstances. Older towns with diversified industrial
structures and skilled workforces could survive, although often at
the cost of relaxing their guild economies. Much depended upon
the dynamics of comparative advantage, including worker resistance to the reduction of labour costs. London's stockingers proved
unable to compete with their counterparts in the East Midlands,
where hosiers were able to tap a cheaper, unregulated workforce
in both town and country. On the other hand, London remained
the leading producer of fashionable goods, despite high rents and
high wages, and it was able to sustain a large silk industry once
international competition from France and India had been eliminated. As soon as any product became part of a mass market, however,
it was liable to leave London or be sweated; that is, turned out to
unregulated workers in their rooms and garrets at deplorable rates

of pay. Fortunately for the London artisans standardized mass markets seldom emerged before the nineteenth century. Even so, quite a few of the labour struggles in London from the mid-eighteenth century onwards were designed to offset the dilution of a trade and the growth of a large, 'disreputable' sector of out-workers.

One of the most violent struggles, in fact, was that of the silk-weavers. Facing widespread wage cuts, unemployment, and competition from provincial workers at lower wages, they fought the large silk-mercers of Spitalfields and Bethnal Green throughout the 1760s and early 1770s. Groups of weavers visited shops, often at night, to intimidate fellow workers, and to cut and destroy silk in the loom when it was that of masters or mercers not abiding by the rates they demanded. Arrests, demonstrations, riots, and destruction of buildings in Spitalfields led to confrontations with troops. Yet these protests achieved their objectives, largely because of the threat they posed to peace in the capital. As we have seen in Chapter 7 they were successful in obtaining legislation that helped protect them for some decades. In contrast, another trade, the buckle-makers of Staffordshire and Warwickshire, responded quite differently to crisis in their trade. They enjoyed flourishing domestic and export markets in the 1760s, but found their trade destroyed within a matter of years when shoelaces came into fashion later in the century. In spite of a successful appeal to the royal family in the 1790s to continue wearing buckles, the decline was irreversible. However, the skills of buckle-makers were equally useful in other small metal trades. They did not riot or get parliamentary protection: they became different kinds of workers.

Industrial disputes

Many things determined whether a trade or industry or local population grew, remained stable, or declined, and whether strikes and riots erupted. The local resource base and comparative costs were important, but so too was the ability to obtain legislative protection by threat or with the support of magistrates and large men in the trade. Many different social circumstances were often important. The prosperity of the rest of the local working population mattered, because poor communities, like those in the East Midlands, could not easily resist sweating, as happened in framework-knitting. The strength of trade organizations (both the degree of unity of small masters with workmen, and also the nature of the labour process, which allowed some trades, through sabotage or riot, greater power) could be determinative for a long time. So too could other social structures. Coventry, for example, preserved its inherited regulation of the silk-ribbon trade (apprenticeship requirements, agreed rates) for a long time, apparently in part because local commoning on lands around the city helped sustain community alliances and discouraged the growth of a competing labour force of the poor. The degree to which the trade was integrated into other community structures could help preserve its workers from dilution by 'dishonourable' unapprenticed labour, and even from the introduction of machinery that threatened unemployment.

The riots against machines that we have noted in the woollen trade later in the century were not uncommon (see Ch. 7). Among many other lesser events, we can cite the destruction of 100 knitting-frames in London in 1710, attacks on Hargreaves' spinning-machines in the Midlands in 1768 and 1769, widespread destruction of the large 'patent' spinning-machines of Arkwright and other Lancashire manufacturers by crowds of 8,000 in 1779 (Arkwright installed cannon to defend some of his factories), the arson and destruction of the factory and machines in Manchester where Cartwright's power loom was first used in 1792, protests against the flying-shuttle in Chippenham between 1801 and 1803, and the widespread machine-breaking of the Luddite protests in 1811–12 in Nottinghamshire and the West Riding of Yorkshire, and earlier in the West Country (see Ch. 12). Faced with massive opposition innovators sometimes moved elsewhere, or delayed the introduction of machinery. But machinery was not resisted everywhere: indeed, in many trades, the resistance was specifically directed at men with very large capital who wished to use a common machine of domestic industry, such as the early spinning-machines, in very large installations, in a 'manufactory'. In the 1779 Lancashire riots, spinning-jennies below twenty-four spindles were not attacked. And in some trades, including metalwork, the introduction of small machines, and constant improvements in them, were entirely integrated into a domestic and small workshop environment.

Two salient features, then, of the English industrial economy emerge from recent work. There was much more industry, particularly in the countryside, earlier than was thought, and that industry was always in flux. Developing regional and trade specializations, changing export markets, and the intrusion of new technology and larger capital into older communities were constants. The result was that industrial trade cycles, competition between regions and within them, and destabilizing technical change were also constants. We now know that primary industrialization was a longer, slower process than it has often been portrayed, but that does not mean that it was peaceful and consensual. The slow secular growth in average output figures conceals a rapidly changing world. The insecurities of markets were disruptive of communities, trades, and individual lives. Communities, trades, and individual workers attempted in many ways to find some protection from such market forces. The claim to custom was one of them, as we have seen in Chapters 6 and 7, as was also the use of force and the threat of violence (see also Ch. 9).

While those modes of negotiating power were to be found in all areas of society, the pervasiveness of industry, its long-standing importance in the economy and in society, meant that industrial disputes shaped much of state policy and social life. Into the familiar and persuasive images of bucolic peace, such as Gainsborough's painting *The Harvest Waggon*, we must put the approaching mob of spinners and weavers prepared to demolish spinning-machines. When we admire Christchurch in Spitalfields or St Matthews in Bethnal Green, we must also remember the hanging nearby of two silk-weavers, surrounded by troops with fixed bayonets, in July 1771. They had been part of a mob of 3,000 who stoned to death an informer, a weaver who had sent other weavers to the gallows more than a year before by informing on them for cutting silk in the loom. In addition to such massive disturbances, we must remember the great frequency of strikes, lockouts, cutting in the loom in all the textile trades, and riot (from small peaceful demonstrations to pitched battles with troops) that occurred throughout the century.

Recent work has extended our awareness of the range of significant industrial disputes in the eighteenth century, but, as is also the case with the food riot, our estimates of the numbers and extent will always be very incomplete (see Ch. 9). Newspaper accounts (one sample gives some 400, for dozens of trades) only begin to count them, usually those that disrupted the public peace. Such estimates are biased over time, becoming more complete as the century progressed and newspapers increased in numbers and coverage. Most disputes concerned wages and hours; others included protests at the use of unapprenticed labour, new machinery, or other innovations by masters or merchants controlling outputting.

Work and freedom

We are concerned here primarily with how work was experienced, perceived, and valued. The first fact about it was that the nature of industry generated experiences of personal and collective freedom, even if it was a freedom beset by the vagaries of trade cycles, harvest failures, and the possibility of destitution. In part a sense of freedom arose from the very nature of innovation and specialization. Areas of growth and industrial concentration, like the metalworking Midlands or the West Riding worsted industry, attracted young populations with high wages, and rewarded skilled and ambitious men and women who mastered new techniques or demanded a share of the competitive advantages of such areas. But freedom also inhered in the nature of work itself, even in areas of relative economic stagnation. As we have seen, there was an immense diversity of industrial organization in the eighteenth century. The factory (with some exceptions noted below) was rare, and the great prevalence of small artisanal workshops and the importance of extensive networks of domestic outputting gave workers forms of purchase, forms of freedom, that dismayed employers but that often were fiercely defended.

Three of these were control of time, control of materials, and control of the nature of production itself. These were most pronounced in artisanal production, at least in trades that were not sweated, but they were also part of many domestic outputting industries. A wool-comber or weaver or nailer working at home was advanced a quantity of raw materials to return, fashioned, within a given period of time. That time was hers, or his, or the family's, to allot; work and social life were fitted together in different ways, depending on trade, locality, decade. The observance of St Monday was widespread; so too were wakes and other local holidays. There were always tensions, of gender and of markets. St Monday was a male ritual; in many trades intensive periods of work by all family members were the only hope in making ends meet. Patterns of changing rhythms of work to suit family and community life were none the less deeply established from the distant past. They could work particularly well when the family both farmed and had an industrial trade.

Secondly, in outputting systems the materials advanced often went through many processes in many different workers' hands. There were many opportunities to collect and use, or resell in other markets, some of the advanced materials. Wastage included brass filings; fents and thrums, which were the pieces of silk attached to the loom; chips, which is what shipbuilders called wood they claimed. There were also the materials that were rejected as imperfect, spillage from casks, defective products. In short, part of the wage paid for their labour was, within narrow limits, literally in their hands. Such appropriation was well understood, often considered to be universal, and had names in each trade: hatters' buggings, tailors' cabbage. Indeed, the merchants advancing materials were often enough among the buyers. Industrial areas were dense with receiving networks. Materials might also be resold in more distant markets: silk appropriated in Coventry was sold in Spitalfields.

Third, the control of production lay in the skills of the worker, even such an elementary skill as that practised by a man or woman who could hand-forge thousands of nails in a day. Nailing was a relatively unskilled trade, with many degraded workers, but when demand was good the nailer working at a home forge determined his income by his strength, endurance, and accuracy. Other trades, either because they were much in demand or because they required great skill (millwrights for example enjoyed both advantages) gave an independence, a self-respect, and a control of much of the working environment that was probably much superior to that of the average curate or schoolteacher or clerk.

There was a congruence, then, of two rhetorics of freedom, and work itself. The constitutional rhetoric of the freeborn Englishman, free from Continental monarchical oppression and taxation ('French slavery and wooden shoes'), was an established trope in national politics. The worker's claim to customary and legal rights at the workplace was attached to that discourse, made part of it, as we have seen in Chapters 6–7. And the realms of freedom in the workplace itself, while contested, narrowed, and often lost, were felt as the freedom which the political claims might protect. It is in these terms that we can understand the profound sense of right, the outrage at lost legal protections or parliamentary indifference, the willingness to use violence against fellow workers or employers. The fear or actuality of unemployment, want, degradation of skills, even starvation were important causes of industrial unrest, but so too was the sense of injustice at freedoms threatened and lost.

Many of the most protracted and violent industrial disputes, particularly later in the century, occurred as men of larger capital sought to control time, the wage, and levels of skill. They brought to bear both the law and new machines.

Coercive law encompassed work in many ways. A long series of statutes in a great many trades penalized the late delivery of work, set limited times for the completion of work, and treated appropriation of part of the product or raw materials as embezzlement. Work practices of too great benefit to the worker could thus be defined as the theft of the employer's time or his property. (There were also statutes that penalized theft of time on his property, by using his machines when they would otherwise be idle.) These were the employer's claims to right, and such penalties were often written by Parliament into the same statutes that recognized worker's apprenticeship or wage rights. But in important instances, notably the worsted trade, Parliament enhanced through special legislation the employer's ability to criminalize and punish by the terms of the law. The worsted employers were empowered to set up a private police force, with extensive powers of search and seizure and prosecution; it was paid for partly at public expense (a drawback on soap tax.)[3] The penalty in all these instances was to make restitution or imprisonment for failure to do so, and then, more and more frequently throughout the century, imprisonment, usually from one to three months. In some trades, mostly poor domestic outputting, the civil law of debt was almost as important. Outputting was, at its core, an extension of credit, and where a workforce was unable to bargain effectively, chains of debt owed to the merchant or master (and debt was imprisonable) tied the worker to his forge or last.

The attack on the claims of skill, particularly in trades enjoying statutory privileges, was effected in other ways. New machinery to supersede older processes was most effective: thousands of female hand-spinners became redundant within a few decades. The contest of established skill with new processes was continuous. Élite hand-workers like shearmen were threatened with shearing-frames, but framework-knitters using an older technology were forced to make lower-quality goods. And, as we have noted, sometimes the attack on the privileges of skill took the form not of more elaborate machinery, but the addition of a large power source. Arkwright's improved spinning-machines could be used in a cottage or small workshop setting, but he insisted on the use of the 'patent' machine only by licence, in large water-powered mills with a thousand spindles. Here the skill was not superseded, but the human being as source of energy was. Finally, in all cases where workers tried to maintain traditional skill levels by demanding formal apprenticeship, they were conscious that masters anxious to expand production or cut costs would try to use unapprenticed labour, especially that of women and children. Both were ubiquitous in industry, their labour cheap.

The employment of women and children in settings where formerly men had claimed the right to work, or in new production processes that undermined older trades, had great (and sometimes contradictory) political resonances. For if work was freedom, everyone agreed that not everyone was equally free. Labour was notionally arranged in a hierarchy of freedoms and unfreedoms, inherited from the medieval past. At one pole was slavery. Englishmen could not be slaves; but Blacks brought to England from the West Indies could be and were (the Attorney-General and Solicitor-General so declared in 1749). A large part of Britain's commerce was in slaves, a fact Burke referred to with approval in the House of Commons in 1787. Her richest colonies, the West Indian sugar islands, had minutely detailed codes of inhuman punishments that legitimated private cruelties: '25 May 1756. Derby catched by Port Royal eating canes. Had him well flogged and pickled [the wounds rubbed with salt], then made Hector shit in his mouth.'[4] This estate steward always whipped offenders, but some of his slaves were branded in the face, and their ears were cut off in serious cases. Dismemberment, provided for by the legislated codes of the British Caribbean until the 1780s, was probably widely practised as an aggravated penalty. In 1759 the attorney of a estate in western Jamaica casually mentioned in a letter to his employer that one runaway lost a leg and another a hand. In England, silversmiths

and blacksmiths advertised collars for slaves brought from the West
Indies; slaves were advertised for sale in England in the newspapers. Runaway slaves in England were captured and resold in the
West Indies, until the Lord Chief Justice reluctantly stopped the
practice in 1772. Slaves in England thereafter (incorrectly but often
effectively) claimed freedom. It was qualified: poor-law authorities
arrested and deported many unwilling free Blacks to Sierra Leone
in West Africa in 1787; what had started out as voluntary emigration by a few became compulsory for many more. In that year
began the first widespread political agitation against slavery (see
Ch. 11). Twenty years later in 1807 Parliament at last enacted
legislation against the slave trade, but it was only in 1834 that
slavery itself finally became illegal in the British West Indies by
Act of Parliament. Compensation to the owners for the loss of
their human property cost the enormous sum of £20 million from
public funds.

Apart from a traditional form of unfreedom among some Scottish miners, repealed in 1775 (although further legislation was
required in 1799), Britons themselves never ever ever would be
slaves (the lyric dates from 1740). Yet the hierarchy of hired servant, domestic servant, covenant servant, journeyman, apprentice,
indentured servant, pauper apprentice, conveyed (with some differences between trades and regions) specific notions of freedom
and unfreedom. The law recognized important rights of maintenance and obligation in the mutual relations of master and a servant under an annual hiring, such as no dismissal without cause,
obligation to labour for a year, obligation to maintain the servant
for a year, even in sickness, three months' notice on either side.
There were fewer such ties or rights in domestic service: a month's
notice was all that was required in London. Written contracts of
service varied greatly. Indentured servants might sell years of their
lives (usually for passage to America). On the other hand, a skilled
artisan might agree, in return for high wages, to be bound to serve
one employer for several years. Boulton and Watt tried to retain
their most valued workers with contracts of three, five, or seven
years.

The biggest range of freedoms occurred within the very old category of apprenticeship. On the one hand, apprenticeship could
be the costly right of entry into a skilled and remunerative trade,

with parents paying a premium, and the apprentice giving his labour to his master for initiation into the skills. On the other, it could be the involuntary committal to servitude of abandoned or orphaned children by parish authorities, the so-called pauper apprentices, to the poorest trades or the factory, often until the age of majority. Between these extremes, apprenticeship, particularly in prosperous artisanal or farming communities, could still function as a significant period of education, instruction, and initiation into adult status and work for many boys and some girls.

In many trades it appears that over time master status was less and less likely to follow apprenticeship and the period of journeyman wage labour as a servant. As larger capital intensified production, it made it harder for small masters to compete. As this happened, in some trades servants were less likely to be children or young adults, more likely to be older men who would never be independent masters of their trade. Eleven-month hirings weakened the protection enshrined in the old law of a year's hiring, including the right to poor relief in the parish. In some occupations, such as the small metal trades of the Midlands, workmen as well as masters came to take, or often more accurately employ, 'apprentices'. Nevertheless, always the hierarchy of skill, of relative privilege, and claims for legal protection under the old law continued. That was the case both where there was a relatively intact juridical and organizational structure in a skilled trade, and in industries in which older skills were being rapidly degraded by new processes or new immigrants.

Women in industry

The connotations of freedom and unfreedom in the different legal categories of labour were intensified when older notions of right were under attack. The widespread use of pauper apprentices in the new mills and factory settings of the textiles and metal trades (Arkwright's mills; Soho near Birmingham) was deeply threatening to adult workers, skilled and unskilled. The metaphor of slavery seemed apt whenever degrading, poorly paid, unskilled work replaced a craft tradition or relative prosperity. The position of women workers in this respect was profoundly ambiguous. In law and much social practice women were less 'free': subordinated to their husbands in marriage, and barred from many roles in civil

life, whether married or single (Ch. 3). In industry their earnings
traditionally were far less than those of men, whether the work
was distinctively female (e.g. spinning) or demanded strength and
stamina (e.g. nailing), or was simply always paid less when performed by a woman. Yet female work was extremely widespread
in early industry; indeed, recent estimates of the degree of wage
labour in industry have been greatly revised upward, in part because
women's work was so rarely counted.

The work of women, so important in early industry, changed
markedly in the course of the eighteenth century, and appears to
have been more radically affected by technological innovation than
the work of men. In the most important sector of early-modern
industry, textiles, three or four female spinners supplied the yarn for
every weaver (usually male). Spinning was the first process to be
mechanized, and with some regional exceptions female employment
in spinning drastically declined. Dexterity and low wages were the
qualities of female labour prized by outputters when women span
(children were similarly cheap and quick at making cards used in
preparing wool). In the silk industry there were fourteen women
and children to every man. As mechanization advanced, large numbers
of women and children were employed in the most dynamic sectors of the economy. In the most advanced textile sector, cotton,
there were as many women and children workers as men, more
in Scotland. In some of the most advanced sectors of the metalworking trades this was also true (including shops at Boulton's
Soho).

Women continued to form an extensive part of the workforce in
those domestic outputting trades that also expanded, with little or
no technical change, during industrialization in the late eighteenth
and early nineteenth centuries. Many women contributed thus to
a household economy, supplementing their male partners' wages
(although there were more all-female working households, which
suffered greatly from the sexual wage differential, than historians
have assumed). The use of female labour in rapidly expanding and
mechanizing sectors was in part recognized by contemporaries to
be an employer's tactic not only to cut costs, but also to subvert
male artisanal resistance to the introduction of technologies and
control of production processes. The factory ('manufactory' in the
eighteenth century; the modern name was old, but its modern sense

dates from the 1830s) under central management, manned by a few men, but many women and pauper apprentices, was recognized for what it was. It was a new kind of place, with potentially enormous significance for social organization, even if it was a rare feature of an industrial landscape still dominated by artisanal workshops and domestic outputting networks.

The factory and the prison

The new manufactory might contain modern machinery, or it might not. It might have a central power source, usually water or horsepower, but that too was not a universal characteristic (and steam power only began to be introduced at the end of our period, and remained uncommon until well into the nineteenth century). More common was highly centralized management and control by those providing the capital. However, as one or several of these characteristics, and eventually all of them, came to characterize places of large-scale production, factory production in its full potential was increasingly realized.

Several of the eighteenth-century manufactories were celebrated architectural, mechanical, and social wonders, attracting foreign tourists as well as admiration, fear, and even hatred in the communities where they were established. Among the first was Lombe's silk-throwing mill on the River Derwent in Derbyshire in 1719; from the 1760s there was Boulton and Watt's great Soho works, on the edge of Birmingham; from the 1770s Arkwright's spinning-mills in Derbyshire, Lancashire, and other counties. Although there are hundreds to choose from, these three well-known examples illustrate some of the ways in which factory manufacture began to change production late in the century, and, even earlier, the ways in which people thought of work and profit.

Lombe's mill for winding silk was celebrated by Defoe, whose account has often been reprinted. Eight hundred workers, in a factory 500 feet long with 460 windows, tended intricate machinery powered by water. The bank of throwing-machines worked over 200,000 yards of silk thread every minute. Smaller versions of the same machinery were built once the patent expired. Centralization helped control embezzlement, an issue in all the textile trades, but of particular concern with silk, given its high value, and the many technical reasons a worker might offer for returning a lesser spun weight. Lombe, the son of a Norwich worsted weaver, gained a fortune from his mill, leaving over £120,000 to his wife and two daughters, one of whom married into the nobility. During his life-time he also won civic honours, becoming master of the prestigi-ous mercers' company in 1727, the year he was knighted, and an alderman of London the following year.

Soho, established by Matthew Boulton and James Watt and their sons in Handsworth near Birmingham, was a concentrated epitome of the engineering and metalworking trades of the region that became known as the Black Country. Starting as a collection of shops in the 1760s, by the end of the century it was one of only three major engineering works in England. What was called Soho Manufactury, a main building of three storeys, with a four-storey tower and cupola, and associated shops in the large yard, housed a workforce in 1770 approaching a thousand people. They worked on a wide variety of specialties of the Birmingham metal trades: plated wares, buckles, boxes, large ornamental buttons, and a wide variety of other products, from cheap mass-produced items to costly single items in silver and gilt. The striking significance of the build-ing to visitors was the concentration, under one management and to a great extent one roof, of all the diverse skills and processes cus-tomarily found scattered through the streets and alleys of the met-alworking towns. Equally striking was the establishment of Soho Foundry in 1795, about a mile away. Boulton and Watt's development of the steam engine had been in the role of consulting engineers: some parts were made at Soho Manufactury, but most were ordered from founders. With the establishment of their own foundry at the end of the century they had become engineering manufacturers. Soho Foundry was carefully planned for maximum efficiency, located on a canal with wharves within the factory itself: contem-poraries were astonished by the degree of planning of the works.

Arkwright's cotton factories in Nottingham and Cromford employed some 600, mostly children, by 1774, but in the 1780s his own fact-ories and those of licencees of his machinery became widespread, particularly in Lancashire. By adding his powered carding-machines, roving-machines, and spinning-machines together under one roof with one source of power, the continuous-process factory began to emerge. His wealth was notorious, and his factories hated by domestic and small-shop spinners:

within the space of ten years, from being a poor man not worth £5, now keeps his carriage and servants, is become Lord of a Manor, and has purchased an estate of £20,000; while thousands of women, when they can get work, must make a long day to card, spin, and reel 5040 yards of cotton, and for this they have fourpence or fivepence and no more.[5]

By the 1780s he was erecting a very large building in Manchester, of the kind that came to characterize the mill towns of the mature Industrial Revolution of the first half of the nineteenth century: his wealth was to vastly increase.

As it happened, Arkwright's patent was overturned in litigation by competitors in 1781, and his Manchester factory was delayed: 'he now swears it shall never be worked and will sooner let it for Barricks for soldiers', Boulton wrote to Watt.[6] The similarity often struck contemporaries: Lombe's factory of the 1720s was compared to a barracks in one of the earliest descriptions of a great manufactory. To many workers displaced by its productivity, or forced out of independent production into wage labour, the great manufactory also brought to mind comparisons to military discipline, the slavish brutalized life of the common soldier. The comparisons of factory and barracks, or factory and workhouse, or factory and prison, occurred to many people.

This was more than simply a changing trope. What seems to be a significant shift in late eighteenth-century England is that many workpeople found their lives to be less free. They perceived that loss as one brought about by large-scale production by men of large capital, by the large manufactory, and the degradation of traditional trades. But they also blamed prisons, increased policing by troops, and war and impressment. There were in fact good reasons for believing that changes in those state structures were important contributors to changes in industrial life.

The homologies between the prison and the factory were noted by contemporaries, as they often have been by historians. Between the 1770s and 1812 about half of the county gaols and houses of correction in England were rebuilt or enlarged. Many simply expanded, but a significant and famous minority were reconstructed to ensure, so far as possible, the enforcement of hard labour. The houses of correction, in particular, founded in Elizabethan times to reclaim the poor to 'habits of industry', were reorganized and rebuilt in a number of counties with the same assumptions foremost.

There, and in reformed county gaols, systems of rules, monitoring of time, and punishments for infractions were elaborated in codes whose only parallels in secular life were to be found in large industrial concerns, increasingly housed in manufactories. It has been suggested that a new theory of discipline, particularly congenial to middle-class radical Dissenters of the class interested in both prison reform and industrial production, was important in both. A belief in rational rules, organized and invariable discipline, certainly fascinated G. O. Paul, who reformed Gloucestershire's prison and workhouse system, and Josiah Wedgwood and other industrialists. But prisons were not simply rather like factories; they were used to compel labour in industry.

Imprisonment was crucial to the discipline of labour. Throughout the eighteenth century Parliament added to the basic law of employment set out in the Elizabethan Statute of Artificers, including its provisions for imprisonment of recalcitrant workers. The statute law punished leaving work unfinished, leaving a master before the end of a hiring or contract, and misbehaviour of a great variety of kinds, all with imprisonment. The law was strengthened: for centuries the maximum sentence had been one month, but in 1766 it became for many trades a minimum of one month, a maximum of three. Not all workers fell under the legislation, depending on how the courts viewed particular trades, and whether they were explicitly named in the legislation. But the law was extremely important. This was the most effective law against strike leaders (who necessarily left work unfinished), but it also was routinely used against labour of all kinds. In the course of the eighteenth century it appears that average sentences became longer, and from the evidence of industrializing counties with good house of correction records we know that the numbers imprisoned rose substantially through the 1790s into the early nineteenth century. During that period, in at least one county (Staffordshire), in some years as many workers were imprisoned for breach of contract as there were thieves punished for thefts of all kinds. In short, penal sanctions were used as often against workers as they were against criminals. During strikes, imprisonment of large numbers became common. In one turnout in Northumberland and Durham in 1810, arrested miners were held in the Bishop of Durham's stables when the gaol (which held 300) proved inadequate.

Increased policing by troops was also characteristic of the end of the century. The war with revolutionary and Napoleonic France led to a huge increase in the number of men under arms. This had two consequences. One was the siphoning-off of unemployed young men into the army, a common characteristic of wartime throughout the century (see Ch. 9). Another was the extensive use of press-gangs in areas where unemployment or industrial unrest were common. But probably more important in the longer term was the greater use of troops stationed permanently, for the first time, in the heart of the new manufacturing districts. It had always been common to use troops when industrial disputes led to widespread disorder, but the barracking of large numbers of soldiers, and their much more frequent use to deal with popular disorder, contributed to the new areas of concentrated industry a dimension of state power, and state policing, hitherto unknown in England. In Parliament Pitt defended the new concentrations of troops:

The circumstances of the country, coupled with the general state of affairs, rendered it advisable to provide barracks in other parts of the kingdom. A spirit had appeared in some of the manufacturing towns which made it necessary that troops should be kept near them.[7]

We have discussed in this chapter industrial development and regional specialization; work and freedom; technical changes and social struggles for control of the consequences of industrialization. The terms of the struggle over work and its conditions changed, and the instruments of repression certainly strengthened later in the century, but, as Pitt and others argued, the manufacturing districts, in their size and temper, represented a dangerous new kind of power that might need to be met with force.

9 The Power of the People

We have seen in preceding chapters how much the early-modern state was concerned with public order. Poor laws, marketing laws, statutes governing trades, all were deeply connected with the 'police' of cities (in the old sense of ensuring food supplies and good order), and with maintaining peace in rural areas, particularly where large numbers of industrial outworkers and colliers might threaten production, order, and even the regime through strikes and riots. Such populations were foremost in food riots (by far the most common disturbances outside London), and in trades disputes, in the countryside but also in London. The threat to the regime itself seemed manifest only in the first and second Jacobite Rebellions (1715; 1745) and in the threat of Jacobin sedition during the French Wars (1793–1815). However, such political crises also took much of their meaning from, and constituted a danger only within, the larger context of consent and coercion that shaped personal and group relations throughout the country, throughout the century, at every level of society.

Power in the lives of both individuals and groups is the product both of enduring structures, when it is taken for granted, and of intermittent or entirely contingent circumstances that may occur annually or only once. Each year, for example, gleaners still entered fields in many parts of England after harvest. Although gleaning was found to be not part of the common law by the courts in 1788, it none the less endured until well into the nineteenth century. Part of the reason may have been continuing local custom, quietly endorsed by some magistrates, but it seems more likely that the harvest calendar was the reason. Gleaning took place immediately after harvest, which was when labour was most in demand, and with that bargaining advantage labourers were able to demand in turn that their wives and children be permitted to glean the stubble.

An instance of unique circumstances is the 1745 Jacobite invasion, and its subsequent defeat. While it was successful, individuals or crowds in towns occupied by the Stuart army could humiliate

their personal and political rivals among Whigs. After defeat, prosecutions for sedition and treason were similarly used to settle scores.

More important are the beliefs and practices peculiar to the eighteenth century which allowed the half of the population which
was almost wholly unrepresented in national and local government to none the less impose its views at many points in the
period. The power of communities and occupational groups to riot,
or threaten riot, was for most of the eighteenth century a constant. It arose from the fact that policing in the modern sense had
not been invented. Organized and paid watchmen, private associations for prosecution, and small contingents of mounted and
armed employees of the justices, particularly in London, were more
common than was once believed. Large landed proprietors still
called out their servants to deal with disorder. However, any large-
scale demonstration or riot could only be met with the force of
troops, and for most of the century there were serious difficulties
in using them for policing. When disturbances were widespread,
as in 1740 or 1757 or 1766, the Secretary at War was unable to
respond to more than a proportion of the demands by magistrates
for military assistance. When troops were called in, they could
exacerbate matters if rioters were killed, and in any case crowds
that formed rapidly and vanished equally quickly were very difficult to engage. Moreover, important constitutional assumptions
surrounding the use of troops were an inhibition to officers and
men alike. Although refusing an order to fire on rioters could result
in a court martial, carrying it out might result in being tried for
murder in the civil courts. Demonstrators sometimes stood up to
troops, daring them to fire, particularly when they felt that opinion, even some magisterial opinion, was on the side of their cause.

In this chapter we discuss three recurring ways in which poorer
men and women sometimes imposed their will or resisted that of
their social and political superiors. These are the riot; anonymous
threats and malicious damage; and popular use of the law. All
three changed in nature and significance over the course of the
century.

Riot

How dangerous was the mob? Opinions among the propertied
varied according to circumstance. One pervasive belief for much

of the period was that firm handling, a confident and robust paternalism, would always govern it. Images of dogs and horses recur
in genteel rhetoric; the JP who rode to hounds should be able to
command obedience in the people by his very appearance. Even
after the food riots of 1766, which transfixed the country, destroyed much property, exercised hundreds of troops, and resulted
in special commissions of the judges that tried scores of rioters
and hanged many, such confidence prevailed. The riots in Norwich
had been among the fiercest, but the following year Wilmot, the
Chief Justice of Common Pleas, hearing evidence in an insurance
case arising from property losses there, observed,

The laws, executed with spirit, will always suppress a mob: the magistrates
did it with ease in this case. The undaunted courage of an individual, or
the personal appearance of a man of credit and reputation, disperses or
assuages these fevers of the people: experience, as well as history, shews it,
according to that beautiful simile in Virgil:

> Ac, veluti magno in populo saepe coorta est
> Seditio, saevitique animis ignobile vulgus;
> Iamque faces et saxa volant; furor arma ministrat:
> Tum, pietate gravem ac meritis si forte virum quem
> Conspexere, silent—arrectisque auribus adstant:
> Ille regit dictis animos et pectora mulcet.[1]

Magistrates and other gentlemen did not consult their pocket
Virgils in the face of a riot, but they did draw on a wealth of experience and observation and common conversation. So too did the
rioters. These were well-understood roles (see Ch. 2). We have
already noted in Chapter 4 some of its political uses to Whigs and
Tories. Riots against Dissenters, Catholics, Methodists, and Jews
earlier in the century, and against Jacobins, and for Church-and-
King at the end all had their uses for political parties and factions.
Riot was part of the repertoire of labour disputes, as well as being
a forum for ethnic conflicts, xenophobia, or alternative economies
(see Ch. 8). Wreckers mobbed troops sent to protect ships, smugglers attacked and sometimes killed excisemen, sailors went for
press-gangs and crimps, enclosure rioters tore down fences, colliers
destroyed turnpikes. There were riots against militia-balloting,
against the price of theatre tickets, against the billeting of troops

in towns. But the paradigmatic mob action, for contemporaries and for historians since, was the food riot.

In the last thirty years historians have come to understand how many things it tells us about social relations in the long eighteenth century. In Chapter 5 we have seen how large a part of most families' budgets was spent on food, and how volatile were prices, especially later in the century. We have also emphasized how central to the concerns of government were such public disorders, and the food riot was by far the most common instance, with large-scale outbreaks almost every decade. Some historians have argued that it was peculiarly backward-looking, a marker of a pre-modern society, in contrast to more 'modern' disorders accompanying demands for higher wages, or for overtly political ends. We argue that this is a misunderstanding of the roots of protest in Hanoverian England.

Some food riots were carried out largely by women and boys, particularly in towns; more commonly they were led by industrial workers in the countryside, perhaps most notably colliers, although weavers, nail-makers, or almost any other trade might be involved. Agricultural labourers and farm servants appear rarely, perhaps because they were more dependent on employers, but probably because they were also better supplied with food by them. In towns riots might be caused by incursions of rural workers, or by local inhabitants, or by both. The common aims of the mob were to seize foodstuffs being exported from the region, to expose and punish hoarding, and increasingly to force the selling of flour, wheat, cheese, or meat at a fair price. In a minority of cases food was destroyed, houses and mills were demolished, or the targets of the crowd were forced to contribute drinking-money. The victims were often carefully singled out, and the violence confined to them. The very few deaths that resulted in eighteenth-century food riots were those of rioters, attacked by troops.

The ritualistic aspects of the food riot were common to many other kinds of popular disturbances: they were conducted with songs, parades, fiddles and cornets and drums, bread stuck on pikes, sprigs of broom or fern, or blue ribbons worn on hats and clothing. Such signs borrowed from local loyalties: Jacobite symbols in the Midlands at mid-century, Jacobinism in many places at its end, and references to local popular and gentry traditions in many places, only some of which have been deciphered. The mobs sometimes declared themselves 'regulators', and they emphasized in shouts and songs, and sometimes in anonymous letters, that their cause was justice. The ritual and symbolic aspects of the riot served two purposes. They not only united participants in common cause, they also expressed a demand for genteel support, particularly that of JPs in the countryside, and the mayor and aldermen of corporations in the towns.

This demand rested squarely on the law. It was effective because it was legitimated by the laws against forestallers, regraters, and engrossers. And a substantial proportion of magistrates, probably a majority until late in the century, shared the mob's belief that dearths were aggravated by buying and selling by middlemen, and that the state should set limits on markets in times of dearth: at such times there was (in Thompson's phrase) a 'moral economy' that took precedence over the right to profit, as we have seen in Chapters 5 and 6. They often shared the crowd's prejudices against Quakers or other dissenters who were likely to be targets if they were middlemen. Even when a JP did not believe that the old marketing offences raised prices, it was expedient to concur, because exemplary prosecutions, or the promise of them (sometimes announced by quarter sessions), could help to persuade rioters to go home. The other means magistrates themselves had for conciliation, or prevention, were the raising of funds for charitable purchase and distribution of food, threats, or exhortations to tenant farmers to bring food to market, and especially (as Mr Justice Wilmot recommended), confident negotiation with the mob on a face to face basis. Many justices (perhaps even judges like Wilmot) had practical experience of the fact that, properly handled, such techniques worked.

When they did not, magistrates wrote to London requesting troops. There was some panic among those facing the 1757 militia riots and 1766 food riots, and other large outbreaks, and on such occasions troops were despatched to the most affected areas by the Secretary at War. But the mid-century consensus among propertied men was that the use of military force against civilians was to be carefully watched. It had, after all, been the basis for revolutionary and republican power in the hands of Cromwell a century before. Hence troops were almost always removed from

assize towns when the courts were sitting, and constitutional concerns surrounded the issue of the place of the army in civil society.
Blackstone stated the received wisdom of mid-century (and classical
precedent) when he wrote,

Nothing then, according to these principles, ought to be more guarded
against in a free state, than making the military power, when such a one
is necessary to be kept on foot, a body too distinct from the people. Like
ours, it should wholly be composed of natural subjects; it ought only to
be enlisted for a short and limited time; the soldiers also should live inter-
mixed with the people; no separate camp, no barracks, no inland fortresses
should be allowed.[2]

Food rioters thus knew that within certain limits they were
unlikely to be prosecuted, unlikely to be shot, and more likely to be
conciliated. The magistracy respected the mob's ability to destroy
property and civic peace, but also shared a common set of values.
This common set of values had deep historical roots, for gentlemen,
not only in the law but in the history of riot, the constitution,
and ideologies of paternalism and patriotism.

The chronology of the food riot is striking. Historians first noted
its importance for the eighteenth century, traced it back to the
seventeenth century, then the sixteenth, and now are exploring
its medieval origins (and classical scholars find it even further
back). The food riot has deep roots; but looking forward from
Hanoverian England, it ends, with the exception of a few scattered
instances, in the early nineteenth century. For that reason some
have argued that it is a peculiarly pre-modern phenomenon, somehow less advanced, in some sense, than strikes for wages, purely
political demonstrations, or other crowd phenomena that continued through the nineteenth and into the twentieth centuries.
The analysis is borrowed from teleological, progressivist assumptions within both Marxism and modernization theory, and although
not always intended, the effect has been to characterize the food
rioter (much as non-European peoples were characterized and
often still are) as somehow lower on a scale of sophistication, or political awareness, or indeed 'civilization'.

We could speculate about what caused the food rioter to become
a more modern person, but a more useful approach to the de-
mise of the food riot lies in an analysis of the changing political

circumstances, and the balance of coercion, at the end of the century. It is worth noting first, however, that a similar dichotomy of traditional versus modern has sometimes been applied to the strikes, industrial sabotage, and riots that punctuated labour demands throughout the century. Thus attempts to defend or extend older protective legislation are said to be traditional, in effect lost causes, products of a different mentality from more modern labour-bargaining. This dichotomy too seems to be misleading, for in the eighteenth century we find organized trades not only making demands for the enforcement or enactment of protective legislation, and destroying machinery (both supposedly older, traditional weapons), but also striking for higher than customary wages, and organizing countywide and indeed nationwide organizations to do so, as West Country weavers did at mid-century (see Ch. 7). Moreover, all kinds of industrial or artisanal workers could be found participating in the food riot.

One conclusion is that the food riot and labour demands for the enforcement or re-enactment of protective legislation both arose commonly in cohesive communities of workers and consumers, especially those centred on industrial and occupational groups with ties of neighbourhood, kin, and trade, and hence common values. For this reason some labour historians have appropriated the term 'moral economy' from the food riot, and applied it to such industrial disputes. The emphasis is on the notion of a shared set of moral values, limiting the right to exploit labour, just as the food rioter and sympathetic magistrate believed in the need to protect the average consumer. However, the similarities are even closer. For at the root of both kinds of supposedly traditional demands, for a moral economy in food and a similar balancing of interests between capital and labour, was the powerful legitimation of law. Even in Parliament, and certainly in the counties, there was a substantial body of élite opinion into the second half of the century, and sometimes much later, that approved protective legislation for labour, both as consumers and as workers, and continued to enact it or to attempt to do so, as we have seen in earlier chapters. It is an anachronism to label it traditional; it could be seen to be traditional only after the tradition ended. Moreover, as we have also seen, the state's repudiation and erasure of both bodies of law was late and (in historical terms) sudden (see Ch. 7).

Agreement between the ruling oligarchy and the labouring poor with respect to the regulation of food- and labour-markets ended, as we have seen, between 1772 and 1814. The end of this agreement also meant an end to the possibility of effective appeal, by food rioters and protesting artisans, to local or national government. Legislation enacted earlier in the century with all the solemnity of parliamentary procedure and royal assent, doctrines declared by the highest judges in the land to be coeval with the common law, came to be termed absurd, ridiculous, oppressive. The food riot and demands for protective legislation, as claims for legal rights, became impossible. From its side, government too now made a different calculation. It had conciliated rioters, whether food rioters or weavers, partly because of shared values, but partly because of fears of their power. With the repudiation of the old law in the name of free markets, the values were no longer shared; but what of the formerly feared power of the mob?

The answer is suggested by the balance of coercive force in the country at the historical moment when the idea of the free market triumphed: they are inseparable. There is no one moment, of course, but if we want an example, a significant one was the night of 15–16 September 1800, in London. A mob, some said the largest group of food rioters seen in the metropolis in the entire century, tore down the house and commercial buildings of Rusby, a leading London corn-factor. They were apparently inspired to do so by his conviction for marketing offences, and the denunciation of his crimes by Lord Kenyon, Chief Justice of England, two months before.

The implications were ominous to government. The partisans of political economy, like the Prime Minister and Home Secretary, were appalled that the most senior judge was ignorant of the benefits of free markets. They were deeply concerned that his enthusiasm for consumer protection might legitimate widespread riot, during the most serious dearth in the century, and in the middle of war with Revolutionary France. However, they were also more confident than many of their predecessors that food rioters were not only wrong, but need not be feared. For the war, and a new concern with crowd control, had turned England into an armed camp. Newly erected barracks in the major manufacturing districts meant that rioters could now be met with a degree of organized and locally available force that had not been available to British governments since 1660. And henceforth there was much less treating with the mob. Throughout the food crisis at the very end of the century, the government castigated magistrates who failed to uphold the new doctrines of free markets, hanged rioters who tried the old tactics, and deployed troops with an efficiency and determination not seen in England since the Rebellion of 1745. Like Jacobitism, the moral economy was destroyed by the forces of law, a competing legitimacy, and armed might.

Anonymous threats and malicious damage

If riot was a public assertion of power by communities confident of their rights and optimistic about their strength, there were also what have been termed the weapons of the weak. This is sometimes an accurate, sometimes a misleading term if extended to Hanoverian England. The repertoire of such actions was wide. Animal-maiming, arson of barns or ricks, the lopping of young oak trees, dismantling of fences and hedges around new enclosures, the killing of favourite hunting-dogs, cutting cloth in the loom, theft of crucial parts of steam engines or other machinery, were all common tactics, and attracted serious criminal sanctions: many of those listed were punishable by death. What do we mean by common? It is difficult to be precise. Historians of the food riot, which was a much more public event, and more likely to be reported, have discovered that many were unreported in the press, and the totals are constantly increasing through research. The much more local, small-scale events we have listed here are even less amenable to quantification. In part this is because the targets of such violence were often anxious that they should not be known, or because the acts were so local in nature that any advertising for information was equally limited in extent. To take one example: we only know about so dramatic an act as the slitting of the throats of the five coach horses of a Midlands landlord and magistrate because he mentions in a letter that he had put up a notice in the local pub. He and other victims often did not advertise an offer of pardons for information in the *London Gazette* or any other newspaper.

We know, however, that some kinds of malicious damage were widespread. Destruction of cloth and looms or other machinery was a very common tactic in eighteenth-century industrial disputes, and

Luddism, its best-known manifestation, was remarkable only in its synchronicity and breadth of organization. Such acts were sometimes carried out anonymously by disguised groups of workers, intimidating other workers from work or masters from introducing machinery. At other times the acts were carried out overtly, at least until specific kinds of attacks on machinery were made liable to the death penalty (as was the case with knitting-frames in 1812). Although intimidation by leaders was not uncommon, it was more often the case that large communities of colliers, or tin-miners, or weavers, or shoemakers, and their families, saw malicious damage and threatening letters as normal and necessary practices in serious industrial confrontations.

In rural settings threats and the malicious destruction of property were more likely to be anonymous. In part this was because rural labourers and farm servants were probably more exposed to prosecution or dismissal for protest. In some cases it probably indicates the relative isolation of aggrieved individuals, carrying out acts of personal, sometimes obsessive revenge. But anonymity is a potentially misleading description. If exactly which individuals were responsible was often difficult to ascertain (and the law, for obvious reasons, was intent upon finding and identifying the writers of anonymous letters, as well as the leaders of riots), it was very often quite clear who was aggrieved. In the cases of tree-barking and fence-breaking after enclosures, commoners who had opposed the Act were natural suspects. In disputes over poaching prosecutions those who killed landlord's dogs or threatened game-keepers were supported by a large proportion of the community. In such circumstances lines were drawn: on one side were the enclosers or landlords and magistrates anxious to prosecute, on the other a community of sympathizers who were unwilling to cooperate with the law. When witnesses came forward in such circumstances, they were ostracized by their communities, and often had to leave.

Were these the weapons of the weak? It is certainly true that some acts of arson and animal-maiming were carried out by individuals, dismissed servants, or others with a personal as opposed to a group grievance, and little power. However, the most common kinds of malicious damage, and those most feared by the gentlemen and millers and farmers who suffered them, were actions fuelled by a large body of outraged popular opinion. Moreover, even when an aggrieved individual committed such an act, a wider constituency watched and was not necessarily displeased. A farm-labourer dismissed, or refused poor relief, who cut off the ears of the farmer's sheep, or barked the magistrates' saplings, had induced the farmer or magistrate to think twice in future whenever considering such a case. Other labourers and poor people could only benefit.

The timing, choice of target, and manner of its execution probably made the intended message clear enough to the victim. When group demands were more complex, and the aggrieved felt the need for greater explanation or justification of their acts, the anonymous threatening letter was a common recourse.[3] It may be an accident of preservation, but there do seem to have been many more of them after about 1790. Since popular literacy probably declined, if anything, toward the end of the century, an increase in the tactic may well indicate worsening social relations, a greater sense of popular grievance. Part of the explanation may be that as the mutual understandings of people and magistracy about markets, poor relief, and paternalism diverged, anonymous letters from the poor represent a desperate attempt to restore a broken dialogue. We should also be aware of the significance of the anonymous threatening letter as artefact. Not only did it convey a disquieting kind of threat, sometimes expressed in drawing or caricature, it also evoked the power of literacy: the power of the text, of the lawbook, of the Bible, and the mode of power characteristic of those with education, status, and influence. The use of biblical language in many anonymous threatening letters at the end of the century was an expression of the belief that the recipient had transgressed, and that on the side of the writer were ranged authority, justice, truth, and the highest law.

Popular recourse to law

As we have seen in our consideration of the food riot, English law as well as the law of God was a significant part of the justification felt by rioters. The law was not being enforced; they would enforce it, or demand that the authorities do so. But to a limited extent, other parts of the criminal and civil law were used by the labouring poor as well as by the middling sort. We should not exaggerate the extent of this form of power: lawsuits and even the cheaper criminal prosecution were used far less frequently, and far less successfully, by the bottom half of the population than by those higher. As always, the poor were the chief target of the criminal law. But in some interesting contexts, poor men and women were able to invoke English law to a much greater degree.

One place in which this was possible was London. The tribes of 'low attornies', with or without formal qualifications, the prevalence of fees contingent on success, meant that even the highest criminal and civil court, King's Bench, where the Lord Chief Justice of England sat, was open to some people of very limited means. It was possible for them even to harass magistrates with suits or criminal prosecutions for magisterial indiscretions. And the immense varieties of courts in London, dozens of them, and the prevalence of justices interested in their income from fees, meant that a highly interested use of the law was available to a wider sector of the population than anywhere else in England.

But even in rural parishes some labourers and paupers could use the law to their benefit. One right that caused some indignation among the farmers and better-off tradesmen who were overseers of the poor was the right of those denied relief to appeal to the justices. A more generous spirit, or the knowledge that the poor rate fell on tenants rather than landlords, could persuade the JP to make a more generous award. There was always a degree of divergence in the interests of rural magistrates and farmers: for the former, public order, a reputation as a generous or fair paternalist, were important considerations; for the latter, maintaining low wages and low poor rates were the desiderata. It was also not uncommon for gentlemen justices to be appalled at individual acts of cruelty by overseers of the poor, particularly when they deported pregnant or ill paupers over parish boundaries. Sometimes they not only castigated the overseers, they prosecuted them on manslaughter charges when deaths resulted.

The same difference of role can be seen in the exercise of the magistrates' power to adjudicate in labour disputes between individual masters and servants. Both under the Statute of Artificers and a number of eighteenth-century enactments, magistrates could order misbehaving or absent workers to gaol, or command employers to pay wages they owed but had refused the worker. In such cases the magistrate often heard the details of complaints from both parties, but the surviving evidence suggests that in the eighteenth century magistrates were far more likely to be awarding unpaid wages than to be incarcerating delinquent workers. The farmers and clothiers and ironmasters who had such cases go against them were the direct employers of labour. The magistrates, whether landed gentlemen or clerics, were able to stand, to a considerable degree, outside, as adjudicators, and when they wished, as paternalists.

The meaning of these specific and limited forms of access to justice in summary hearings before JPs, and, in London, even in the royal courts, is a matter of current debate among historians. One common interpretation is that by using the law, the poor showed that they assented to it. We very much doubt the value of this generalization. The use of law could be, and often demonstrably was, highly instrumental, limited to the current case, motivated by an individual's quest of power over another. Even when acts with common moral valuations were at issue—notably thefts and murders—individuals and communities made judgements about the law that were highly specific. Smuggling communities might not all support the murder of excisemen, but they could understand how it could happen (and might be necessary if smugglers were risking the death penalty if detected). Weaving and coining communities understood the ironic ramifications of local economies, where respected and wealthy manufacturers participated in receiving embezzled yarn or in processing clipped guineas. There was not a common moral assent to all the criminal law, particularly when so large a part of it criminalized the weapons labour used to bargain, and poverty and homelessness itself.

The changing balance of coercion and consent

Two significant changes in eighteenth-century commissions of the peace affected the balance of coercive power in many counties toward the end of the century. One lay in their composition; the other was the geographical distribution of magistrates.

The most active magistrates were increasingly likely to be clerics. Early in the century this was rare: fears of Jacobitism among the clergy made Walpole loath to appoint many to the bench, and it is likely that a smaller proportion of Anglican clergymen had the property and status deemed necessary for a magistrate than was true later. Moreover, political considerations dominated appointments, and the most powerful gentlemen and peers were deemed most appropriate to be named. Tithe commutation at enclosure, mostly after mid-century, enriched many livings; Jacobitism and indeed party-political conflict became much less significant a threat in the same period.

Most important, wealthy gentry seemed less and less willing to act as justices, even when they accepted appointment. Thus in the later eighteenth century governments met the common complaint that too few justices were willing to act by appointing more and more clergymen and other 'marginal gentlemen'. And many of the clerics took on the greatest part of county judicial business, especially in the Midlands and the east. Four of the ten most active justices in Staffordshire in the second half of the century were clerics, and they committed well over half of prisoners to trial and summary imprisonment. By the period of the French Wars, 40 per cent of those sent to the Stafford House of Correction were committed by Anglican clergymen in their capacity as magistrates.

There were probably several causes for this development. The easing of Whig and Tory political tension early in the century meant that it was less crucial to be on the Bench to protect one's personal and party interests, and the higher gentry appear to have hence become less willing to serve (see Ch. 4). It may also be the case that gentlemen were increasingly deterred by the scale or temper of disorder and indigence with which they would have to deal if they became active justices. For it appears that long-term changes in the economy, and in social inequality, had pervasive effects. In the sixteenth and early seventeenth centuries poverty, vagrancy, and lawlessness were matters of deep concern to the central and local state. In contrast, the period of the late seventeenth and early eighteenth century was, as we have seen, one of higher real wages and greater prosperity for most of the labouring poor, due to good harvests and limited population growth. With some exceptions, riots were less common and operated within a set of mutually understood limits; and dealing with theft, poverty, and some of the other more burdensome judicial duties was less onerous than it had been a hundred years before. But as harvest failures, poor rates, and prosecuted crime all increased later in the eighteenth century,

wealthy country gentlemen preferred to leave enforcement of the
law to less prominent gentlemen, some quite marginal, and many
of them clerics.

The second main change in many county benches was an old
but continuing pattern of residential change, accelerated by the
population growth of the later part of the eighteenth century.
Gentry justices tended to leave their former residences in newly
populous and disorderly parts of the country where rural and
urban industry was expanding. In many manufacturing districts it
was extremely difficult to find a magistrate, even a clerical magistrate. There was therefore an evolution in local government that
reinforced some of the developments we have described in national government. Recognition in Parliament of the traditional
claims by labour and the poor, and face-to-face dealings with their
disputes by wealthier gentry and peers, both declined in the second half of the century. The poor became less known to the rulers
of England at the same time as their traditional claims to equity and
paternalism came to be scorned. Population growth and the concentration of new trades probably accentuated such divisions. The
pullulation of peoples in the new manufacturing districts astounded contemporaries. Defoe in the 1720s had remarked on it with
pride, but the density of the Potteries or emerging Black Country or
Manchester later in the century began to seem like the most alarming parts of London to many country gentlemen. In the food riots
in the Midlands at the end of the century, magistrates were often not
to be found residing for many miles around the most populous
industrial areas. The letters from the few who did, beseeching the
government to send troops, sound like the voices of colonizers surrounded by dangerous, and dangerously unknown, foreign tribes.

In part this tone was also a product of the fear of Jacobinism.
Both central government and local magistrates invested in spies
throughout the French Wars, an investment that probably increased
the fears and credulity of many JPs, even when the reports they
forwarded were discounted by the Home Secretary. But whether
cause or effect, the belief in conspiracies, in danger, in the unknown
intentions of workmen and food rioters, was different in quality
and kind from assessments earlier in the century, except perhaps
during the Jacobite scares. The kind of confidence in the ability
of any proper gentleman to handle a mob that was expressed by

Chief Justice Wilmot in 1767 was less common. Even before the beginning of the wars with Revolutionary France in 1793, the political intentions of the mob had come to seem more dangerous. The destruction of property, threats to Parliament, and insults to its members that accompanied the five days of anti-Catholic London riots named after Lord George Gordon in 1780 also reshaped opinion (Ch. 11). When Gordon continued to encourage recalcitrant Blacks, debtors, and condemned criminals by proclaiming the injustice of government and law through the 1780s, and specifically denounced the capital law against theft, the government prosecuted and imprisoned him for the rest of his life for undermining the consent of the governed on which civil society depended.

We are suggesting a slow but significant sea change in social relations and the exercise of power in the last quarter of the century. It appears in part to be related to the kinds of economic changes we have already noted: poor harvests, greater indigence, more riot and crime. It also may be partly due to increased uneasiness and a lack of confidence at the top of the political regime. The loss of the American colonies after a humiliating military defeat in 1782 had a profound impact. The first alarming appearance of insanity in King George III in 1787 compromised the legitimacy of the very embodiment of the state (see Ch. 1). And as the ideology of markets penetrated parliamentary opinion, force seemed more necessary, more likely of success, than conciliation in dealing with the power of the people. The 1780s, in part because of increased want but almost certainly also because of an increased intolerance for disorder and crime, saw the highest rates of prosecutions, death sentences, and hangings in England up to that point in the century.

By the early 1790s the Professor of Laws at Cambridge questioned Blackstone's traditional constitutional strictures on 'barracks' and 'inland fortresses':[4]

Since this was written, with a genuine love of liberty, by the author, experience has proved, that the most formidable enemy which the people of England have to dread, is their own lawless mobs. Care ought therefore to be taken, that soldiers may never become familiar with the people in great towns, lest they should be more inclined to join, than to quell, a riot. *Nam neque quies gentium sine armis, neque arma sine stipendiis, neque stipendia sine tributis, haberi queunt.*[5]

In the 1790s press-gangs and want drove a very significant proportion of the most desperate workers and labourers into the
armed forces, where much harsher discipline prevailed (see Ch.
10). Within the forces themselves it seems likely that a greater
gulf, and more coercion, marked relations of officers and men.
Naval historians have noted the relatively consensual nature of discipline at mid-century. The great naval mutinies of 1797 probably
changed things for decades. We know that on Nelson's flagship
Victory in the first seven months of 1804, 105 out of a complement of about 800 were flogged. That is about fifteen a month.
On average, then, the crew of the *Victory* saw a man whipped with
a cat-o'-nine-tails, often until his back was a bloody pulp of lacer-
ated tissue, every other day.

In the years of the French Revolution the rhetoric surrounding
reference to the people was increasingly suffused with blood. 'We
are sorry to hear that you have had symptoms of Rioting in your
quarter', wrote the great engineer James Watt to the great iron-
founder John Wilkinson on 10 April 1791; 'the madness seems
very prevalent over all at present, and I doubt will not be allayed
without a copious bleeding. . . . This comes of preaching up the
Soveraignty and Majesty of the people, we cannot say their Maj-
esties are very gracious.' There was similar language from the other
side, particularly in the great dearth at the end of the century. An
anonymous letter to the officers and privates of the Bromwich
Association in April 1800 informed the former, who gloried in
scarlet waistcoats,

this is to you damnation blasted & dam'd red faced devils that have your
lessons taught you, yes perish your lims and sever your joints, we don't
care a dam for your big Devils as wear that damnation bloody bloody rag
about your damn'd paunch bellys. Blood shall be spilt from you like a
butcher sticking a pig.[6]

What significance can we attach to such statements? We can
gloss that of James Watt. He was probably slyly twitting Wilkinson,
who was suspected of Jacobin sympathies. But Watt did not shy
from coercive measures: he advocated the press-gang for recalcitrant workers in the 1780s, and his partner Boulton had offenders
whipped at the factory gate, and prosecuted under capital statutes.
So too did Wilkinson. The medical image of 'bleeding' is perhaps

appropriate to their class (as dogs and horses were to country gentlemen) but it was also suggested by common public events, whether
of capital punishment or the whipping of rogues, vagabonds, and
petty thieves. But what are we to make of the anonymous correspondent of the Bromwich Association? He is one of a host of
such writers, men and women with personal or political grievances,
or with biblical visions in their heads, of whom we can only say
(since we must often guess the context) that they had rage, fear,
or despair in their hearts. Their misspelt letters litter the Home
Office papers late in the century, and crop up from year to year
in many large collections of estate and personal correspondence
through the entire period. However, in their fiercer language and
greater frequency at the end of the century, their frequent evoca-
tion of revolution and the end of monarchy, they announced a
new social temper, a new politics.

10 War and Peace

Britain was at war for much of the long eighteenth century. In the 126 years between 1689 and 1815, Britain was under military arms for no less than 65; in other words, roughly one year in every two (see Fig. 8). This meant that the fall of James II in 1688 inaugurated the longest period of English/British warfare since the Middle Ages. Impressive as this might seem, historians have not considered its broader implications until quite recently. One reason for this neglect was that the eighteenth-century mode of warfare appeared very different from the modern notion of total war; that is, one that actively involved the energies and resources of the nation as a whole. By comparison with modern wars, the participation of the populace at large appeared slight, the extent of government intervention, meagre; and its political ramifications seemed modest. Britain, so the argument ran, experienced some sort of industrial 'take-off' in the eighteenth century. Its economy and society did not appear to be ravaged by war. Its government remained relatively decentralized, with many functions, particularly those pertaining to law, order, and welfare, delegated to local authorities. And for all the political instability that war drew in its wake, the rule of the landed aristocracy and the oligarchical structure of politics continued unchecked. In the Great War of 1914–18 approximately 55 per cent of all men aged 15–49 joined the armed forces; in the American and Napoleonic Wars, the proportion was under 15 per cent. The Great War saw important collectivist experiments: a government pegging prices, imposing wealth taxes, supervising industries, bargaining for industrial peace with major unions, and generally intervening in the economy. It also witnessed a striking mobilization of women in the workforce and the promise of democracy in return for citizen participation. No eighteenth-century war seemed so portentous in its effects upon society.

There is an important element of truth in this comparison, but it is misleading to the extent that it obscures the critical developments in Hanoverian society that resulted from war. The cumulative effect of war in the long eighteenth century was formidable and structurally significant. The century marked the coming of age of Britain as a major military power in Europe, whose navy, in particular, safeguarded major trading routes and interests. The state's military role made it the most formidable actor in the domestic economy. At the height of every war, the army and navy sustained an establishment whose population was larger than every city save London. The royal dockyards each employed a workforce of 2,000 men at a time when few businesses employed 200. And the capital investment in the fleet was by 1800 over five times the total fixed capital of the West Riding woollen industry, whose 243 mills cost approximately £402,000.

War and money

In order to pay and supply this increasing military establishment, Britain needed money and an expanding state bureaucracy to collect it. This was especially true of the departments of Customs and Excise, whose numbers nearly tripled (to over 7,100 officers by 1783) in the century after 1690. Taxes alone, moreover, became insufficient to pay for persistent war for which average annual expenditure rose sixfold from 1693–7 to 1812–15. Britain had continually to borrow money to meet the shortfall in revenue, and the long-term debt rose from £16.7 million at the end of the Nine Years War in 1697 to over £238 million by 1780 to as high as £1,003 million by 1816. Within 120 years the National Debt had grown 60 times, a very formidable increase in an economy with small growth rates, less than 1 per cent per annum of GNP in the years 1700–80 and no more than 1.5 per cent per annum thereafter.

The ability of the government to borrow money from a broadening range of investors, both domestic and international, was indispensable to its success in waging so many wars on such a formidable scale. But that success was very dependent upon a secure and viable tax base to repay the long-term debt and to finance new wars. Despite the relatively low rates of economic growth for a burgeoning industrial economy, that tax burden significantly increased as the century wore on. Allowing for population growth and price inflation, historians have calculated that the per caput income appropriated as taxes rose from 16 per cent in 1716, to 23 per cent at the end of the American War, to as much as 35 per cent at the turn of the century. In real terms it nearly doubled under the first three Georges. Indeed, Britons appear to have borne a tax burden that was arguably twice as heavy as the French, despite the ingrained belief that Britain's traditional enemies groaned under huge taxes within an oppressive *ancien régime*. Only the Dutch, Prussians, and Austrians appear to have paid more.

Who actually paid? Or, more specifically, on whom did the incidence of war-driven taxation fall? The answer is, increasingly on the consumer. Although the landed class paid a significant proportion of the taxes required for the wars of the late seventeenth and early eighteenth century through the direct taxation of their estates, after 1713 its contribution in this area declined in importance. Thereafter the land tax rarely made up more than 20 per cent of governmental income, partly because ministers wished to placate members of their own class whose rents did not keep pace with taxation before 1740, and partly because the tax assessments were internally policed by the county property-holders and increasingly bore no relation to their actual market value. Only with the introduction of income tax in 1799 was this trend reversed, and then briefly (see Fig. 6). In the place of direct taxes came a modest increase in customs duties and more importantly, a substantial rise in excise duties on commodities such as beer, malt, hops, soap, salt, candles, and leather. Customs duties on tea, sugar, spirits, and tobacco became important sources of revenue for the government, but they were cumbrous to collect and perennially evaded through smuggling. Excise duties, on the other hand, were collected at the point of production by a veritable juggernaut of administrators. Because of the legal powers invested in the Excise Office, the duties were difficult to evade and were routinely passed on to the consumer in the form of higher prices.

Britons thus increasingly paid for war through indirect taxation, taxation that was also socially regressive. Like the landed gentry, merchants and West Indian planters were powerfully placed to resist substantial tax increases on their commodities. And manufacturers in some of the expanding sectors of the economy, most notably cottons, woollens, metal and wood products, pottery, also derived benefits from the fact that their products were exempted from the excise. The result was that the middling sort and the labouring classes in general bore a disproportionate part of the tax burden. Politicians sometimes made a great parade of the fact that they were prepared to tax the luxury items of the rich such as carriages, silver plate, servants, wig powder, and dogs, and at the same time declined to tax the necessities of the poor. With the exception of salt, which Sir Robert Walpole deliberately introduced in 1732 as an alternative to a reduced land tax, basic foodstuffs and plain clothing were exempted from the excise. Moreover, in periods of very high taxation, poorer varieties of a taxed commodity, table as opposed to strong beer, for example, or tallow as opposed to wax candles, were given token concessions.

None of this substantially altered the attempt to tax the poor as far as was politically feasible. By the 1790s this included items that had become necessities or semi-necessities, such as tobacco, sugar, and tea. For the bulk of the labouring classes the burden of taxation rose faster than wages, and indeed became heavier at precisely the time that non-monetary forms of income (in the shape of customary rights and privileges) were in decline. Sir Frederick Eden's sample budgets for labouring families in the 1790s suggests that coal, tea, sugar, candles, soap, and starch, all items subject to tax, represented over 20 per cent of a family's expenditure. And this did not include shoes and clothing, both items that were likely taxable, which accounted for a further 10 per cent of plebeian budgets. For families whose income seldom exceeded its expenditure, whose rights to gleaning and so forth were being whittled away, this was a hard burden to bear.

Recruiting for war

The burden of war upon plebeian families did not simply extend to taxation. It also involved 'personal service'. Throughout the eighteenth century the demand for troops and seamen grew faster than population supply, with the result that the government had to scour the streets and lanes, the pubs and fairs, for suitable recruits. Because the pay was meagre, discipline harsh, and disease rampant, armed service generally appealed only to the reckless, the adventurous, and the indigent: to those whose heads might be turned by the blarney and booze of the recruiting sergeant; to men who wished to evade family responsibilities; and to those who were driven into the armed forces 'by necessity'.[1] As a Northamptonshire man remarked during the dearth of 1801: 'People can scarce live here. The young ones go for soldiers and the old ones starve at home.'[2]

As war progressed bounties had to be offered to sustain the voluntary complement of men. This often amounted to as much as three or four months' wages, and under the Quota Acts could constitute as much as a labourer could earn in eighteen months. Even so, governments had to use coercion to man the regiments and fleets. Vagrants were routinely enlisted into the armed forces on the grounds that their disorderly behaviour and masterless status merited such action. Criminals were sometimes reprieved on condition they joined up. In 1782, for example, Mr Justice Willes of King's Bench recommended a pardon for William Chatterlin who had been found guilty of horse stealing at the Warwickshire assizes, on the grounds that 'some favourable Circumstances' had been discovered in his case and that he was 'a Young healthy Man' who was very willing to escape the noose by serving in the marine. Similarly, Lord Loughborough recommended a pardon for three men found guilty of grand larceny at the Rutland and Leicestershire assizes who preferred to enlist rather than face transportation or imprisonment.

In the case of the navy, the government reserved the right to enlist the services of seamen in wartime, recognizing the importance of seafaring experience to the effective manning of the fleet. This selective form of conscription was also extended to all men between the ages of 18 and 55 who 'used the sea', a liberal definition that gave press-gangs licence to pick up just about any straggler or quay- and riverside-worker. Just as the 'noble and most opulent of the nation' contributed taxes and governance to the public welfare, wrote Charles Butler in the first sustained defence of naval impressment, so should the poor man in 'personal labour and service'.[3] Such an argument ignored, of course, the very real contribution that the poor made to war-driven taxation. At the same time it invoked older notions of 'unfree' labour to legitimize the conscription of the seafarers, fishermen, keelmen, dock-workers, and sometimes even artisans.

Naval impressment was a constant hazard for portside workers as the few nautical autobiographies of the era remind us. It was also more intrusive than historians have assumed. From the mid-century onwards, when the Admiralty established a network of rendezvous in the major ports and seafaring towns, impressment extended beyond the southern ports to encompass those of north Britain and Ireland. By 1795 it embraced the country as a whole, for three Acts specified minimum quotas of recruitment for all counties in England, Scotland, and Wales, moving in effect upon territory hitherto reserved for the army. Naval impressment was also deeply resented, not only because it undermined a seaman's capacity to profit from higher wages in the merchant marine, but because it subjected such men to long voyages without leave and flouted their rights as free-born Englishmen. As David Hume recognized, it was a state-sanctioned act of 'violence' carried on 'amidst the greatest jealousy and watchfulness of the people'.[4]

Sailors sought to evade impressment by taking temporary employment inland and by pretending they belonged to those categories of seafarers that had gained official protections from the press. Sometimes they even had themselves arrested for debt to escape the foul holds of the press-tenders. Beyond these forms of legal prevarication seamen were also prepared to confront the gangs head-on. Violent affrays between press-gangs and seamen were frequent and bloody, with the latter quite ready to use pistols, cutlasses and knives to ward off their assailants. In the opening months of mobilization, in particular, anti-impressment riots were quite common. In the months before the Seven Years War, at least eighteen major riots were reported in the press and in letters to the Admiralty. In the Nootka Sound crisis of 1790, thirty-three affrays were reported in the newspapers alone; while in the opening months of the French War three years later, sailors openly confronted the gangs in several ports by attacking the rendezvous; that is, the headquarters of the press-gang. At Liverpool, for example, where the press-gang had killed the master of a sloop whom they sought to impress, 'a large body of sailors' besieged the rendezvous in Strand Street and demolished another at New Quay, leaving 'scarcely anything but the walls, floors and roof undestroyed'.[5] At Whitby, Whitehaven, and Greenock, collective resistance was such as to make these ports virtual 'no-go' areas for the impress service. At Whitby, Rear-Admiral Pringle reported that the service could not operate without military intervention to 'disperse Riots and protect the Officers and their Gangs in the execution of their duty'. At Greenock, he stated that 'when the Gangs have attempted landing on different parts of the Shore, they have been driven off by the People, and rescues have taken place more than once upon the Quays'. All that could be done here, he concluded, was to recruit men from vessels in the Firth of Clyde.[6]

Manning the fleet remained a vexatious and troublesome problem for the government, who continually had to jockey local authorities into cooperating with the Admiralty. It was only because impressment allowed those authorities and their mercantile allies the opportunity to sift out the rebellious and recalcitrant and retain some control over their more reliable workers, that the system worked at all. Even then, local authorities had to come to terms with the domestic repercussions of impressment and of wartime recruitment in general. In times of war or of pre-war mobilizations, family separations increased by 40 per cent or more as men were impressed or sought refuge from unhappy or poverty-stricken marriages in the relative anonymity of the armed forces.[7] Poor relief sometimes rose by an even larger margin. In Sunderland in 1793 the overseers of the poor estimated that their poor-relief expenses would triple as the 'families of impressed men' fell on the parish. In Newcastle, too, poor relief shot up to accommodate the families of impressed or volunteer seamen. Sir Frederick Eden found a similar pattern in North and South Shields. Once the principal breadwinners had departed and the bounty money had gone, the families of servicemen had no other recourse but begging or parish relief. The first major inquiry into mendicity in the metropolis in 1796 found that the majority of poor were married women who alleged that their husbands 'are gone away from them into either the army or the navy'.[8]

War, demobilization, and crime

An increase in the poor rates in wartime was something that the propertied classes could accept with a certain equanimity. To begin with, the increase was counteracted by the fact that recruitment mopped up a large part of the male population who might otherwise have been underemployed or unemployed and a potential burden on the rates. In any case, a higher poor rate was a small price to pay for the potential long-term effects of war: the security of overseas markets; the fillip to war-related industries; the windfalls of privateering; and the profits that might accrue from government loans, whose terms were generally more favourable as the war progressed. Further, manufacturers like Boulton and Watt believed that wartime exigencies tended to increase social discipline, especially if a few timely impressments removed the recalcitrant from the workforce.

The prospect of demobilization, on the other hand, was more frightening. War tended to reduce serious propertied crime, especially in years of low food prices. The onset of peace, by contrast, tended to increase crime as troops and seamen returned to face the prospect of unemployment and poverty. In Staffordshire, for example, the average annual rate of indictments for theft was 26 per 100,000 in wartime, but 35 per 100,000 in peace, an increase of 35 per cent. In East Anglia and what is now the Greater London area, too, the pattern of prosecutions for theft appears to follow the rhythms of war and peace, although high and low bread prices complicate the picture. In London especially, the immediate years of peace saw a conspicuous spurt in prosecutions for major property crime, virtually doubling in the years 1763–5 and again 1783–5, and moving upwards again in the aftermath of the Napoleonic Wars.

The surge in indictments for property crime in the aftermath of war could reflect the determination of prosecutors to take their cases to the courts, just as the fall in wartime might reflect the disposition of judges to reprieve criminals by pushing them into the armed forces. Certainly the tremendous publicity given to propertied offences during the first years of peace cast criminality as a major social problem of escalating proportions, one that caused something of a moral panic among the propertied classes. Yet the significant rise in prosecutions for theft after war, especially in London, had some material basis. It reflected not only the general insecurity of the propertied, but the effects of demobilization; a fact that can be simply illustrated by noting that in the aftermath of the War of Austrian Succession, a disproportionate number of those hanged at Tyburn were servicemen, over half in 1749. Within a relatively short space of time the army and navy disgorged thousands of men upon the streets: 70,000 in 1749, as many as 200,000 in 1763, 130,000 in 1783, and an alarming 350,000 in 1815. These were men whose prospects of employment were often slight and whose arrears in pay or prize money were often whittled away by the usurious credit they had received from crimps and ticket-brokers. Hardened by war, and sometimes physically disabled from getting 'any other support than what they can obtain from extorting charity in the streets', as one seamen's petition reminded the King in 1783,[9] it is not surprising that they took to crime.

Contemporaries were certainly aware of the dislocating effects of demobilization and sometimes took steps to address them. The 1744 Vagrancy Act specifically allowed servicemen to beg. At the end of the War of Austrian Succession legislators hoped to employ discharged seamen in the newly formed British herring industry, one that could service as a useful nursery for the navy. They also offered every serviceman the opportunity to resettle in Nova Scotia, providing each applicant with 50 acres of land rent-free for ten years, with an additional grant of 10 acres for every member of their family that accompanied them. In 1763, as earlier, demobilized veterans were permitted to work at trades without requiring the customary apprenticeships, and plans were mooted to employ them in the Scottish fishing industry and to settle them on the uncultivated commons, heaths, and forests. Yet such projects scarcely addressed the magnitude of the problem, and what compassion might have been felt for men who had risked their lives in the service of the country wilted before the spectre of rising crime rates. The *London Evening Post* of 12–14 April 1763 reported that a confectioner passing through Marylebone 'was assaulted by four men, dressed in sailor's habits, who knocked him down, treated him in a very cruel manner, and robbed him of 15s. in money, his coat and waistcoat . . . and likewise his pocket-book, containing a silver pencil and sundry papers'. It was accounts such of this, of middling men of property being robbed in broad daylight by ruffianly veterans, that captured the public imagination. What the newspapers chose to emphasize in the immediate post-war years was the high incidence of violent crime against property, the vulnerability of the wealthy, especially those whose conspicuous consumption marked them out as enviable prey, and the impunity with which such robberies were conducted. The poor 'starve, and freeze, and rot among themselves,' remarked Henry Fielding in 1753, 'but they beg, and steal and rob among their betters'.[10] Henry Pelham's eldest daughter Catherine, the wife of the Earl of Lincoln, was so troubled by the reports of street robberies that upon one scheduled Court appearance in 1749 she hid her diamond earrings under the seat of her hackney chair 'for fear of being attacked'.[11] It was these ruling-class anxieties that framed the way in which the 'crime wave' would be perceived.

War and social reform

The debate on post-war crime tended to concentrate less upon the problems of demobilization and more upon the broader question of 'luxury', especially the 'immorality' and 'insubordination' of the poor. In the years 1749–53, and again in the aftermath of the American War, social critics wrestled with the general problem of how they might reform and regulate the plebeian classes and bring them to honest labour. Such an enterprise was by no means new. The earlier part of the eighteenth century had seen a successive wave of campaigns to reform the poor, to regulate their morals and their drinking habits, and to improve their work discipline. Some of these efforts had been given legislative and institutional effect in the form of workhouse tests, gin Acts, new vagrancy laws, charity schools, foundling and magdalen hospitals. But from the mid-century onwards, the dynamics of war and demobilization tended to bring these reforming drives into sharper focus, prompting broad-ranging discussions about the nature of the criminal law, penal and poor law reform, and even popular education. Historians have often seen the social reform of the Hanoverian era as quintessentially local, voluntarist, and incremental, prompting few discussions of broad social policy. Yet in fact social reform was the product of an expanding public sphere of propertied opinion, élite and middling. In the aftermath of wars, or in anticipation of large-scale demobilization, it could generate debates of national significance.

We can see this in the 1750s and again in the 1780s. On both these occasions there was a broad review of the poor laws, whose current operation was widely perceived to be both expensive and conducive to crime, in the sense that it had failed to inculcate values of thrift and industry among the poor. Radical critics would have overhauled the poor laws quite dramatically, eliminating the settlement laws and transferring the administration of poor relief to larger, more accountable bodies. Bills to do this were publicly mooted, but all that was achieved was permissive legislation to incorporate parishes into larger units under Gilbert's Act of 1782, so that larger workhouses might be built to aid the deserving poor, to bring pauper children under stricter institutional control, and to instil greater social and industrial discipline. Accompanying this initiative was an Act to tighten up the administration of bridewells, and another to mobilize the Vagrancy Act of 1744 as a preventive strategy against crime. In some counties such as Yorkshire, associations were formed to crack down on vagrants, night-poachers, pawnbrokers suspected of receiving stolen goods, and the 'idle and disorderly' who congregated at alehouses, wakes, and fairs. In the capital, efforts were launched to promote a new police Bill to consolidate the forces of law enforcement and revivify prosecutions under the Vagrancy Act, but this proposal was opposed by the City of London which feared some erosion of its chartered privileges. Rather more successful was the campaign to promote Sunday schools as a counterpoint to crime and idleness. By fostering a culture of religion, deference, and respectability, social reformers, whether merchants or country gentlemen, hoped to rescue future generations of the poor from a life of crime and indolence and perhaps even inculcate a better work ethic among their parents. Although there had been precedents for the Sunday school before 1785, it was no accident that the movement took off when it did.

In the context of post-war crime, these regulatory drives necessarily encompassed some reconsideration of the criminal code and punishment. Confronted with escalating crime rates, contemporaries questioned whether the traditional practice of judicial terror was working. One spokesman in the 1750s suggested that Britain should introduce a system of galley slaves to strike terror in a liberty-loving populace. Others wanted to eliminate the counter-culture of Tyburn fair, where criminals were applauded for dying 'game' and where crowds strenuously defended the right of the executed to a Christian burial rather than suffer the humiliation of dissection at the hands of the surgeons. 'Instead of making the Gallows an Object of Terror,' complained Henry Fielding, 'our Executions contribute to make it an Object of Contempt in the Eye of the Malefactor; and we sacrifice the Lives of Men, not for the Reformation, but for the Diversion of the Populace'.[12] As a result, Parliament passed a Murder Act in 1752 to reaffirm the right of the surgeons to the bodies of the condemned. In 1783 the London gallows was relocated before Newgate Prison rather than at Tyburn in an attempt to counteract the irreverent rituals of hanging-days. At the same time, there was a growing debate about whether judges and juries should implement the full rigour of the law against felons convicted of capital offences and minimize the discretionary effects of the pardon. By the 1780s many reformers, following Cesare Beccaria, felt that punishments should be more strictly calibrated by the offence, thereby offsetting the tendency among jurors to 'downsize' offences or recommend mercy. Generally speaking, however, judges and juries responded to the crime wave with increasing severity, hanging a higher percentage of the condemned and reducing the likelihood of a pardon by doing so quickly. Yet the ending of transportation to America forced lawmakers to reconsider the secondary punishments to hanging. As a result, the promise of the penitentiary in reclaiming criminals was taken up with gusto. There had been precedents for this in the 1750s, most notably in Henry Fielding's project for a Middlesex House of Correction, but it took John Howard's tract on prison reform to publicize the rehabilitative potential of incarceration with its solitary cells, work regimen, standardized clothing, and salaried staff. By the mid-1780s, pursuant to the Penitentiary Act of 1779, prisons on this model were taken up in a number of counties, either by adapting existing bridewells or building new ones.

War and political reform

War had the effect of concentrating the energies of the propertied upon the problems of social reform. It also had the effect of concentrating them on political reform. Historians have had a tendency to view political reform as a post-1760 problem: either a consequence of the American Revolution, when the question of taxation without representation came dramatically to the fore, or a result of growing urbanization and industrialization, revealing the skewed nature of Britain's political representation towards the old chartered towns and the agricultural south-west. While these factors certainly fuelled the movement for political reform, it could also be argued that the demands for a reform of Britain's political structure emerged fundamentally from the interplay of domestic and imperial politics in the eighteenth century. The first significant movement for the purification of Parliament from executive influence occurred in the wake of the War of Jenkins' Ear in 1739, when the government was widely perceived as compromising with the Bourbon powers over the rights of British shipping in Caribbean waters and impeding the growth of the Atlantic economy. The second occurred after the loss of Minorca to the French in 1756, when Newcastle's administration was criticized for diverting the responsibility for failing to safeguard Britain's commercial routes to the Levant upon the hapless Admiral Byng. Neither of these episodes are normally accorded the status of reforming 'moments' because they were concerned with ministerial influence over Parliament rather than with a redistribution of seats and an expansion of the franchise. Yet the contrast between these episodes and the association movement of the American War, when urban radicals and disgruntled manufacturers and gentry championed parliamentary reform, can be overplayed. All three moments addressed the issues of the public accountability of Parliament to a broad propertied public. All prompted petitions or instructions from a fair array of counties and large towns. And the signal achievement of the last, 'economical' reform, was in essence the old Country programme of place and pension Bills designed to recapture the independence of the Commons from ministerial management. It was when the government neglected or threatened important trading links and disrupted business cycles and the flow of credit that the debate over political reform became most focused and intense, generating patriotic projects to revivify domestic politics and to render government more accountable to its propertied public.

War and patriotism

To what extent did war engender political instability? Could not statesmen and citizens, by invoking libertarian, anti-papist, and imperialist imperatives, consolidate the nation; indeed, construct a national indentity out of Britain's traditional rivalry with the Bourbon powers, especially France? Such an argument has been offered in recent years, particularly in the context of the French Wars, when unprecedented numbers of men were mobilized against a potential Napoleonic invasion.[13] It demands some engagement.

Patriotism was an ambiguous word in the Hanoverian era. Throughout much of the eighteenth century, it referred not to a narrow chauvinism but to an aspiration to place the *res publica*, however defined, above considerations of self-interest. As such it frequently presented itself as a critique of oligarchical government, particularly under the first two Hanoverian monarchs, whose preference for their German electorate made them something of a popular liability. During the American War radicals described themselves as patriots ready to defend liberty both at home and abroad. They were bitterly critical of the government's coercive policy towards the colonists, seeing the conflict as an unnecessary and impolitic civil war against fellow Protestant brethren and a violation of hard-won constitutional freedoms. Roughly one-third of the formal political nation sympathized with this view, although not necessarily with American Independence; and George III, hailed as a patriot king at the inception of his reign, was excoriated for his foolhardy destruction of the first British Empire. By this time however, patriotism was already being claimed by ministerial supporters, who used the Declaration of Independence and America's alliance with Britain's traditional enemies to unhook national sentiment from radical moorings. The court martial of Admiral Keppel in 1779 revealed something of the volatility of patriotic signifiers at the high point of the war, for the cause of this Whig admiral against a seemingly malevolent ministry bent on destroying him for an ineffectual engagement with the French, was defended in terms that were radical, anti-Gallican, anti-papist, anti-ministerial, and sometimes nostalgically hopeful of a reconciliation with America.

Radical patriotism expressed strong support for the goals of international freedom and national self-determination at the outset of the French Revolution, but it found itself increasingly upstaged by a loyalism that was anti-Gallican, pro-monarchical, and conservatively libertarian as the war with France in the 1790s got under way. To what degree loyalism penetrated the populace at large remains a disputable point, for the loyalists monopolized public space in ways that made political dissent hazardous beyond the highest circles. The initial success of the loyalist associations proved of short duration; their command over popular allegiances elusive. The volunteer movement that succeeded it proved more successful, with no less than 300,000 on its rolls by 1802. But the volunteer movement was never a genuine *levée en masse*. Its tone was snobbish and exclusive, and many poor men must have joined it to evade more onerous forms of military service. Certainly by 1803, when there was a growing political consensus for the need to defend the country from a potential Napoleonic invasion, an impressive number of men testified their willingness to take up arms. Yet some areas of the country showed little enthusiasm for volunteering and the returns for the capital were quite imperfect. Furthermore, employers and landowners used their influence over tenants and workers to persuade them to enlist. And an unknown number of volunteers probably calculated that joining a corps was the best safeguard against conscription as the long war against France resumed. In short, the defence-of-the-realm figures are an imperfect index of popular patriotism. They certainly do not signify any mass endorsement of the status quo.

We can get a glimpse of the complexities of patriotism during the Napoleonic era by considering the two principal war heroes, Nelson and Wellington. In both cases the political establishment sought to draw capital from their exploits, celebrating their victories with appropriate hoop-la. Yet of the two Nelson was incomparably the more popular. Partly this was a question of timing. Wellington's principal victories came at a point when the country as a whole was weary of war and their commemorations were correspondingly celebrated with less enthusiasm. But partly it was a question of style. Wellington lacked Nelson's common touch; his aristocratic hauteur was always a bar to fulsome popularity. Nelson was an admiral with whom the populace could readily identify. He was successfuly represented as a plucky British tar, flamboyant, courageous, recklessly honest about his infatuation with Emma Hamilton, and ever ready to acknowledge the contribution of both officers and men (as well as have them flogged). Nelson, moreover, was a war commander who stood above the political fray in a way that Wellington manifestly did not, and the difference was tellingly told in the differential honours that each received from the state. As the war ground to a halt, and as servicemen returned home with some hope that their contribution to the war effort might be recognized, Wellington's Toryism and endorsement of the European *ancien régime* signified how little things would change. It took all David Wilkie's ingenuity to cast Wellington as a popular hero in *The Chelsea Pensioners*. In the month before he revised his painting to commemorate Waterloo and to suggest that the veterans greeted the victory with rapturous applause, his patron had been pelted with mud and jostled by crowds for supporting George IV in his determination to bring Queen Caroline to trial and for generally supporting the government's repressive policies against popular demands for political reform. According to one account, the crowd shouted out 'The QUEEN for ever! . . . No military despotism!'[14] Different kinds of patriots wanted different kinds of change.

11 Popular Beliefs and Popular Politics

Methodism and popular belief

In March 1791 John Wesley, the most charismatic preacher of the eighteenth century, died at the age of 87. Ten thousand people are reported to have passed his coffin at City Road chapel to pay their last respects, testimony to the strong appeal that this founding father of Methodism drew from sections of the public at large. From its small beginnings as a penitential group of pious young gentlemen at Oxford, Methodism had grown into a vigorous religious movement by Wesley's death, poised to secede from the Anglican Church and to join the ranks of Nonconformity. How are we to explain its extraordinary appeal? What impact did it have upon the lives of ordinary people?

Methodism's success owed much to its accessibility and temper. Drawing inspiration from the pietistical sects of continental Europe, Methodism was quintessentially a revivalist religion that stood in stark contrast to the latitudinarian and élitist ethos of the Established Church. From the Moravians Wesley understood the value of salvation through faith in terms of inward experience, a demotic version of the Lutheran ideal that placed great emphasis upon individual conversion, the inner certainty of being saved. From George Whitefield, the son of a Gloucester innkeeper who galvanized the 'Great Awakening' in America, Wesley learned the techniques of mass evangelism, preaching in the lanes and open fields when people were coming and going to work and sometimes using barns and sheds as makeshift meeting-places. Methodism was open to all believers, of whatever social status, religion, or sect. It was a message of hope to the poor, who through personal faith and strict moral example, could find love in Christ and save themselves. As such it was infinitely more attractive to ordinary people than its gentrified alternative, whose formality, condescension, and overriding sense of hierarchy, both within church and without, vitiated its popular appeal. For this reason some traditional parsons found Methodism a disturbing counterpoint to Anglican practice, one that was socially and even politically subversive.

Methodism's evangelizing campaign was initially directed at the most marginal members of society. Its preachers went out of their way to save convicts and those awaiting execution. But it quickly reached those outside the pale of Anglican governance, gaining ground in the more densely populated industrial parishes of England and also in the dispersed rural settlements outside squire-archical control. By 1791 72,000 people were formally affiliated to the Methodist Connexion and circuits had been established in most parts of England. In the next thirty years the movement would grow dramatically, so that by 1830 there were over 320,000 'hearers' of the Wesleyan Connexion and a further 100,000 members in the various splinter groups that seceded from the central body after John Wesley's death. Throughout this period of growth, Methodism's greatest appeal continued to be among craftsmen, miners, and to a lesser degree unskilled labourers. Over 75 per cent of the Methodist membership hailed from these ranks in the eighteenth and early nineteenth centuries. Although the Wesleyan Connexion had attracted proportionately more merchants and manufacturers by the 1830s, Methodism as a whole remained emphatically a religion of the people.

Methodism's success was not only attributable to its demotic ideology of salvation and its accessibility. It also strove to close the cultural gap between rich and poor by addressing the irrational and superstitious elements in popular culture. While the Enlightenment had made magical cures and explanations increasingly unacceptable to the more prosperous elements in society, such views remained vigorous at the popular level. The belief in witchcraft survived its legal proscription, as a 1751 incident of witch-hunting in Hertfordshire revealed, and omens and talismans were strenuously endorsed. In an age of demographic and economic uncertainty, poor people still had recourse to magical healing and cunning men and women to ward off sickness, to exorcize evil spirits, to interpret dreams, to bless crops and animals. At certain times of the year, St Agnes's Eve or Hallowe'en for example, rituals of divination were practised to ascertain the identity of a future spouse, the fortunes of children, or the portent of death. Methodism spoke to this structure of belief in its emphasis upon diabolical possession and exorcism by prayer; in stressing the hand of providential punishment upon reprobates and backsliders, who could be struck down by lightning or epilepsy. Wesley himself produced a medical handbook of popular remedies, emphasizing at the same time the power of prayer and clean living as an antidote to sickness and reaffirming popular prejudices against an emergent medical profession whose practices precluded the poor from the advances in medical knowledge. Methodist practice thus intersected with popular belief in important ways, and in communities where workers were highly dependent upon luck or changes in the seasons for their survival, could strike deep roots. Thus in Cornwall, where miners and fishermen faced high risks of death or injury and were vulnerable to sudden fluctuations in wind or tide, or chance discoveries of good ores, Methodism took hold, translating folk beliefs into a religious idiom.

On the other hand, Methodism declared holy war on many popular pastimes. It was opposed to drink, hurling, wrestling, bull-baiting and cock-fighting, to feasts, festivals, and fairs. It exhorted its followers to find love in Christ through a rigorous asceticism, through love feasts,[1] watch-nights, and hymn-singing. It also took a dim view of various forms of plebeian self-activity such as rough music, wife-sales, and popular interventions in defence of the moral economy of provision. In 1739 John Wesley's brother Charles, hearing of a bread riot at Kingswood, rushed into the midst of it and hauled out a number of his converted colliers. He 'marched with them singing to the [Kingswood] school', he recalled in his journal, where they held a two-hour prayer-meeting 'that God would chain the lion'.[2] Such interference did not always endear Methodist preachers to their potential congregations. In his early days of open-field preaching John Wesley was regularly confronted by hostile mobs, who, in league with threatened clergymen and squires, opposed his efforts to convert their community and revolutionize their pastimes. Nor were his proselytizers exempt from popular wrath. At Leeds a crowd complained to one intinerant preacher that Methodists 'make people go mad: and we cannot get drunk or swear, but every fool must correct us, as if we were to be taught by them'. 'After May Day' complained one Yorkshireman upon the appearance of another Methodist zealot, 'we shall have nothing but praying and preaching.'[3] To preclude this possibility crowds pulled down meeting-houses, attacked worshippers, and in the case of the Norwich disturbances of 1752, ran the ranter out of town.

Methodism was thus a controversial and sometimes divisive force in eighteenth-century society. Its revivals did not go unopposed, and John Wesley's own determination to root out 'triflers or disorderly walkers' from his fledgling congregations, for drunkenness, 'idleness and laziness', even for 'lightness and carelessness', meant that the turnover in membership was considerable. For these reasons one should not make too much of the actual numbers affiliated to the Connexion at any one time. In an adult (aged over 15) population of 6.7 million in 1821, 400,000 hearers does not seem a significant following; just under 6 per cent. But when one ponders the actual number who came into contact with the new evangelism, then its influence was considerably greater than its regular congregations suggested. One historian has speculated that perhaps 20 per cent of the most politicized sections of the labouring classes were associated with chapel communities of one sort or another by the early nineteenth century.[1] Indeed, it is likely that radicals appropriated some Methodist modes of organization for their own needs; most notably its division of congregations into 'classes' for discussion and debate.

One of the more interesting aspects of Methodist historiography is its relationship to politics; specifically whether it encouraged or inhibited change of a radical or reformist character. The evidence on this is still ambiguous, largely because it is difficult to determine the political aspirations of the rank and file from the official pronouncements of its leaders, but also because splinter groups of different political persuasions kept breaking from the main body. Few historians would now argue that Methodism saved Britain from revolution by diverting zealots from politics. But some would still argue that Methodism absorbed energies that might have been directed towards more secular political goals, despite the fact that after 1790 there was some geographical correspondence between areas of radicalism and revivalism, and in the north-east coal-fields at least, some close linkages between the two movements.

In Wesley's own lifetime it is also possible that some Methodists courted politics in a manner that veered from their leaders' official stance. That stance was clear. As far as possible Wesley strove to endorse a 'no politics' rule among his congregations and insistently proclaimed his loyalty to the Hanoverian regime. Yet because Methodism made its appearance during the Jacobite scare of the 1740s, its demotic, emotive character made it suspect among the more paranoid members of the ruling class. Methodists were sometimes accused of fomenting Jacobitism. Wesley himself was forced to take the oaths of loyalty to the King and to sign a declaration against popery, despite the fact that he and his brother were vehement anti-Catholics, even to the point of supporting the Protestant Association in its opposition to the Catholic Relief Act of 1778, on the grounds that Catholicism's persecuting spirit was undeserving of religious toleration. Indeed, Methodism never entirely lived down its reputation as a clandestine, subversive religion, notwithstanding Wesley's protests to the contrary.

Wesley was none the less outspoken in his opposition to popular political practice. He detested the hurly-burly of eighteenth-century elections and the 'Bedlam' of mob activity, just as he detested other aspects of popular licence and profanity. In 1772 he openly deplored the popularity of John Wilkes, whose name and visage, he regrettably speculated, was 'more celebrated than that of any private man . . . in England for these thousand years'.[5] In his opinion the cry for liberty had become an 'Epidemic Madness' that needed to be curbed. The press, in particular, had created 'a royal monster of a king'; its freedom had degenerated into a licentiousness that threatened to culminate in political anarchy.[6]

Wesley's views on this score were not dissimilar to those of the counter-revolutionary Vice Society of the 1790s. They were out of touch with the popular pulse. Despite the decline of party strife and the reconfiguration of political oligarchy in the mid-century decades, extra-parliamentary politics remained vociferously vibrant. Public opinion had been mobilized against the Jewish Naturalization Bill of 1753 and against Admiral Byng during the Minorca crisis three years later. And as popular exuberance for the Seven Years War gave way to a post-war depression and deep misgivings about the direction of the government under the influence of Lord Bute, especially its generous treaty with the French and its widening search for new revenues to refurbish Britain's depleted coffers, popular sentiment moved against the ministry. Crowds demonstrated against the cider tax of 1763 and burnt symbolic Jack Boots and petticoats to show their contempt for George III's favourite and first minister. John Wilkes captured the mood when he lambasted the Peace of Paris in the *North Briton*, No. 45 as an 'odious' measure and 'the most abandoned instance of ministerial effrontery ever attempted'.[7]

Wilkes and Liberty

Wilkes was a social adventurer schooled in the cut-and-thrust of unreformed politics, but he had a canny eye for popularity and for transforming political feuds into issues of constitutional importance. Having failed to assert his parliamentary immunity when he was prosecuted for seditious libel for his remarks in the *North Briton*, No. 45, he took the government to task for issuing a general warrant for his arrest on the grounds that such a legal process was inimical to English freedom. When the government rejected his election as MP for Middlesex in 1768 because he was technically an outlaw, Wilkes rallied his supporters to denounce the decision as a repudiation of the rights of the electors. When the government attempted to shut down the pro-Wilkes newspapers, Wilkes's supporters defended the liberty of the press in new and capacious terms. They affirmed the people's right to political information as a necessary corollary of its representative status in Parliament, questioned the government's use of ex-officio informations to avoid the hazards of a trial before jury, and demanded that juries deliberate upon the matter as well as the fact of libel. By expanding the meaning of traditional liberties in these and other contexts, Wilkes and his supporters campaigned for a more open politics.

'Wilkes and Liberty' appealed pre-eminently to the small man of property in eighteenth-century society; to those who resented the intrusive presence of the grandee in law and politics and demanded greater accountability (and greater commercial security) from the ruling class. It is no accident that Wilkes was able to mobilize the smaller freeholder in his struggle to represent the metropolitan-dominated county of Middlesex, generating a nationwide petitioning movement in his favour, nor that his name was cherished by the clubs and Masonic lodges of middling tradesmen who were anxious to link his cause with their own anxieties about the laws against debt. Yet at the same time Wilkes's support reached beyond this bourgeois world. Seamen and petty artisans identified with his campaign against naval impressment. Striking seamen, silk-weavers, hatters and coal-heavers found Wilkes a useful signifier for their own struggles. And the very ethos of the Wilkite movement, with its

raucous festivals of Liberty, its defiant parading of boot and petti-
coat, its flags representing the Bill of Rights and Magna Charta, its
play on the ubitiquous number 45, which commemorated Wilkes's
first confrontation with the government and became a metonym
of Wilkite causes, drew thousands to its fold. Wilkite festival stood
in stark contrast to the orthodox cycle of royal and national celebration. Indeed, Wilkes's own anniversaries commemorating his
struggles with authority for a time eclipsed the official calendar in
popularity, scale, and revelrous exuberance. It was precisely this
sort of behaviour that John Wesley deplored, even if some of his
supporters did not.

Popular politics and America

The Wilkite movement did not simply address domestic issues
of contemporary significance. It quickly acquired a transatlantic
dimension. While Wilkes challenged ministerial power at home,
liberty-lovers in the leading ports of North America resisted the
fiscal policies of the Crown and its efforts to tax the colonies
despite the fact that the colonies were not formally represented
in Parliament and, so they argued, had chartered privileges and
assemblies that exempted them from such exactions. To radical
'patriots' on both sides of the ocean, the government seemed bent
on the occlusion of liberties both at home and abroad. This shared
sense of grievance was expressed in tokens of support for one
another, even financial aid. American Sons of Liberty regularly
toasted Wilkes, corresponded with him, and financed his cause; a
few even named their sons and one Pennsylvanian town in his
honour. English radicals made a conciliatory approach to America
an integral part of their platform, and as the struggle escalated
after the Boston Tea Party contributed money to relieve Bostonians
suffering under the Coercion Acts.

Not all Britons of an anti-ministerial temper, of course, uncon-
ditionally identified with the American cause. While most sympathized with the opposition to the Stamp Act, successive acts of
colonial resistance troubled many, especially the Americans' denial
of parliamentary sovereignty. Even so, the pro-Americans were able
to mount an impressive campaign for peace in 1775. No less than
seven counties, eleven medium-to-large boroughs, and over ten
unrepresented industrial towns petitioned for peace in that year,

amassing over 44,000 signatures, nearly as many as voted in the general election of 1761.[8] And while the onset of war, the Declaration of American Independence, and the entry of France into the conflict fragmented the pro-American constituency, there were many who continued to blame the ministry for what was widely believed to be an impolitic, fratricidal war. The court martial of Admiral Keppel in 1779 revealed the rancorous and volatile state of British politics and the popular detestation of ministerial policies. Across the country there were popular demonstrations of support for Keppel, a well-heeled and well-connected admiral who had refused to fight the colonists (although not the French). In London and the provinces mobs burnt effigies of ministers and their clients in effigy. In the capital itself troops had to fend off attacks upon the residences of Lords Bute, Sandwich, and North, all politicians closely identified with the war effort.

The bitter divisions over the American War had even more dramatic consequences the following year. This time popular passions focused upon the Catholic minority in England who in 1778 were formally given the liberty of inheriting property, founding schools, and openly practising their religion in return for their contribution to the war effort. The Catholic Relief Act was viewed with deep misgivings in many quarters. It was seen not only as a slight to British liberty, which had traditionally been defined in opposition to the 'foreign incubus' of Catholicism, but as exemplary evidence of the authoritarian tendencies of George III and his ministry at home and abroad. In Scotland, the Catholic Relief Act had drawn violent protests in 1779, and the same was to prove true of England in the wake of a mass petitioning movement to repeal the act organized by the Protestant Association under the leadership of Lord George Gordon. Once Parliament refused to attend immediately to the petitions for repeal, mobs ransacked the Catholic chapels in London and attacked the houses of leading supporters of the Relief Act. As the riots escalated, gaols were broken open, toll-bridges and crimping houses were smashed, and an assault was launched on the Bank of England. For nearly a week London was at the mercy of the mob, and the riots were only finally repressed with military violence, with over two hundred people dying in the street from gunfire. The Gordon riots were the most formidable and complex disturbance of the century, raising vexed issues about the nature of British liberty, the legitimacy of mass petitions and political associations, and the political maturity of the London crowd. They were to haunt British politics for decades.

Three long-term developments are worth stressing in the era of Wilkes and Gordon. The first was the dramatic expansion of political space. This can be seen in the burgeoning growth of the press, not only in London but also in the provinces, where there were approximately fifty newspapers by the end of the American War, more than double the number of the early Hanoverian decades. By 1775 the circulation of the press had reached 12.6 million, that is, roughly 34,700 a day. It was a press, moreover, that increasingly specialized in political critique and proto-editorial commentary, supplanting the pulpit and rivalling the pamphlet as the prime medium of political discourse, so that a copiously reported and annotated event like Keppel's trial was brought into the coffee-houses and alehouses of the nation in an unprecedented fashion.

Accompanying this expansion was the growing sophistication of extra-parliamentary association. Prior to 1760 political clubs were not unknown in London and some of the larger provincial towns such as Norwich and Bristol. But the two decades after 1760 saw a significant expansion of club life. Newcastle, for example, saw the appearance of the Revolution Society, the Constitutional Club, the Independent Society, the Lumber Troop, and the Sidney Society, all of which helped to nurture the distinctive radical politics of the town. With the proliferation of such clubs and a more self-confident press, politicians of all colours were in a position to create a commercially freer, politically more self-reliant public than was hitherto possible.

This was especially evident in the metropolis, where weekly debating societies afforded men and women the opportunity to discuss all manner of topics—social, political, religious, and philosophical—at 6*d*. a session. This development of the public sphere, largely made possible by the middling demand for credit facilities and organized recreation, allowed politicians to create movements whose dimensions and dynamic were unknown to their forebears. Extra-parliamentary associations were not unprecedented before 1760—the Walpolean era had witnessed some notable instruction campaigns by the large cities and counties—but few could compare in scale and organization to the mass petitions and large-scale associations of the period 1768–1784, in which virtually every English county and large town was involved. In these years more than a quarter of a million signatures were solicited for loyalist and anti-ministerial petitions to Crown and Parliament, a number roughly comparable to the total number of people who voted in the four general elections of the period. By eighteenth-century standards this was an unprecedented mobilization of the political nation.

Another manifestation of this growing intensification of popular politics was the movement to abolish slavery. Prior to 1787 and the formation of the first London Abolition society, the most active abolitionists (aside from exceptional individuals like Granville Sharp) were Quakers. It was this sect that first petitioned parliament and canvassed the political élite to abolish slavery, winning over important converts like John Wesley, whose *Thoughts on Slavery* (1774) persuaded many Methodists of its iniquities. After 1787, however, abolitionists effectively exploited the techniques of popular politics, generating two impressive mass petitioning campaigns in 1787–8 and 1792 and a boycott on slave-grown sugar that won a wide swathe of support from the urban public, especially in the industrial towns of the North. Although this movement was temporarily stalled by the French Revolution, it convincingly transcended its initial sectarian base and bridged political differences, with conservative evangelicals allying themselves with radicals on this particular issue. It also made an important breakthrough in gender politics. Women not only debated the cause of abolition in 1788 and wrote on its behalf, but four years later signed public petitions for the very first time, even though doubts were raised about the propriety of their doing so.

Abolition was not the only movement to avail itself of the expanding public sphere of discussion, debate, and popular mobilization. Parliamentary reform also become a salient part of the public agenda. Parliamentary reform had been mooted earlier in the century in opposition to the intrusion of moneyed wealth in the Commons and to the sinews of power that consolidated the rise of Whig oligarchy. But the experience of the American Revolution pushed it to the foreground. The demand for no taxation without representation laid bare the anomalies of the electoral structure at home and induced some to argue for universal male suffrage on the grounds that all taxable income should be represented. Only a handful of radicals were prepared to follow this logic until the French Revolution. Sceptical of the political maturity of the masses and the eat-and-swill temper of some popular constituencies, most propertied Radicals resisted giving the vote to a dependent and venal electorate. Most rested their case on a more equal representation of Parliament, a claim that envisaged a modest extension of the franchise but, more importantly, an increase or redistribution of seats to accommodate a broader spectrum of propertied interests within the political nation. Together with annual parliaments, more frequent elections, and a Country programme of place and pension bills, it was hoped that this would make parliament more accountable to the political nation and undermine the political paralysis that many felt was responsible for the loss of the American colonies. Even these object-ives proved difficult to advance in programmatic form. In the after-math of the American War, the disgruntled gentry of the counties were prepared to support 'economical' reform, that is a trimming of executive power through the elimination of petty offices and sinecures, but it drew the line at more radical solutions. Hopes for reform that went beyond old Country panaceas remained stillborn even if they were strenuously advocated in the forums of urban radicalism.

What did emerge strikingly from the American crisis was the political rebirth of Protestant Dissent. During the early Hanoverian era the Nonconformists, who were well represented among the urban middling class, remained riveted to the Whig party, mindful of the damage that the Schism Act would have inflicted upon their social and political fortunes. Dissenters well entrenched in local politics sometimes continued this allegiance, but the American crisis saw the gravitation of many to the ranks of the opposition, at least in towns like Bristol, Northampton, Norwich, and Yar-mouth. Here Dissenters helped revitalize electoral independence, if not radicalism. Here their preachers brought the Commonwealth tradition into the mainstream of radical thought, popularizing the language of rights, especially the rights of resistance to unjust or illegitimate authority. As the Presbyterian minister James Murray stressed in his political début in Newcastle politics, in lines reminis-cent of Rousseau's *Social Contract*: 'A nation of slaves is a kingdom of asses. All Europe—yea the greatest part of the world—have couched down between these two burdens of civil and religious oppression.'[9] It was no accident that it was a Dissenter (James Burgh) who first propounded the idea of a 'Grand National Association' or anti-parliament as the appropriate forum for drawing up a programme of radical, constitutional reform.

Dissenting discourse was of enormous importance in legitimizing opposition to the government's coercive policy in America, in demystifying monarchical authority, and in questioning unconditional deference to social superiors. Its spokesmen inveighed against corrupt patronage as energetically as their Country predecessors, but they focused more sharply on the ways in which political privilege had frustrated talent as well as enterprise. In the aftermath of the American War it was predictable that the Protestant Dissenters would seek to rectify their own civil and religious disabilities by renewing the campaign for the repeal of the Test and Corporation Acts, and, on the centenary of 1688, that they should reframe the Revolution settlement in contractual terms, asserting the legitimacy of constitutions that were founded on the consent of the governed and revindicating the right of resistance to unconstituted authority as the true legacy of the 1688 *coup d'état*.

Popular politics and the French Revolution

In 1789 the Protestant Dissenters welcomed the French Revolution in much the same terms as they had come to accept the American, as a justifiable revolt against a corrupt and morally bankrupt regime. At the November meeting of the London Revolution Society, Dr Richard Price, one of the best-known spokesmen for Dissent and one of the first to recognize American Independence, recalled with pleasure that he had lived to see 'nations panting for liberty, which seemed to have lost the idea of it'. He then moved that congratulations be sent to the newly formed French National Assembly and expatiated upon the prospect that the Revolution gave to both Britain and France 'of a common participation in the blessings of civil and religious liberty'.[10] Not all Britons were prepared to follow Price in linking the French Revolution with the hope of further reform at home, but many welcomed the event as a Continental replication of 1688. Bastille Day was celebrated in 1790 and 1791 in many British cities, and in London various theatres staged representations of the Revolution's most symbolic act. In its commercial rendering at least, Liberty's victory in France was derivative of England's long-standing constitutional heritage.

Yet the totality of the French Revolution inevitably gave rise to misgivings, and Burke's pre-emptive attack upon developments in France and their promotion in Radical Dissenting circles in his now-famous *Reflections* helped shape the conservative response. Bastille-Day celebrations were banned in a number of towns in 1791 and at Manchester a mob was encouraged to pull down the tavern where the local Constitutional Society had met to celebrate the event. This did not happen, but the cultivation of Franco-phobia and sectarian animosity by Anglican ministers and magis-trates was sufficient to generate a swathe of violence against the Dissenting bourgeois élite of Birmingham on the anniversary of the fall of the Bastille. Liberal, presumptuous, and socially aloof, hostile to the moral economy and the customary expectations of the poor, the rich Dissenters of Birmingham were easy targets for populist rancour, and their principal spokesman Joseph Priestley, Dissenting divine, scientist, and educator, had his house and valu-able laboratory ransacked for his Francophile sentiments and pro-gressive views.

What deepened the alarmism of the conservative establishment was the evident popularity of Tom Paine's *Rights of Man*. Framed as the response to Burke's *Reflections*, Paine's Radical denunciation of the British constitution, his audacious support of the Americans and the French as the pathbreakers of freedom, fortified demo-cratic rhetoric and the imperative of reform. By 1792, his forthright defence of the 'rights of the living' to frame their own consti-tution and to reject Burkian tradition had emboldened small master artisans, journeymen, and shopkeepers to form their own political associations. In about twenty towns throughout Eng-land and Scotland, popular democratic societies emerged, open to 'members unlimited'. In London, Norwich, and Sheffield, they rapidly proliferated, forming 'divisions' or 'tythings' that spread into the countryside. According to one hostile observer, such soci-eties reached 'the very lowest order of society . . . such wretched looking blackguards that it requires some mastery over that innate pride, which every well-educated man must necessarily possess, even to sit down in their company'.[11] At Newcastle-under-Lyme, where Paine's writings found an enthusiastic audience, it was reported that 'more than two thirds of this populous Neighbourhood' were 'ripe for revolt, especially the lower class of Inhabitants'. The same was said of the Durham coal-field, where the accessibility of Paine's works had raised the tempo of protest against high taxes, coal duties, and the extravagancies of the Prince of Wales.[12]

Conservatives were alarmed by these developments on two accounts. The rather sedate revolution societies of the Dissenters and their allies were easily visible; the newcomers were more difficult to locate and their mushrooming was correspondingly more disturbing because it was imponderable. Further, the phenomenal popularity of Paine's writings—250,000 copies of the *Rights of Man* had been sold or distributed by radical societies by 1793—appeared ominously subversive. Not only was Paine's work unequivocally republican, it was also stridently egalitarian, anticlerical, and quite original in its advocacy of redistributive taxation to finance public education and welfare. How far these ideas were assimilated into the outlook of the popular societies remains a moot point. There is evidence, for example, that Paine's republicanism was not wholeheartedly accepted by the new radical clubs and that his hostility to organized religion was divisive. But the endorsement of French republicanism after the King's flight to Varennes, the celebration of the French army's early victories against its Continental foes, and the flamboyant parade of *tricolors* and planting of Liberty trees, inevitably suggested that Paine's views were striking deep roots in the populace at large. 'Payne is a dangerous book for any person who does not share in the spoil to be left alone with,' wrote one London merchant to Dundas, 'and it appears that the book is now made as much a standard book in this country as Robinson Crusoe & the Pilgrim's Progress, & that if it has not its effect today, it will tomorrow.'[13]

The conservative response to this activity was the formation of loyalist associations to curb the contagion of plebeian radicalism. Encouraged by royal proclamations against the spread of seditious writings, loyalist associations sprouted all over the country, often taking their cue from John Reeves's Association for the Preservation of Liberty and Property against Republicans and Levellers. The object of these associations was threefold. In the first instance they sought to enforce public conformity to the campaign against republicanism and sedition by mobilizing local authorities and employers against radical sympathizers, sometimes to the point of pressuring all local householders to declare their allegiance to King and Country. This strategy was buttressed by a strict surveillance of taverns and alehouses, whose landlords were threatened with the loss of their licences if they allowed radical clubs to meet on their premises. This essentially policing operation was accompanied by the active propagation of loyalism, by address, sermon, tract, and festival. In the penny tracts that were distributed in their thousands, plebeian readers were enjoined to consider that Britain's constitution had brought palpable gains for everyone: a rule of law, security of property, religious concord, domestic and commercial felicity. By contrast, the French Revolutionary experience, so the argument went, had engendered scarcity, atheism, specious aspirations of equality, unparalleled political violence, and the spectre of mob rule. If this was not compelling enough, plebeian audiences were indulged with Christmas doles, New Year's parades, and ceremonial burnings of Tom Paine in effigy, with the richer inhabitants rolling out the barrels of beer to lubricate the proceedings.

In reviewing this evidence historians have recently stressed the sympathetic response of the populace to these manifestations of popular conservatism. They have generally done so by playing the numbers game; that is, by emphasizing the sheer volume of loyalist tracts distributed, the number of associations formed (2,000 according to Reeves's own calculations), and the degree to which Friendly Societies or local lodges were prepared to join them or to participate in a Church-and-King festival. Yet this evidence should be read more sceptically. The vast majority of loyalist associations were organized by men of property powerful in their own neighbourhoods, and the climate of surveillance and intimidation was such that dependants were induced to collaborate, however unwillingly, in loyalist displays of solidarity. In some areas, whole villages were mustered to hear diatribes against Tom Paine and his works and house-to-house enquiries into loyalty were not unknown. Even in market towns like Halesworth in Suffolk, the few men who refused to sign loyalist declarations were singled out for their nonconformity.

With examples such as these we should be wary about reading too much into the displays of loyalism that were enthusiastically reported in the press. Popular loyalism made some headway among

Wesleyan communities. In urban centres where the religious rivalry between Anglicanism and Dissent was especially rancorous, it also drew upon the same populist hostility that marked the Priestley riots of 1791, with Tom Paine burnings being accompanied by attacks on meeting-houses. Sometimes it drew successfully on the politics of rumour and fear, especially in the wake of the September massacres in Paris. One correspondent reported to Dundas that he had heard 'Common Labourers at their work, nay women and children, on repeating the Cruelties of the French to them, vow vengeance and utter imprecations against these murderers'.[14] Yet in other areas the common people went along with loyalism for the incidental benefits that accrued from it. One pamphlet recalled that several men who were hired to burn Tom Paine in effigy waited on the Devonshire gentleman who employed them to ascertain 'if there was any other *gemman* among his friends who [*sic*] he wished to have burned, as they were ready to do it for the same quantity of beer'.[15]

On balance, the loyalist associations of 1792–3 were more successful in seizing political space than they were in mustering a genuinely popular clientele. Perhaps their most significant contribution was in severing the links between liberal reform and Painite radicalism. While some of the more liberally inclined property-holders attempted to hold fast to a loyalism that stressed allegiance to a constitution still open to reform, they were basically swamped by the sheer weight and presence of a more conservative Church-and-King movement. The panic of the propertied classes and the partial retreat of the reformers left the popular radical movement dangerously exposed, but it did not destroy it. Although a few popular societies faltered in the face of loyalist harassment, others regrouped, and in the ensuing years of spiralling prices and food shortages actually increased their membership. Loyalism stiffened radical resolve rather than the contrary, and paradoxically may have stimulated radicalism by making politically-marginal people more conscious of the language of rights. Certainly, the Jacobin temper of the radical societies became more visible and confrontational despite Britain's declaration of war with France. Radicals adopted *bonnets rouges* and egalitarian styles of address. They teased loyalists with their own paranoid rhetoric. They held the first National Convention at Edinburgh in 1794, and staged dramatically large public meetings under the very nose of government. The Establishment's response to this subversive flamboyance was repression. Leading delegates at the Edinburgh Convention were sentenced to transportation and other prominent radicals were subjected to treason trials. These backfired, but the suspension of Habeas Corpus and the passing of two 'Gagging' Acts in 1795 enabled the government and the magistracy to crack down on sedition and public meetings; or at least, to prosecute judiciously *pour encourager les autres*. As a result, the radical societies were largely driven underground. The most prominent, the London Corresponding Society, lost roughly half its members in the immediate aftermath of the Gagging Acts but enjoyed a shaky and sometimes shadowy existence until 1799, when it was specifically prohibited by name under an 'Act for the more effectual suppression of societies established for seditious and treasonable Purposes'.

It is difficult to determine the depth and nature of disaffection to King and Constitution in the decade of the French Revolution. Some 200 cases of sedition were prosecuted in the major courts, but these carefully formulated prosecutions, most of which were successful, were only the tip of the iceberg. In the 1800–1 food riots, seditious handbills and outbursts against the King and government litter the Home Office papers in a way they had never done before, and bloody loaves were raised alongside pointed messages of 'Bread or Blood'. As one Maldon rhymster warned:

> On Swill and Grains you wish the poor to be fed
> And underneath the Gullintine we could wish to see your heads.[16]

Disaffection against the government was rife until the Peace of Amiens in 1802, especially if one adds Scotland and Ireland to the picture. The political disposition of the populace was volatile, with radical hopes sometimes giving way to chiliastic despair and unsettling Methodist congregations, particularly those splinter denominations that had broken with Wesleyanism after 1791. Popular protests took a wide range of forms: spontaneous imprecations against the King and ruling class; millenarian prophecies by Richard Brothers and his ilk who saw the French Revolutionaries striking down Babylon; radical constitutional reform in an English idiom; insurrectionary plans for a Jacobin republic. The latter surfaced dramatically through the activities of the United Irishmen and their English allies who sought to shape and capitalize upon the naval mutinies of 1797, and who, after the abortive Irish Rebellion of 1798, conspired to stage a *coup d'état* in London and, if necessary, to assassinate the King. Revolutionary cells for this purpose were not only to be found in London, the mecca of the migratory Irish, but also in the industrial districts of Lancashire and Yorkshire. Here, in the context of significant changes in the productive relations of the textile industries and the blanket prohibition of combinations after 1800, ultra-political and industrial militancy were combined. Such an illegal tradition, with its secret oaths and clubs, its belief in armed resistance to 'tyrants', would surface in the activities of the 'Black Lamp' in 1802, in northern Luddism a decade later, and in the Pentridge rising of 1817. It was still visible in 1820. Amid the bitterness of post-war distress and political repression, there were three abortive risings in that year: at Glasgow; in the textile districts around Huddersfield and Barnsley; and in London, where ultra-Radicals, in what became known as the Cato Street Conspiracy, planned to assassinate members of the cabinet as a prelude to a general insurrection in the capital. Whether the three were linked is unclear; certainly the insurgents of the northern textile districts were in contact with one another through an extensive network of clubs and delegates. But there is no denying the explosive rage that welled from these Radical centres, as the efforts to build a mass democratic movement were thwarted at every turn.

The birth of the mass platform

By 1820 popular Radical activity was losing its Jacobin flavour. Once the Jacobin era of the French Revolution gave way to the imperialist designs of Napoleon, many British Radicals lost faith in the French dawn of freedom and turned their thoughts towards more indigenously patriotic projects: universal manhood suffrage; the recognition of full citizenship for those who had risked their lives in the war effort; the reform of the war machine and a corrupt state; a lasting peace. Increasingly, these demands were articulated through discussion groups and a mass platform; that is, within public modes of agitation that stressed the moral and unassailable power of the 'people' to voice its claims, to educate its public, to seek a lawful restitution of its grievances. In the immediate post-war years political societies, or Hampden clubs as they were frequently called, sprouted up across the country for the purpose of buying, reading, and discussing Radical tracts and newspapers such as Wooler's *Black Dwarf* and Cobbett's *Register*, whose circulation in 1817 was running around 40,000 to 60,000 copies a week. By that time, the clubs numbered 500 with a total membership of over 450,000.[17] Concentrated in the textile areas of Glasgow, Manchester, and the West Riding, these clubs served as an organizational base for the mass platform, the meetings of working people to demand political democracy, an end to 'Old Corruption', and the redress of their grievances.

Such a political enterprise was deeply threatening to a ruling class that was happy to mobilize the people for the war effort but unwilling to recognize its status beyond that of dutiful subjects. Legislation against federated political societies remained in force; legislation controlling 'seditious' meetings was periodically revived; and prosecutions against public 'agitators' were stepped up as the mass platform advanced. Public meetings took place in the presence of spies, with cavalry regiments at the ready in case of disorder. In the aftermath of the war the battle for public space resumed with a vengeance, leading to tense confrontations and ultimately to the tragedy of Peterloo, when the yeoman cavalry cut down hundreds at St Peter's Field, Manchester, in its determination to arrest Henry Hunt and his colleagues and to capture the Radical flags of 'sedition' that were topped by red caps of liberty.

The Manchester meeting of 1819 encapsulated many of the features of post-war popular political activity. It was, to begin with, part of an all-out national Radical effort that centred on meetings at Birmingham, Leeds, and London as well as at the centre of the cotton industry. The selection of towns was indicative of the degree to which democratic radicalism had outgrown its old artisan centres to encompass the rapidly expanding industrial centres of the Midlands and the North, towns that were collectively a synecdoche of the classic 'Industrial Revolution'. The meetings themselves were remarkably orderly, revealing not only the degree to which the emergent working class had given up mob politics, but the depth of popular self-activity and organization. Deputations from outlying districts, organized by local union societies, marched peaceably into town carrying flags, banners, and caps of liberty.

Such deputations were also gendered, acknowledging the degree to which working women had become formally involved in the mass platform, although largely as mothers, daughters, and putative educators of the next Radical generation rather than as citizens in their own right. The mass platform represented the people assembled; it signified the advances in popular political organization and the ways in which the industrial experience and the war had transformed popular political consciousness. In 1819 one 'nation' faced another. At Birmingham, where the first meeting had been held, radicals elected their own 'legislatorial attorney'. At the second, in London, it was resolved that from 1820 onwards the people would not feel themselves bound 'by any persons styling themselves our representatives, other than those who shall be fully, freely and fairly chosen by the voices and votes of the largest proportion of the members of the state'.[18] In a manner redolent of the revolutionary experience and the calling of congresses, conventions, and anti-parliaments, the politically excluded asserted the rights of popular sovereignty as a condition of its compliance with the Hanoverian state. It was an issue that would haunt Britain's governors until 1848.

12 Class and Power in Hanoverian England

The historiography of Hanoverian England is currently in a state of remarkable flux. There are very few generalizations that command any degree of consensus. Hanoverian England has been conceptualized as both traditional and modern, aristocratic and bourgeois. It has been viewed as an *ancien régime* virtually untouched by industrialism, a regime whose capitalist imperatives were accommodated within a non-capitalist order, an acquisitive society in which wealth mattered more than lineage, a modernizing, industrial society, and yet a society in which vertical solidarities subsumed horizontal, in which religious, patron–client, and national identities still counted for more than class. The permutations seem almost endless. In this chapter we consider some conclusions that flow from these divergent interpretations.

The notion that Hanoverian England was an *ancien régime* fails on several accounts. The patriarchal mystique of monarchy survived only among a minority of Jacobites, and although the radical contractual implications of 1688 were glossed by conservative Whigs, everyone knew that the prerogatives of kings had to conform to the realities of parliamentary power. Furthermore, England lacked the juridical distinctions that separated Continental estates; even those privileges accorded the peerage were less formidable than those of Continental nobilities. No English peer could claim tax exemptions by virtue of his rank; nor could he dispense justice in private courts. While English peers could sometimes profit from manorial privileges, as did the Duke of Beaufort in the seigniory of Gower and Kilvey (although not without a good deal of political contention and legal prevarication), the great source of their wealth came from the rentals of their landed estates within what was an agrarian capitalist order. It was these rentals that made English peers part of a larger landed élite and distinguished them from Continental nobilities, whose wealth derived in the first instance from the commercialization or commutation of seigniorial dues. The fact that the nobility on the Continent invested in finance and industry and was more vulnerable to the dilution of honours than in Britain, in the sense that a trade in titles was competitively waged for the purposes of tax evasion, does not really detract from the fact that their wealth was derived from fundamentally different sources. In Britain the power of the landed aristocracy rested on its ability to exploit its estates through efficient management, larger tenancies, and increasingly through the enclosure of the open fields, and to consolidate and enhance that wealth through legal instruments, advantageous marriages, and wherever possible, the windfalls of political office and influence.

The dynamics of power among the propertied

Britain's landed élite was never as reliant upon state favour as its Continental counterparts. It could afford the luxury of open opposition to King and Court because it could translate its wealth into parliamentary power. Indeed, the formal political power of the landed élite, and of the peerage within it, has been one of the salient features of the aristocratic interpretation of the age. The landed aristocracy monopolized the high offices of state and dominated county government and the armed forces, particularly the army. Relative to its wealth and numbers, it also dominated Parliament. Between 1734 and 1820 at least 30 per cent of all MPs were Irish peers, English baronets, or the sons of titled familes; at least 40 per cent could be described as landed gentry, including some of those in the first cohort. By contrast the number of bankers, manufacturers, merchants, nabobs, and West India planters in the Commons numbered 11 per cent in 1734, rising to 23 per cent by 1820. Clearly the Commons was not impervious to forms of new wealth, but it remained overwhelmingly a house of established landed families and its affines, some of whom entered Parliament after careers in the armed forces or the law. Well over half of all MPs had relatives who had been in Parliament before them and well over half belonged to identifiable family groups even if they did not always vote the same way. The relative ease by which landed grandees entered the Commons can be registered by the age of first entry: on average 24 years for the eldest sons of the peerage; 27 for younger sons; 31 for all 'descendant' MPs;[1] the mid-to-late thirties for career officers and lawyers; the early forties for men of commerce.

In terms of political experience, the landed grandees who had seats as heirlooms had a demonstrable advantage.

Yet it would be wrong to infer from this evidence that the landed aristocracy monopolized political power. If commercial and middling interests, broadly defined, were underrepresented in Parliament, they could certainly have an impact upon policy at the national level. Successive governments had to court the powerful constellation of moneyed men in the City who were so critical to the funded debt and the promotion of short-term loans in wartime. In the middle decades of the century, the Duke of Newcastle spent as much time worrying about the disposition of the City as he did the factional politics within the House, well aware that it was vital to Britain's foreign and imperial policies. Moreover, politicians in general constantly had to attend to the powerful local or sectoral interests that besieged Parliament with special demands. During the eighteenth century interest politics expanded dramatically as the fiscal requirements of the state and its active promotion of industrial protection involved a wide variety of business enterprise and as Parliament's status as a regulatory body grew. Between 1690 and 1790 over 15,000 Bills were laid before Parliament, and the number of public and private Acts that were actually passed increased dramatically, averaging 58 a session in the reign of George I, 81 a session in that of George II, and as many as 254 a session in that of George III. In these circumstances lobbying Parliament became an increasingly sophisticated art, carried on by a bewildering variety of groups, from powerful mercantile bodies, local corporations, to manufacturers, shopkeepers, and, as we have seen in the case of the Spitalfields Act, even artisans. Powerfully placed mercantile groups with representatives in the House or permanent agents were more likely to corner the attention of Parliament, of course, but more modest men of property could sometimes successfully mobilize on a national scale against taxes or concessions injurious to their trade. Over 100 different bodies petitioned for the repeal of the leather duties between 1697 and 1699, for example, some of them tanners in small market towns. In the 1730s and again in 1785 shopkeepers across the country petitioned against measures that advantaged street-hawking, in the latter instance forcing Pitt to amend and ultimately repeal his retail tax. Their success was testimony to the acumen and vigour of the middling sort in defending their livelihoods in an oligarchic political system.

That system itself was not inpenetrable. Although the electoral structure of the eighteenth century showed signs of increasing ossification, with as many as two-thirds of all seats under private patronage and the industrial regions of the country grievously underrepresented, the middling electors could make their presence felt in the more open constituencies. This was less the case in the counties, where grandee compromises had virtually eliminated electoral contests; although even here the lesser freeholders could chalk up some victories, as in the eastern counties in 1784, where one spokesman complained that 'the Yeomanry and common freeholder are only considered as a pack of hounds, and as such are to be obedient to the whistle of some neighbouring squire'.[2] But the middling voice was palpably audible in the larger urban constituencies that had opposed Walpole and supported Pitt in the mid-century decades and, if anything, increased their electoral vibrancy thereafter. Indeed, it was precisely these open constituencies that were at the vanguard of the mass petitioning movements of the second half of the century, and before 1790 at least, at the forefront of the campaigns for parliamentary reform. In the eyes of the press, they were often seen as a barometer of public opinion, whose real foundations, it was argued, lay with the middling men of property.

This reformist discourse contained a latent anti-aristocratic bias in the sense that it espoused an open, accountable politics that could be set against aristocratic pretensions to rule. It was complemented by the publicity given to upper-class fashion and sexuality, most notably its macaroni manners and criminal conversation trials, which reinforced the conviction that the aristocracy was a decadent, self-absorbed élite, unfit to rule. Yet this anti-aristocratic critique was not without its ambiguities. Many of those who deplored aristocratic vice and demanded a moral regeneration of society often retained quite conservative notions of how society should be organized, notions that stressed the appropriate reciprocities between ranks and the need for Christian stewardship, whether aristocratic or bourgeois. Similarly, reformers who denounced the stultification of political life and the occlusion of popular liberties did not necessarily target the aristocracy as a class. They were mainly concerned with the accretion of vested interests that surrounded the state, the beneficiaries of what later became known as 'Old Corruption', whatever their class background. Within this framework, individual aristocrats or aristocratic factions could arguably serve as a counterpoint to overweening state power, provided they acted as genuine trustees of the national interest—a position adopted by Charles James Fox in his role as the Westminster tribune of the people. Even as Radical a man as Joseph Priestley could endorse an enlightened aristocracy as an antidote to political and moral corruption; at least until the Anglican-cum-aristocratic hierarchy refused to support the Dissenters' demand for full citizenship. It was only in the wake of the French Revolution and Burke's call for a revitalized aristocratic order to combat the contagion of democracy and the ambition of Dissent that Priestley began to have his doubts, believing that the intrinsic arrogance of the nobility was a disbarment to political leadership, if not true citizenship. 'There is not only most virtue and most happiness, but even most true politeness in the middle class of life', Priestley reflected. Their social interactions made them more tolerant than the aristocracy, whose hauteur and brittle code of honour undermined its self-control and compromised its statecraft.[3]

If the Radical spokesmen of bourgeois Dissent were rapidly moving towards an anti-aristocratic critique of society by the 1790s, there were powerful undercurrents that were working in different directions. Merchants and manufacturers were sometimes piqued by the insouciant manner in which gentlemen handled their petitions. The Midlands ironmaster, Samuel Garbett, for example, complained in 1766 that the 'old country families look upon themselves as patrons of the trade in the neighbourhood, and really have an inclination to serve it when they understand the subject. But . . . we sorely want somebody who is not only intelligent but hath enlarged views to take the lead in considering our commerce as a subject of politicks.'[4] Yet the relative success of middling lobbying tended to temper such irritations and in any case seldom promoted the clash of broadly-based economic interests. Most of the economic issues brought before Parliament were local and particular, disclosing tensions within sectors as much as between them. Even in those cases where economic policies broached palpable class interests, strenuous efforts were made to harmonize them. Disagreements about the corn bounty, for example, an issue which potentially raised wage costs for manufacture and pitched industry against agriculture, were seldom articulated in class terms. Nor were the debates over the export of wool in the 1780s. The only plausible exception to the rule was the battle between landed and financial capital over the funded debt in the early eighteenth century, and this conflict was mollified by lower land taxes and lower rates of interest upon annuities and by broadening the social base of the funded debt itself. By the mid-decades, in fact, leading London businessmen were as likely to marry daughters of the landed gentry as landed gentlemen were to seek out city heiresses, facilitating a new symbiosis of landed and merchant capital that was to survive well into the nineteenth century.

The pragmatic pursuit of economic interests, then, by and large allowed for the reconciliation or coexistence of different fractions of capital in the eighteenth century. Merchants, manufacturers, professionals, peers, and gentry all invested in the turnpikes and canals that mushroomed in the second half of the century.[5] The same was largely true of the varied schemes for urban improvement, for paving, lighting, sewage, or the construction of neat terraces and squares that were an intrinsic part of the urban renaissance. Many of the statutory bodies set up to administer these concerns had a broad propertied representation, as did the voluntary associations, such as hospitals and educational trusts, which were also part of the new urban landscape. Such associations, for which there was no religious disqualification, gave many members of the middling classes a stake in the social order and allowed them to combine 'patriotic' endeavour with self-advancement. It made them part of a pluralistic, propertied endeavour for improvement. Perhaps the most numerous and popular of all these organizations were the prosecution associations that were formed to deal with a broad spectrum of propertied crime, from industrial embezzlement and petty larceny to highway robbery, housebreaking, poaching, and the theft of horses and sheep. Judging from the Staffordshire and Essex evidence, there was a significant growth in these associations in the aftermath of the American War, paralleling the course of recorded propertied crime at the quarter sessions and assizes. Although the game associations were inevitably dominated by landowners and the anti-embezzlement societies by manufacturers, others had a broad propertied membership. They signalled the growing concern within the propertied classes about the breakdown of law and order and the need to discipline the lower orders into habits of industry and propriety. They help explain why the middling classes joined the loyalist reaction of 1792/3, when plebeian Jacobin notions of equality sent a *frisson* of fear among the propertied classes in general. Whatever reservations the middling sort may have had about aristocratic leadership, these were set aside in a common defence of property against the potentially destabilizing forces of popular radicalism.

Patrician–plebeian relations

If the relationship between the landed aristocracy and the middling sort generated broad affinities of interest based on a common defence of property and a deepening anxiety about crime, the relationship between the propertied classes and the plebs became more antagonistic over time. Historians who contend otherwise have tended to stress the degree to which the landed aristocracy was able to sustain lower-class loyalty through the traditions of landed paternalism and how the small-scale, face-to-face milieu of industrial enterprise buoyed up patriarchal authority. Certainly there is no doubt that patriarchalism survived as a social gospel even though its importance as a political creed declined. Anglican spokesmen made much of the notion that eighteenth-century England was a society of interdependent orders, ordained by Providence, in which some 'should be Masters, others Servants' bound by relations of duty, subordination, and mutuality. Moreover, landowners were regularly depicted as genial paternalists who cared for their people, especially in times of distress, and administered the law with a fitting compassion and impartiality. Indeed, this wealthy, leisured class was sometimes seen as a necessary arbiter of social discord, the only group whose education and material security enabled them to stand above the fray of trade and productive relations, to view society's problems in broad, dispassionate terms.

Yet to endorse these images of the eighteenth century is in the first instance to endorse the landed hierarchy's self-legitimation. The point is underscored by recognizing that there were competing definitions of how society could best be arranged. For example,

Hanoverian England was increasingly portrayed by political economists as an aggressively commercial society in which the maxims of the market and the virtues of independence, industry, and self-reliance could best address its social problems, largely through the exigencies of economic growth. In view of this it is worth while exploring the country-house ideal of paternalism further, and asking ourselves whether the small-scale nature of industrial enterprise, let alone other employment settings, really promoted the sorts of vertical identities upon which conservative interpretations of the century have set so much store.

The inference that paternalism was continually reinforced by the slow, uneven process of industrialization in the eighteenth century is misleading in two important respects. It completely overlooks the fact that the economic historians who have advanced this view of industrialization have not denied that there were long-term structural changes in the economy and productive relations. It also ignores, quite ironically, that this interpretation of industrialization is predicated upon the salient fact that England was an industrial society at the very beginning of the period spanned by this book. The revision of Gregory King's figures now reveals that a very substantial proportion of the workforce was engaged in cottage industry, albeit on a seasonal part-time basis at the beginning of the century but becoming regionally denser and more specialized over time. This predominantly putting-out workforce was not under the eye of the employer; it worked on a contract basis for merchant suppliers and retained considerable control over the labour process itself. This relative freedom gave rise to continual complaints about the so-called leisure preference of workers and about the potentially damaging effect of embezzlement upon suppliers' profits. In the West Country textile industries, where specialization was most advanced in the early Hanoverian era, it gave rise to a good deal of hard collective bargaining between clothiers and weavers over piece-rates, truck, and the existence of combinations; a pattern that was repeated in other areas as their economies matured.

Productive relations in the large putting-out industries could hardly be described as 'patriarchal'. As we have already seen in Chapters 6 and 8, the battles between labour and capital occurred within a customary framework of labour regulation that had endured since the sixteenth century. The same was increasingly true of craft-workers within the older urban centres. Here the trend was towards the disintegration of guild economies, and in the face of combinations or incipient combinations, an increasing resort to the courts or even Parliament to settle labour disputes about wages, piece-rates, perquisites, the dilution of labour through an infla- tion or evasion of apprenticeship regulations. Only in the relatively settled parishes of rural England was there anything approximat- ing a paternalist timbre to work-relations, and even here such con- ventions were undermined from the 1770s onwards by the decline in living-in servants and farmer hospitality and by the elimina- tion of female labour from the harvesting of corn. Even among domestic servants, where one might expect to find paternalism in full bloom, one finds instead little loyalty to masters and mis- tresses. Servants remained in a household long enough to secure a poor-law settlement. Thereafter, as the Church court interrogat- ories reveal, they frequently moved around at a rapid rate. In the big houses, leading servants bargained hard for their perquisites and were deeply resentful when vails (customary tips from vis- itors) were eliminated in the 1760s. In cases of marital breakdown between milord and milady, they might use their intimate know- ledge of the household to their own advantage. Lawrence Stone has recently noted the 'casually exploitative attitude of both mas- ter and servants' at Stockfeld Park during the 1790s, where the lady of the house, Clara Louisa Middleton, developed an unfortu- nate, and ultimately disastrous, infatuation with the groom.[6] The cosy mutualities of upstairs–downstairs dramas hardly reflect the intrigue and self-interest that surrounded master–servant relations in polite society.

Master–servant relations at any level were seldom very harmo- nious in the eighteenth century and they certainly do not merit the assumption that patriarchal authority was willingly accepted. Yet we have argued that during the first half of the century at least, the landed gentry did often endorse the claims of popular custom in the interests of social and political peace. Gentlemanly JPs were prepared to arbitrate labour disputes in labour's favour, often because they resented the way in which manufacturers might arbitrarily reduce wage or piece-rates during an economic slump, thus throwing workers on the poor rates and increasing the eco-

nomic burden on their own tenants. Confronted with angry consumers and fearful of public order that would challenge their own
authority, JPs would also support the moral economy of provision
in times of dearth; although as the 1756–7 bread crisis revealed,
landed gentlemen were reluctant to consolidate its legitimacy by
adding new legislation to control profiteering, preferring instead
to use their powers under the old Book of Orders. This was sometimes backed up by paternalistic gestures to the poor. Although
gentlemen organized themselves into armed posses to contend with
the roving bands of rioters who attacked mills and unloaded barges
of grain during the crisis of 1756–7, they also opened subscriptions to sell corn under the market rate and encouraged their tenants to bring corn to the pitched markets where it might be sold
on reasonable terms.

From the mid-eighteenth century, we have suggested, this endorsement of custom weakened in favour of market values. The
statutory legitimacy of the moral economy disappeared after 1772,
even if judges briefly reactivated its common-law status in 1800.
Labour legislation, or the lack of it, increasingly favoured employers. Customary rights in agriculture and industry were regarded
with increasing disfavour, as were freeman rights of access to town
commons. After 1770 a new wave of parliamentary enclosure pared
down and often eliminated common right. This attack upon custom, with the attendant social dislocations, was increasingly
encouraged by clerical JPs and *ad hoc* prosecution societies; or by
pro-manufacturing magistrates in urban courts of request. As the
beau monde gravitated to London for the delights of the season,
so the landed aristocracy renounced rural duties and spent more
of its time and money in the capital or at aristocratic spas like
Bath. By the end of the century the landed gentry resembled an
urban *rentier* class whose contact with the countryside was principally associated with genteel summer retreats and weekend visits
to their own gaming-parks. Contact with country tenants and
labourers became increasingly ceremonial, reserved for a carefully
choreographed royal jubilee, peace thanksgiving, or coming-of-age
party. Paradoxically the pretensions to benevolent landlordship
increased at precisely the point that their realities waned, so that
new model villages and rococo cottages accompanied enclosure.
As the landscape gardener Humphry Repton self-interestedly

remarked, if the cottages of the poor 'can be made a subordinate part of the general scenery, they will, so far from disgracing it, add to the dignity that wealth can derive from the exercise of benevolence'.[7]

Alongside the model villages and game parks the social land-scape of the countryside was visibly changing. After 1770 custom-ary tenancies and medium-sized farms began to disappear under the impact of agricultural improvement, accentuating the gulf between the larger tenant farmers and the mass of the rural poor. An enquiry in the late 1780s concluded that farm-workers could 'scarcely with their utmost exertions' supply their families with bread, a sentiment repeated throughout the following decade. Agricultural labourers in the south did attempt to raise their wages in the years 1792–4, but whatever few gains they made were quickly offset by sky-rocketing food prices. Predictably there were protests against food shortages in 1795 and 1801; in fact it is likely that the visibility of rural workers in the food riots of these years was unpar-alleled. Some of these confrontations were accompanied by demands for more adequate poor relief, a critical issue for farm labourers whose meagre wages were increasingly being subsidized from the rates. Yet JPs were quick to deter collective protests in these years of political radicalism and Revolutionary war and routinely used the volunteer regiments to suppress them. The overpopulated, pau-perized south became a cauldron of smouldering discontent, period-ically surfacing in acts of malicious damage, incendiarism, assaults upon unpopular poor-law administrators and at the end of the war, in attacks upon threshing-machines in East Anglia.

Although farm-workers were not altogether isolated from the mainstream of political radicalism, they seldom strayed from the traditional repertoire of collective protest. Other workers did. West Country textile-workers had strike funds and combinations at the very beginning of the century, and by the end most industrial trades were organized in some manner. A few, like the hatters who held a 'congress' to discuss their grievances in 1777, were even organized on a national scale. More generally there appears to have been a rise in labour militancy. Certainly there was a discernible increase in the number of reported strikes or labour disputes after 1760 (fifty-five per decade), virtually double the number reported in the first half of the century. Employers retaliated with more prosecutions under the master and servant act as time went on, with no less than 900 prosecutions in Staffordshire in the final two decades of the century. At the same time there was a call for tougher legislation against combinations, thought by William Wilberforce in 1799 to be 'a general disease in our society' meriting a 'general' remedy. The government obliged, passing a Combination Act which outlawed all collective bargaining and allowed employers speedy summary action against workers' combinations. Protests from artisans across Britain followed, and some modifications were made to the newly enacted labour law, the chief of which was to reform the rules governing the prosecution process. Even so, the law was heavily weighted against the workers and signalled the government's abandonment of the old mercantilist machinery for regulating labour issues, although it was subsequently prepared to pass Acts to allow for limited arbitration agreements.

The Combination Acts were designed to crush the workers' capacity for collective action. They had contradictory effects. While the acts did intimidate some trades, they proved difficult to enforce, and workers were more often tried under the old common law of conspiracy and 5 Eliz. c. 4 than under the new legislation. At the same time, the general interdict under which all trades laboured encouraged their ongoing cooperation. In London there was regular contact among seventeen trades by 1800; in the Manchester area there was a secret trades council in existence by the turn of the century, linking textile-workers to tailors, shoemakers, bricklayers, and joiners. Here were the foundations of the burgeoning class consciousness that was to inform the strike wave of 1818 in the cotton district, when the demands went beyond a dissatisfaction with wage cuts and high prices to address the broader changes in capitalist exploitation and the widening gulf between masters and men.

The critical catalyst for this shift in social relations was the spate of machine-breaking known as Luddism that broke out in the textile districts of the Midlands and the north in the years 1811–12 and smouldered on until 1816. The crisis was brought on by a poor harvest in 1811 and a Napoleonic blockade that severely disrupted export markets, but it was accentuated by the government's commitment to industrial *laissez-faire* and its persistent refusal to countenance any statutory regulation of industry. Indeed, these were the years when the last vestiges of industrial paternalism were dismantled. In each area the machine-breaking followed the failure of workers to secure any legislative or judicial redress for their grievances. In the hosiery districts of Nottingham and Leicestershire, the protests against cheap stockings or cut-ups made by unapprenticed labour generated a remarkable spate of machine-breaking in 1811–12 in which over a thousand frames were destroyed by redressers acting under the mythic leader General Ludd. Further north, in Lancashire and the West Riding, Luddite targets centred upon the introduction of machinery (power looms and shearing-frames) that threatened the livelihood of hand-loom weavers and croppers (or shearmen). Here the protests tended to be more dramatically confrontational, involving a good deal of clandestine planning and oath-taking and full-scale attacks upon mills and mill-owners. Here Luddism moved beyond its industrial objectives to embrace political revolt. Although the evidence is circumstantial and heavily dependent upon the reports of spies, it seems likely that Luddism developed an insurrectionary *élan* through its links with Painite clubs and the United Englishmen. Certainly the Luddite areas of the north brimmed with sedition and talk of a general rising. One Leeds handbill urged croppers to bring down 'all Nobles and Tyrants' and 'follow the Noble Example of the brave Citzens of Paris'.[8] At Bolton the news of the first minister's assassination in 1812 was openly applauded. On West Riding walls notices were chalked offering 100 guineas for the Prince Regent's head. At the same time, Luddites killed in their attacks upon mills were treated like martyrs, while a general conspiracy of silence shielded those on the run from the thousands of troops sent to capture them. As Lord Byron understood, Luddism had a quasi-insurrectionary dimension, brought on in part by the Establishment's indifference to workers' grievances and its refusal to consider industrial protection as a solution to their woes.

The experience of Luddism and Parliament's endorsement of industrial *laissez-faire* left a legacy of class bitterness that survived the war. As the victory peals of Waterloo died away, working people contemplated the consequences of a long, exhausting war against France from whose death toll few families were spared. Relative to the size of the armed forces, a higher percentage of men died in the French Wars of 1793–1815 than in the Great War of 1914–18; and the privations at home, with the near famines of

1795 and 1800–1 and the heavy regressive taxation, were indisputably more severe. The sacrifices made by ordinary people, moreover, were hardly recognized beyond a few celebratory ox-roasts and a smattering of soup kitchens in the years of distress and demobilization. Combinations continued to be outlawed; the corn laws confirmed landed rentals and inflated bread prices; and payment by truck eroded real wages. Demobilized servicemen confronted the 'rationalities' of the market, not government aid; and mass protests were constrained by laws against popular assembly and the ominous mustering of cavalry regiments. It was hardly surprising that people were bitter and that demobilized soldiers sometimes renounced their Waterloo medals to public applause. At Blackburn in 1819 one Waterloo veteran begged the pardon of a reform meeting 'for having fought in so bad a cause'.[9] At Stockport, a soldier who had been nineteen years in the army exclaimed 'he once thought he was fighting for liberty, but now found to the contrary'.[10]

The birth of working-class radicalism

The pattern of protest in the years 1815–20 was significantly different from that which occurred in the aftermath of the War of Spanish Succession. In the earlier period the protests centred upon a disputed succession and a bitter party conflict between Whig and Tory, scarring national anniversaries with revelrous insults and effigy-burnings, seditious ballads, and the parading of treasonable colours. Although these protests ebbed and flowed to the rhythm of national politics, they were largely local in nature and sometimes covertly choreographed from above—in the case of the anti-Hanoverian, Jacobite demonstrations, by disaffected Tory clergy and gentlemen. Social grievances were sometimes embedded in these overtly political protests. The attack upon Dissenting meeting-houses in the summer of 1715, for example, was prompted in part by the fear that the newly formed Whig ministry would embroil Britain in another arduous Continental war. But social and political grievances did not always go hand in hand. Riotous weavers in Devon (1717) and in London and Norwich (1720), for example, pursued economic goals that were never annexed to opposition politics. In fact, they publicly disavowed Jacobitism in order to stress the legitimacy of their grievances against clothiers and calico imports.

The pattern of protest in 1815–20, on the other hand, was more more national and more self-activating, in the sense that it was seldom dependent upon upper-class support or sympathy in the same way that protests had been a century earlier. Early eighteenth-century strikes, riots, and other trade protests were accompanied by a sharp awareness of opposed economic interests (on the part of clothiers and weavers, for example). Indeed, Parliament's interference was often grounded in the belief that its role was to mediate. But such struggles were usually contained within the boundaries of specific industries, and often confined to particular parts of the country. By 1820, however, there were the beginnings of a knitting-together of a working-class consciousness that would come to fruition in the 1830s and 1840s, a new sense of collective identity among workers in different trades based on their common experience of economic exploitation and political exclusion. While crowds continued to force down the high price of provisions within their own localities, and while national anniversaries such as George IV's coronation still served as a focus of revelrous discontent, the repertoire of protest was more programmatic and institutionally more complex. The final years of war had seen the birth of a national reform movement, beginning with Major Cartwright's petitioning tours of the Luddite counties. His Hampden Clubs significantly broadened the boundaries of political literacy and association beyond the old Jacobin, artisan centres, shifting the centre of gravity in radical politics towards the industrial north. 'Orator' Hunt was able to build on these foundations, mobilizing working people around a Radical mass platform that demanded full political citizenship for all male adults as well as annual parliaments and a secret ballot. In its call for national conventions or anti-parliaments of elected deputies, such a platform sought to create an alternative structure of democratic politics that might subvert the normal channels of propertied politics if its demands were not recognized. Together with exclusive dealing[11] and strike action across a spectrum of trades, Radicals sought to create a working-class movement of unassailable proportions, one where the line between popular constitutionalism and more militant forms of mobilization was deliberately blurred.

Government authorities, and the propertied classes in general, found the mass platform doubly threatening. Not only did it invoke political strategies that had been forged in the crucible of the democratic revolutions of the late eighteenth century, but it also sought to mobilize workers whose grievances challenged the post-revolutionary capitalist order. The last point is critical, for while the rhetoric of the platform was grounded in a Radical democratic discourse that pitted the people against the bastions of privilege and was thus potentially open to a variety of populist reconstructions, it went beyond a straightforward demand for political inclusion. Parliamentary reform was a means to an end, to the rectification of working-class grievances, as the 1818 strikes in the Lancashire cotton district make very clear.[12] These grievances included discriminatory taxation, the corn laws, the game laws, the legal ban on union activity, the repeal of statutory regulations governing apprenticeship, truck, and hours of work. Radical newspapers even talked of workers being denied a 'sufficient competency' for their labour, of 'perishing for want' while 'the great and middling classes' indulged in 'excessive luxury, dissipation and waste, produced by legal robbery'.[13] Parliamentary reform thus challenged the power of the landed gentry and the industrialist. The socio-economic priorities of reform varied from place to place, as befitted a society of uneven industrialism, but there was an abiding sense that the parameters of political power had to be radically altered if this body of grievances was to be adequately addressed.

The mass platform of the post-Napoleonic years sought to redress working-class grievances by staking out Radical claims for the enfranchisement of working-class men. Whether for strategic reasons or out of personal conviction, male Radicals did not assert the same freedom for women, whose role remained predominantly one of class allies and regenerators. Feminist historians have rightly pointed to the problematic nature of women's involvement in the Radical movement and to the overwhelmingly masculine definition of full citizenship despite the efforts of Wollstonecraft and others. At the same time, women's participation was not as cosmetic as is sometimes claimed. It drew on women's traditional role as the preservers of life, as the gatherers and distributors of social resources within their communities. Through the formation of new female political societies, most notably in Lancashire, it gave women a special voice in the articulation of working-class grievances, dramatizing their impact upon hearth and home and extending the promotion of Radical ideas in the industrial districts. Women's activism was also critical to the expansion of political space so necessary to the Radical platform, especially at a time when such space was subject to legislative and military repression. The spectacle of women marching *en militaire* in Radical parades, dressed demurely, bearing flags and flamboyant liberty caps, helped to underscore the communal basis and respectability of the platform while at the same time reasserting its militancy. 'Who is there but must admire and wish to see emulated the noble example of these worthy descendants of Boadicea', ran one Wigan handbill, 'that Boadicea, who, hundreds of years ago, led on her countrymen, and defeated the country's invaders.'[14] Far from being marginal or inconsequential, the brand of 'female consciousness'[15] and class solidarity that women espoused proved of vital importance to the fledgling radical movement of the post-war years.

The mass platform was a mobilizing force in its own right, helping to create a new working-class presence in the political landscape. Certainly there were areas of the country that were unaffected by it. The agricultural south was largely untouched by political radicalism. As late as 1830, as the Swing riots revealed, rural labourers remained largely outside the working-class mainstream. On the other hand, the years 1815–20 saw a significant efflorescence of working-class politics in the industrial north and the Midlands and among the London trades, where the traditional leadership provided by the London Livery and the Westminster committee was being contested by Spencean ultra-radicals, shipwrights like John Gast, and flamboyant figures like the diminutive shoemaker-printer Samuel Waddington. In a series of trials he defended himself with a panache that enraged judges and magistrates and afforded his Radical supporters much merriment.

The changing class character of British politics can even be seen in the Queen Caroline affair of 1820. The attempt by George IV to strip his estranged wife of her regal rights on account of her adultery with her Italian valet-cum-chamberlain has conventionally been seen as a royal soap opera, a diversionary episode conducive to the theatrical, factional politics of an earlier era. To some extent this is true. But the agitation for the Queen did not only generate political space for the opposition Whigs, nor for the middle-class matrons who identifed with Caroline's marital ordeal and vulnerability, nor indeed for the wags who relished the sight of two royal incorrigibles playing holier than thou. It also allowed the fledgling working-class movement the opportunity to regroup after Peterloo and the Cato Street conspiracy, to test the boundaries of political legitimacy circumscribed by the Six Acts, to vindicate the order and discipline of their own organizations, to regain the momentum of the mass platform. To a large degree it was successful. In the industrial north, pro-Caroline demonstrations were inextricably bound up with protests against Peterloo and the imprisonment of Radical leaders, so that the Queen's cause became as much a parable of political iniquity as of royal or marital persecution and hypocrisy. In London demonstrators hoisted the cap of liberty and reasserted the place of the 'industrious classes' as the 'chief energy of the nation'. To underscore the point, the London trades continually kept the Queen's cause before the public eye with their processions and addresses, and in her British finale, her funeral procession from Brandenburg House to Harwich, forced the cortège to pass through the City, much to the disgust of King and ministry. As one member of the crowd told Lord Stowell: 'Ay, you gemmen thought you could carry everything your own way; but we'll show you the difference.'[16]

England after the Napoleonic Wars sometimes resembled an armed camp. The army was only slowly disbanded. In 1820 there were roughly 120,000 men on effective duty, half the number at the time of Waterloo, but significantly more than in previous demobilizations. The great majority were now barracked about the country rather than billeted on the population, largely to insulate them from disaffection. This was all the more necessary because troops were routinely brought in to police public meetings, even public anniversaries. At the celebration of George IV's coronation at Carlisle, some Radicals crowned an ass while the onlooking crowd assailed the military commander with shouts of 'Manchester, Manchester'. The troops were predictably brought in, striking 'the populace with the backs of their swords very forcibly'.[17] For the remainder of the night Carlisle 'exhibited the appearance of a place subject to martial law'. The situation was little better in the metropolis itself, where the town appeared to be under a 'military occupation' during the coronation. 'Had a stranger . . . approached at that moment', the *Champion* remarked, 'he might have mistaken London for a conquered city, in which the governing powers were at war with the people.'[18]

The presence of the troops was only part of the machinery designed to curb popular disaffection and inhibit public redress. As we have already noted, the law itself placed severe restraints upon the capacity of ordinary people to organize, whether in labour disputes or on matters pertaining to political and social reform. Combinations were outlawed; so, too, were corresponding societies, making it very difficult for working people to embody their democratic ambitions in institutional form. The pauper press was hamstrung with increasing stamp duties and public meetings were subject to magisterial approval and surveillance, the only exceptions being the legal constituted assemblies convened by sheriffs. The battery of legal sanctions against the emergence of the mass platform and its allied clubs and societies was very formidable, and Radical leaders were constantly subjected to legal harassment. It is no accident that by 1820 many Radical or union leaders were in prison or awaiting trial.

Three general observations may be ventured in the context of this constellation of military and legal power in the post-war years. The first pertains to the language of radicalism and its relationship to emergent class loyalties. In recent years historians have argued that the language of radicalism was pre-eminently a language of political exclusion that did not frontally address the realities of class power in that it did not embody a critique of capitalism per se. Indeed, because the language of radicalism was sociologically unspecific, it cannot be read as a language of class. Yet the language of radicalism did not only excoriate 'Old Corruption', the parasitic crew of pensioners and placemen that bled the taxpayer. It was often accented to address the changing social relations of production. We have given some examples in this chapter; there are many others. In the cotton strike of 1818, local leaders talked not only of misgovernment but of the 'Tyranny of their masters', those 'petty monarchs' whose 'whole time is occupied in contriving how to get the greatest quantity of work turned off with the least expense', whose endeavours were turning artisans into 'bondsmen'.[19] At the same time radicalism was a pertinent language because it addressed the warp and weft of state and class power that disabled workers and denied them redress. In other words, if the language of working-class radicalism was principally preoccupied with relations of political power, it was because the state and the law were seen as fundamental obstacles to working-class emancipation.

If radicalism shaped the working-class critique of power, so, too, paradoxically did nationalism. Normally nationalism is seen as a solvent of working-class identities, enjoining workers to embrace a commitment to nationhood that transcended, or at the very least accommodated, class loyalties. In framing this argument historians have pointed to the volunteer movements of the French Wars, and to the ecstatic celebration of royal anniversaries and victories that accompanied them. This interpretation of the evidence, we would argue, is suspect. There were a medley of reasons why men might volunteer including unemployment, pressure from landlords, the evasion of more onerous forms of service; all of which make it difficult to determine its reliability as a register of nationalism. Similarly, the celebrations of military victories or royal jubilees provide much evidence of the promotion of majesty and token paternalism, and of the choreography of public space, especially in those villages and market towns where huge open-air dinners were put on for the inhabitants in an attempt to immobilize crowds and to reassert traditions of ruling-class noblesse oblige. What they meant to the poor beyond a good meal and a bumper of beer is another matter.

What is interesting about the discourse of nationalism during the French Wars and its aftermath is the contradictory postures of the ruling class. On the one hand the landed aristocracy were very keen to have working men join up or volunteer in the event of an invasion from France. On the other hand they were not prepared to acknowledge their contribution as citizens. As the debate on the Seditious Meetings Act of 1819 revealed quite explicitly, the unrepresented were accorded no legitimate claim to citizenship; as Canning explained, they were not part of the deliberative nation or people at all, and had no legal right to assemble publicly. Fighting for King and Country was commendable; having even a modest voice in the country's future was not. Such sentiments were seldom challenged in the eighteenth century, but they now rankled with a public that had suffered immeasurably during the war. Certainly they fuelled the demand for political inclusion. As the Radical James Fitton reminded his audience at a reform meeting at Rochdale in July 1819, during the war they had been called 'British Heroes—Brave Lads—and the finest Fellows in the World'. But, he asked, 'What do they call you now? Scum, Rabble &c. A set of People who have no Rights. Is not every Man equal? He ought to be ... We are all made of the same materials ... We are all equal in the sight of God—have all an equal right & Privilege— Ponder well on these things when you go home tonight.'[20]

Two nations faced one another in the post-war years and the divide between them was immense. What the post-war crisis revealed most clearly was that the ruling class was losing the capacity to govern. In the first half of the century, we have argued, there had been an equilibrium of power between rulers and ruled, one in which the landed gentry were largely tolerant of the customary expectations of the people and prepared to negotiate them in the mannered style of patrician paternalism, even to the point of sometimes compromising the aspirations of middling employers. By 1820 those social reciprocities had greatly weakened. In a new social order in which custom and paternalism were marginal, in which new working-class identities were emerging alongside the growing economic power of the industrialist and the rule of the market, laws denouncing workers' associations and the haunting shadow of the military featured more conspicuously in the theatre of rule.

Notes

The following abbreviations are used in the Notes:

PRO	Public Record Office, London
BL	British Library
Add. MS	Additional Manuscript
Adm	Admiralty papers
HO	Home Office papers
SP	State Papers
TS	Treasury Solicitor papers

Chapter 1 (pages 1–16)

1. C. Vancouver, *General View of the Agriculture of Hampshire* (1813), 496.
2. Oliver Rackham, *The History of the Countryside* (London, 1986), 4–5.
3. *Tour through the Whole Island of Great Britain* (1724), ed. Pat Rogers (Harmondsworth, 1971), 176–7.
4. *Journeys of a German in England*, trans. Reginald Nettel (1965; repr. 1983), 113.
5. See Ch. 3. Some recent work suggests that state policy toward dearth, poverty, and markets may have been important in explaining the differences between England and France: see Ch. 5.
6. Son of James Francis Edward, the 'Old Pretender', who was the only son of James II, and the younger brother of Queen Mary and Queen Anne. See Ch. 4.
7. Silas Neville's diary account, quoted in Christopher Hogwood, *Handel* (London, 1984), 238.

Chapter 2 (pages 17–36)

1. Robert Owen, *The Life of Robert Owen, Written by Himself* (London, 1857; repr. New York, 1967), ii. 209. The date of the incident was sometime before 1820.
2. Social inequality has considerably increased in Britain since 1985.
3. T. Malthus, *Essay on the Principle of Population* (London, 1798; Penguin edn., Harmondsworth, 1970), 144; Henry Fielding, *The History of the Life of the Late Mr. Jonathan Wild the Great* (London, 1743; Everyman edn., London, 1976), 41–2 (both cited by P. J. Corfield, 'Class by Name and Number in Eighteenth-Century Britain', in ead. (ed.), *Language, History and Class* (Oxford, 1991), 118–19); Adam Smith, *Lectures on Jurisprudence*, ed. R. L. Meek, D. D. Raphael, P. G. Stein (Oxford, 1978), 208.

4. The argument disappeared later in the century: see Ch. 7.
5. On party politics in the early eighteenth century, see Ch. 4.
6. See Chs. 4 and 11 for the role of the mob in politics. See also Ch. 9 for the evolution of gentry–mob relations later in the century.

Chapter 3 (pages 37–53)

1. Cited by John R. Gillis, *For Better, For Worse: British Marriages, 1600 to the Present* (New York, 1985), 140.
2. On this case, see Lawrence Stone, *Broken Lives: Separation and Divorce in England 1660–1857* (Oxford, 1993), 82–116.
3. *Spectator*, 9 Sept. 1712, cited in Bridget Hill (ed.), *Eighteenth-Century Women: An Anthology* (London, 1984), 89.
4. John Gregory, *A Father's Legacy to his Daughters* (London, 1774), 115–16, cited in Hill (ed.), *Eighteenth Century Women*, 77–8.
5. Randolph Trumbach, *The Rise of the Egalitarian Family* (New York, 1978), 191.
6. Ibid. Trumbach admittedly qualifies the import of his title, but the progressive bias of his treatment is nevertheless very evident.
7. 'Colonizing the Breast: Sexuality and Maternity in Eighteenth-Century England', *Journal of the History of Sexuality*, 2/2 (1991), 215–16.
8. (1791; London, 1950 edn.), 61–2.
9. For the emphasis upon fertility-dominated, marriage-driven population growth in England, see E. A. Wrigley and R. S. Schofield, *The Population History of England 1541–1871: A Reconstruction* (Cambridge, 1981), 450–3.
10. Peter Laslett, 'The Bastardy Prone Sub-Society', in Peter Laslett, Karla Oosterveen, and Richard M. Smith (eds.), *Bastardy and its Comparative History* (London, 1980), 217–39.
11. Cited by E. P. Thompson, *The Making of the English Working Class* (London, Penguin edn. 1968), 60.
12. Gillis, *For Better, For Worse*, 206.
13. *The History of Women*, 2 vols. (London, 1779), ii. 179, cited in Hill (ed.), *Eighteenth-Century Women*, 79.
14. *The Autobiography of Francis Place*, ed. Mary Thale (Cambridge, 1972), 80–1.
15. *London Evening Post*, 4–6 July 1748.
16. *Hampshire Chronicle*, 20 July 1795.

Chapter 4 (pages 54–70)

1. They were also remembered for other reasons. 4 November was the birthday of William of Orange; 5 November was the anniversary of the discovery of the Gunpowder Plot, 1605, when the Catholic Guido Fawkes planned to blow up the Houses of Parliament.
2. *Newcastle Chronicle*, 8 Nov. 1788.

3. The figures on the contested elections come from John Brooke (ed.), *The House of Commons 1754–1790: Introductory Survey* (Oxford, 1964), 95; those on private patronage from John A. Phillips, 'The Structure of Electoral Politics in Unreformed England', *Journal of British Studies*, 19 (Feb. 1979), table 1, 80.

4. John Cannon, *Aristocratic Century: The Peerage of Eighteenth-Century England* (Cambridge, 1984), 106–7, 111–12. Oldfield's early calculations are comparable to Cannon's, his later figures more expansive. Calculations for the number of MPs under private patronage in the early 19th cent. range from 65 per cent to 72 per cent. See John Wade, *The Black Book* (London, 1820), 423; A. Aspinall and F. A. Smith (eds.), *English Historical Documents* (London, 1959), 216–36; Frank O'Gorman, *Voters, Patrons, and Parties* (Oxford, 1989), 18–21. O'Gorman rightly points out that the calculations depend upon the more problematic category of 'influence' as opposed to 'nomination'. He is interested in prising the two apart in order to downplay the importance of territorial influence in the Commons, although he concedes that it increased during the eighteenth century.

5. John Brewer, *The Sinews of Power* (New York, 1988), 71.

6. BL Add. MS 32735, fo. 268.

7. *Whitehall Evening Post*, 8–10 Apr. 1784.

8. BL Add. MS 32867, fo. 8.

9. BL Add. MS 32874, fos. 161–2.

10. BL Add. MS 32873, fos. 311–12.

Chapter 5 (pages 71–83)

1. Henry Legge to John King 13 May 1800, PRO HO 42/50.

2. The dearth occurred in the middle of a period of disease, notably typhus and enteric fever, and very high mortality resulted in the Midlands.

3. Anon., *Account of workhouses for employing the poor* (1732), cited in A. F. J. Brown, *Essex At Work 1700–1815* (Chelmsford, 1969), 148.

4. Birmingham Reference Library, Boulton and Watt, Assay Office Papers, Birmingham Box 2, 'Facts . . . 1789'.

5. *An Appeal to Manufacturers on the Present State of Trade* (1795).

Chapter 6 (pages 84–96)

1. Quoted in John Rule, *The Experience of Labour in Eighteenth-Century Industry* (London, 1981), 194.

2. W. Nelson, *The Office and Authority of a Justice of Peace* (1745), i. 404.

Chapter 7 (pages 97–113)

1. Edmund Burke to Arthur Young, May 1797, *The Correspondence of Edmund Burke*, ed. R. B. McDowell and John A. Woods, ix (Cambridge, 1970), 361–2.

2. Staffordshire Record Office, D603, 1763 to 1776 *passim*.
3. Quoted in A. P. Wadsworth and J. de Lacy Mann, *The Cotton Trade and Industrial Lancashire 1700–1780* (Manchester, 1931), 374.
4. Quoted in G. D. H. Cole, *A Short History of the British Working-Class Movement, 1789–1947* (London, 1948), 51.
5. Quoted in Wadsworth and Mann, *Cotton Trade*, 367.
6. Quoted in T. K. Derry, 'Repeal of the Apprenticeship Clauses of the Statute of Apprentices', *Economic History Review*, 3 (1931–2), 78.
7. Published four years later, in *The Wealth of Nations*.
8. *Thoughts on Scarcity*, in *Works*, vii. 404. 'Presented to . . . William Pitt, . . . November, 1801', it was reprinted in the even greater dearth of 1800–1. See also the quotation at the head of this chapter.
9. For a more detailed account of the evolution of the food riot, and the issue of public order, see Ch. 9.

Chapter 8 (pages 114–133)

1. *A Tour through the Whole Island Of Great Britain*, ed. Pat Rogers (Harmondsworth, 1971), 85, 105, 141, 256, 367, 370, 408, 454, 493–8, 535.
2. Urban here means centres with populations of 5,000 or more. If one interpreted urban to mean centres with 2,500 inhabitants or more, then the urban population would have constituted 18.7 per cent of the total in 1700 and 30.6 per cent in 1801.
3. A variant of these powers was in use in the Hebrides in the twentieth century.
4. Quoted in J. R. Ward, *British West Indian Slavery, 1750–1834: The Process of Amelioration* (Oxford, 1988), 27–8.
5. [R. Mather], *An Impartial Representation of the Case of the Poor Cotton Spinners in Lancashire* (1780), 5, quoted in Wadsworth and Mann, *Cotton Trade*, 500.
6. 7 August 1781, quoted in Wadsworth and Mann, *Cotton Trade*, 491.
7. *Parliamentary Debates*, 22 Feb. 1793.

Chapter 9 (pages 134–151)

1. In *Drinkwater* v. *Royal Exchange Assurance Company* (1767), Wilmot 281; 97 English Reports 114. The quotation is from the *Aeneid*, i. 148–53:

> Just as so often it happens, when a crowd collects, and violence
> Brews up, and the mass mind boils nastily over, and the next thing
> Firebrands and brickbats are flying (hysteria soon finds a missile),
> That then, if they see some man whose goodness of heart and conduct
> Have won their respect, they fall silent and stand still, ready to hear him;
> And he can change their temper and calm their thoughts with a speech . . .
>
> (trans. C. Day Lewis)

2. *Commentaries* (12th edn., 1793–5), i. 414.
3. As, of course, it was in the case of personal blackmail, a different issue.
4. Above, n. 2.
5. Tacitus, *Historiae*, iv. 74. Edward Christian's editorial note to Blackstone's *Commentaries* (12th edn.), i. 414 n. 6: 'for you cannot secure tranquillity among nations without armies, nor maintain armies without pay, nor provide pay without taxes . . .'.
6. PRO HO 42/49, Lord Gower to Lord Portland.

Chapter 10 (pages 152–167)

1. As C. Dalrymple described army recruits in 1761. See Roderick Floud *et al.*, *Height, Health and History* (Cambridge, 1990), 55.
2. Quoted in D. Hay, 'War, Dearth and Theft in the Eighteenth Century: The Record of the English Courts', *Past & Present*, 95 (May 1982), 141.
3. *An Essay on the Legality of Impressing Seamen* (London, 2nd edn., 1778), 6.
4. *Essays Moral, Political and Literary*, ed. Eugene Miller (Indianapolis, 1971), 375.
5. *Derby Mercury*, 31 Oct. 1793.
6. PRO Adm 1/579. The Whitby riots were the subject of Elizabeth Gaskell's novel *Sylvia's Lovers* (1863).
7. David A. Kent ' "Gone for a Soldier": Family Breakdown and the Demography of Desertion in a London Parish, 1750–1791', *Local Population Studies*, 45 (1990), table 1. Our own figures for St Clement Danes echo those of Kent for St Martin-in-the-Fields. In St Clements, the number of desertions reported in the parish examinations rose from 8.55 per cent in the years 1752–4, to 11.53 per cent in the years 1755–62, falling with the peace (1763–70) to 8.3 per cent, and rising again during the Falkland Island crisis of 1770–1 and the American War.
8. British Parliamentary Papers, iii (1814/15), 238.
9. Cited in the *Leeds Mercury*, 29 Apr. 1783.
10. *A Proposal for making an Effectual Provision for the Poor* (1753), in *Complete Works*, ed. William E. Henley (London, 1903), xiii. 141.
11. *Yale Edition of Horace Walpole's Correspondence*, ed. W. S. Lewis (New Haven, 1960), xx. 114.
12. *Covent Garden Journal*, 28 Mar. 1752.
13. Linda Colley, *Britons: Forging the Nation 1707–1837* (New Haven, 1992).
14. *British Press*, 19 Aug. 1820.

Chapter 11 (pages 168–187)

1. Originally a meal in token of brotherly love among early Christians, the Methodists designed a religious service to imitate this practice.
2. Charles Wesley, *Journal*, i. 242, cited in Rev. L. Tyerman, *The Life and Times of the Rev. John Wesley*, 3 vols. (New York, 1872), i. 295.

3. Cited by John Walsh, 'Methodism and the Mob in the Eighteenth Century', in G. L. Cumming and Derek Baker (eds.), *Studies in Church History*, viii. *Popular Belief and Practice* (Cambridge, 1972), 223.

4. A. D. Gilbert, 'Methodism, Dissent and Political Stability in Early Industrial England', *Journal of Religious History*, 10 (1978–9), 381–99.

5. John Wesley, *Thoughts upon Liberty* (London, 1772), 7.

6. Ibid. 19.

7. *North Briton*, 45 (26 Apr. 1763).

8. See James Bradley, *Popular Politics and the American Revolution in England* (Macon, Ga., 1986), tables 1, 3.1, 3.3.

9. *Sermons to Asses* (London, 1768), 4–5, cited in James Bradley, *Religion, Revolution, and English Radicalism* (Cambridge, 1990), 129.

10. Cited by Albert Goodwin, *The Friends of Liberty* (Cambridge, Mass., 1975), 111.

11. TS 11/3510/A (3), cited by E. P. Thompson, *The Making of the English Working Class* (Harmondsworth, 1968), 171.

12. BL Add. MS 16927 fos. 45–6; PRO HO 42/22/474.

13. PRO HO 42/22/623.

14. PRO HO 42/24/286.

15. *Tom Paine's Jests* (London, 1794), 35.

16. Cited by Clive Emsley, *British Society and the French Wars 1793–1815* (London, 1979), 86.

17. PRO HO 40/3/72–3, 81, 92.

18. Cited by Joyce Marlow, *The Peterloo Massacre* (London, 1971), 105.

Chapter 12 (pages 188–208)

1. i.e. those with ancestors who had been MPs in the Commons.

2. *Public Advertiser*, 7 Apr. 1784.

3. *Memoirs to 1795* (London, 1809), 74.

4. PRO SP 37/5/7a, cited by J. M. Norris, 'Samuel Garbett and the Early Development of Industrial Lobbying in Great Britain', *Economic History Review*, 10 (1958), 451 n.

5. On the broad investment in canals, see G. R. Hawke and J. P. P. Higgins, 'Transport and Social Overhead Capital', in Roderick Floud and Donald McCloskey (eds.), *The Economic History of Britain since 1700*, 2 vols. (Cambridge, 1981), i. 233, table 12.1.

6. *Uncertain Unions and Broken Lives*, 504.

7. G. Carter, P. Goode, and K. Laurie, *Humphry Repton: Landscape Gardener, 1752–1818* (Norwich, 1982), 116, cited in Paul Langford, *Public Life and the Propertied Englishman 1689–1798* (Oxford, 1991), 386.

8. E. P. Thompson, *The Making of the English Working Class* (Harmondsworth, 1968), 609.

9. *The Times*, 27 July 1819.

10. PRO HO 42/188/193.

11. Exclusive dealing was a form of popular consumer pressure upon shop-keepers, buying only from one's political sympathizers.

12. See Robert G. Hall, 'Tyranny, Work and Politics: The 1818 Strike Wave in the English Cotton District', *International Review of Social History*, 34 (1989), 433–70.

13. *Sherwin's Weekly Political Register*, 22 May 1819.

14. PRO HO 42/189/106.

15. For the concept of female consciousness, see Temma Kaplan, 'Female Consciousness and Collective Action: The Case of Barcelona, 1910–1918', *Signs: Journal of Women in Culture and Society*, 7 (1982), 545–66.

16. G. Pellew, *Life and Correspondence of First Viscount Sidmouth*, 3 vols. (London, 1847), iii. 356.

17. *Champion*, 28 July 1821.

18. *Champion*, 21 July 1821.

19. See Hall, 'Tyranny, Work and Politics', 450–1.

20. PRO HO 42/190/127–8.

Chronology

*serious riot and/or sedition

**1688 William of Orange challenges James II's rule; Gregory King's social survey.

1689 Bill of Rights; Nine Years War (to 1697)

1691 Entitlements to poor relief changed by Settlement Act

1702 Accession of Anne; War of Spanish Succession to 1713

*1710 Impeachment of Dr Sacheverell; strike and riot of keelmen, Tyne and Wear

1713 Peace of Utrecht

*1714 Accession of George of Hanover; coronation riots

*1715 Bolingbroke, Oxford, and Ormonde impeached; Riot Act; Jacobite rebellion

1716 Septennial Act

*1717 Exeter woollen weavers riot

1718 Abortive Jacobite invasion

*1719 Colchester, Norwich calico riots, Lombe's silk-mill riot in Derbyshire

*1720 South Sea Bubble; London calico riots

*1721 West Country weavers riot

1722 Sir Robert Walpole becomes first minister; impeachment of Bishop Atterbury

1723 Workhouse Act

1724 Defoe publishes his *Tour*

1726 West Country weavers riot; Act for wage-setting

1727 Accession of George II

1733 Walpole forced to withdraw the Excise Bill

1738 (to 1740) Extensive riots, West Country

1739 War of Jenkins' Ear begins

*1740 Food riots; War of Austrian Succession (to 1748)

*1742 Resignation of Sir Robert Walpole; Portsmouth shipyard riot

1743 Henry Fielding publishes *Jonathan Wild*

1744   Tyne and Wear keelmen riot; Deptford and Woolwich shipyards disputes; Vagrancy Act

**1745   Last Jacobite rebellion

1746   Defeat of Jacobites, subduing the Highlands

1748   Peace of Aix-la-Chapelle

1749   Law officers say Black slavery is legal in England

*1750   Tyne and Wear keelmen riot

1752   Murder Act

1753   Hardwicke's Marriage Act

*1755   Impressment riots

*1756   Seven Years War (to 1763); Act for rating of West Country textile wages; food riots, Lancashire strikes

*1757   Admiral Byng court-martialled and executed; Textile Act repealed, food riots and militia riots

1759   Joseph Massie's social survey; conquest of Canada

1760   Accession of George III

1763   Peace of Paris; Wilkes prosecuted for seditious libel, *North Briton*, no. 45

*1765   Stamp Act passed; strike by NE Colliers

*1766   Stamp Act repealed

1768   Wilkes elected as MP for Middlesex

1769   Petitions protesting Luttrell's status as MP for Middlesex

*c.*1770   Approximate beginning of major wave of parliamentary enclosures

*1770   Boston massacre; weekly market prices begin to be published; impressment riots (during Falkland Islands crisis)

*1771   The 'printer's case'; Spitalfields silk-weaver riots

1772   *Somersett's Case* (slaves); marketing offence statutes repealed

1773   Spitalfields Act

*1775   Life bond for Scottish miners abolished; violent seamen's strike, Liverpool

**1776   War with Revolutionary America (to 1783); Smith's *Wealth of Nations* published

1778   France enters war in support of America; Battle of Ushant

*1779   Keppel court-martialled; Association Movement for parliamentary reform; large attack on Arkwright's mill; Penitentiary Act

**1780 Gordon riots in London

*1783 Peace of Paris; food riots; Nottingham weavers riot

1789 George III recovers from first bout of madness (probably porphyria); outbreak of French Revolution; colliers riot in NE.

1790 Edmund Burke's *Reflections on the Revolution in France*

**1791 Tom Paine publishes part 1 of the *Rights of Man*; death of John Wesley; Priestley riots

1792 Founding of London Corresponding Society; also first loyalist association; colliers and weavers riot

*1793 War against France declared; Tyne and Wear keelmen riot; impressment riots

**1795 Gagging acts against seditious meetings and publications; establishment of Soho founding; serious and widespread food riots

**1797 Naval mutiny at the Nore and Spithead

**1798 French invasion and rebellion in Ireland; suspension of Habeas Corpus

*1799 General laws against combinations introduced.

**1800 Extensive food riots in London and provinces

*1801 First Census; food riots

*1802 Shearmen (or croppers) attack gig mills; Peace of Amiens; Colquhoun's social survey

1803 War against France resumed; Parliament suspends apprenticeship in wool trades

1809 Apprenticeship in woollens repealed

1810 Regency established

**1811 First outbreak of Luddism

**1812 Food riots

*1814 Parliament abolishes apprenticeship provisions in all trades

1815 Corn laws; Waterloo

1816 birth of Hampden Clubs and Political Unions; Byron publishes *Song for the Luddites*

1817 March of the Blanketeers; suspension of Habeas Corpus

*1818 Strikes throughout the Lancashire cotton district

**1819 Peterloo; Six Acts

1820 Accession of George IV; Cato Street and Grange Moor conspiracies; trial of Queen Caroline

Figures

1. Farming regions of England, *c.*1700
   Source: J. Thirsk, *England's Agricultural Regions and Agrarian History, 1500–1750* (1987).

2. Counties and regions of England

3. Fastest travel from London, 1750 and 1821
   Sources: Pawson, *Transport*, fig. 41a, and Freeman, 'Transport', 82, from M. J. Freeman and J. Longbotham, 'The Fordham Collection at the Royal Geographical Society: An Introduction', *Geographical Journal*, 146 (1980), and *Bradshaw's Railway Companion for August 1845.*

4. Population growth and change in England
   Source: E. A. Wrigley and R. S. Schofield, *The Population History of England 1541–1871* (1989).

5. Estimates of income inequality, 1688–1985
   Sources: Peter H. Lindert and Jeffrey G. Williamson, 'Revising England's Social Tables 1688–1812', *Explorations in Economic History*, 19 (1982); L. Soltow, 'Long-run Changes in British Income Inequality', *Economic History Review*, 2nd ser., 21 (1968); Anthony B. Atkinson and John Micklewright, *Economic Transformation in Eastern Europe and the Distribution of Income* (Cambridge, 1992).

6. Proportion of direct to total taxes, 1650s to 1820s.
   Source: P. K. O'Brien and P. A. Hunt, 'The Rise of the Fiscal State in England, 1485–1815', *Historical Research*, 66, 160 (1993).

7. Wheat prices 1690–1820
   Source: B. R. Mitchell, *British Historical Statistics* (1988).

8. Proportion of adult men in the armed forces, 1691–1820
   Sources: Christopher Lloyd, *The British Seaman* (1986); Roderick Floud, Kenneth Wachter and Annabel Gregory, *Height, Health and History* (1990); E. A. Wrigley and R. S. Schofield, *The Population History of England 1541–1871* (1989).

9. A Lincolnshire parish before and after enclosure in 1766
   Source: Rex C. Russell.

10. Industrial change

Sources: P. D. Glennie in R. A. Dodgson and R. A. Butlin (eds.), *An Historical Geography of England and Wales* (2nd edn., 1990); Nick von Tunzelmann in Langton and Morris (eds.), *Atlas of Industrialising Britain 1780–1914* (1986).

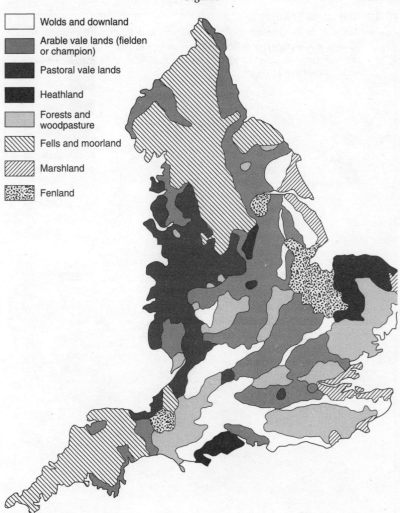

Wolds and downland

Arable vale lands (fielden or champion)

Pastoral vale lands

Heathland

Forests and woodpasture

Fells and moorland

Marshland

Fenland

Fig. 1. Farming regions of England, *c.* 1700

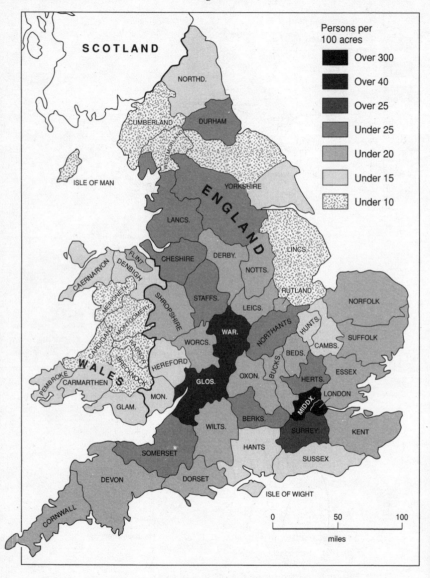

Fig. 2. Estimated density of population in England and Wales in 1750 (shown by counties)

(a) 1750 (stage-coach)

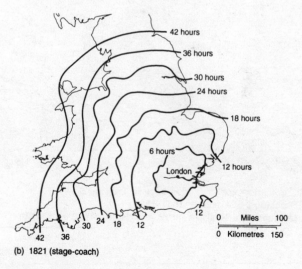

(b) 1821 (stage-coach)

Fig. 3. Fastest travel from London, 1750 and 1821
  (a) 1750 (stage-coach)
  (b) 1821 (stage-coach)

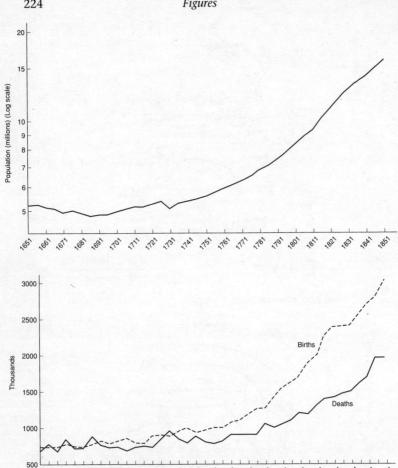

Fig. 4. Population growth and change in England
   (a) Population of England, 1651–1821
   (b) Quinquennial totals of births and deaths, 1650/4 to 1820/4

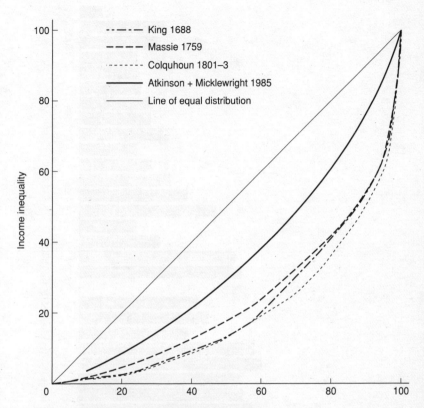

Fig. 5. Estimates of income equality, 1688–1985
Note: The diagonal line denotes an exactly equal distribution of income.
The curves map incremental shares of income: for example, in 1759, the
poorest half of the population received about 18% of total income (and
therefore the richer half, 82%; in 1985 the comparable figures were
about 30% and 70%).

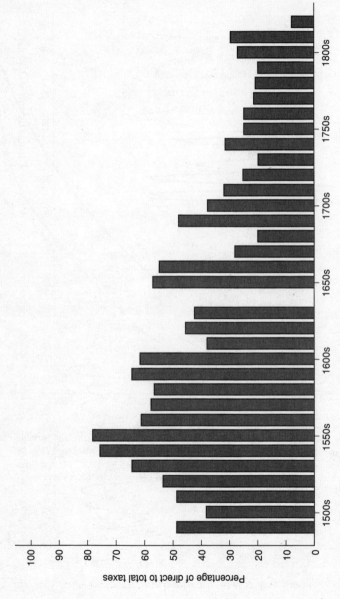

Fig. 6. Proportion of direct to total taxes by decade, 1650s to 1820s

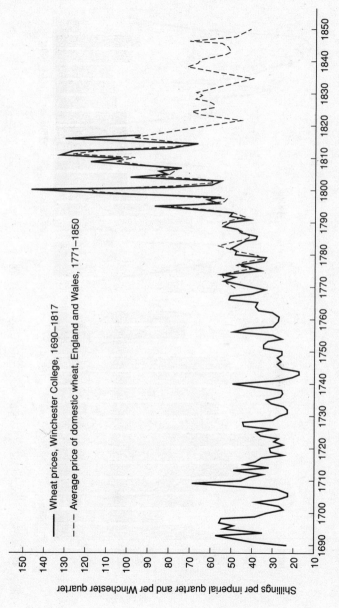

Fig. 7. Wheat prices, Winchester College, 1690–1817, and average price of domestic wheat, England and Wales, 1771–1820

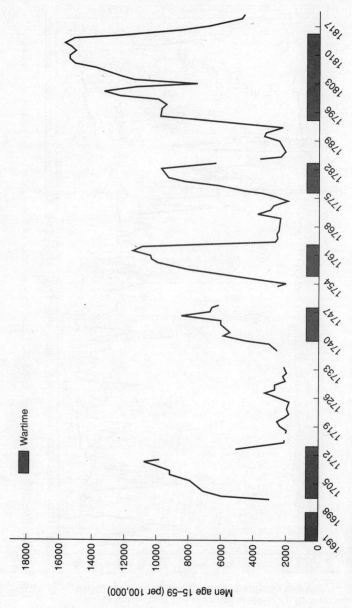

Fig. 8. Proportion of males age 15–59 in the armed forces, 1691–1820

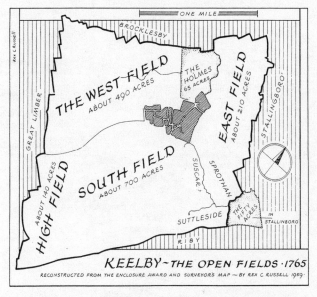

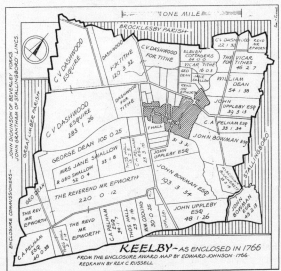

Fig. 9. (a) A Lincolnshire parish, 1765, before enclosure, the village still surrounded by large open fields (strip holdings not shown)

(b) The same parish after enclosure: surveyed, divided, and with roads running between fenced parcels of land

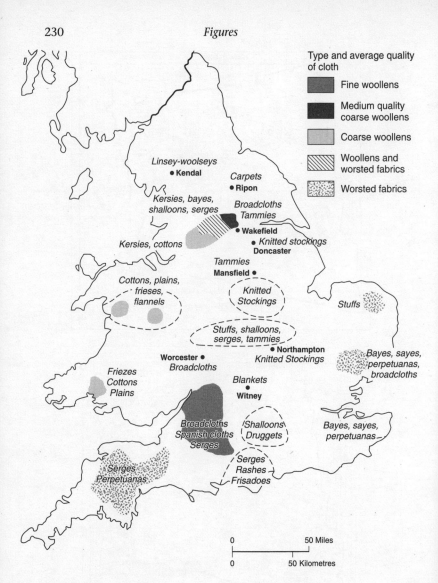

Type and average quality of cloth

Fine woollens

Medium quality coarse woollens

Coarse woollens

Woollens and worsted fabrics

Worsted fabrics

Linsey-woolseys
● **Kendal**

Carpets
● **Ripon**

Kersies, bayes, shalloons, serges

Broadcloths Tammies

● **Wakefield**

Kersies, cottons

● *Knitted stockings*
Doncaster

Tammies
Mansfield ●

Cottons, plains, frieses, flannels

Knitted Stockings

Stuffs

Stuffs, shalloons, serges, tammies

Worcester ●
Broadcloths

● **Northampton**
Knitted Stockings

Bayes, sayes, perpetuanas, broadcloths

Friezes Cottons Plains

Blankets
● **Witney**

Broadcloths Spanish cloths Serges

Shalloons Druggets

Bayes, sayes, perpetuanas

Serges Perpetuanas

Serges Rashes Frisadoes

0 — 50 Miles
0 — 50 Kilometres

Fig. 10. Industrial change
   (a) Textile specialization, England and Wales, *c*. 1700

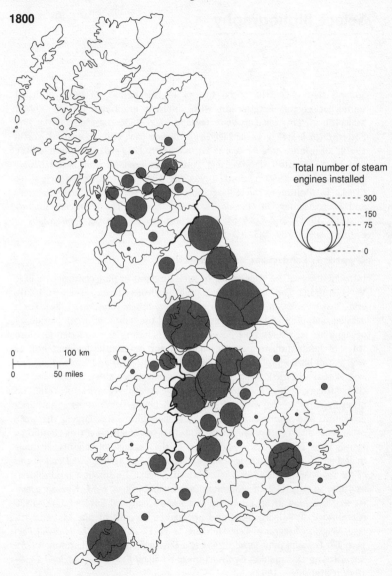

1800

Total number of steam
engines installed

----- 300
----- 150
----- 75

----- 0

0   100 km

0   50 miles

Fig. 10. Industrial change
   (b) Steam engines installed by 1800

Select Bibliography

Surveys that cover the social history of this period, or parts of it, at somewhat greater length and with different emphases include Robert Malcolmson, *Life and Labour in England 1700–1780* (London, 1981); Roy Porter, *English Society in the Eighteenth Century* (rev. edn., Harmondsworth, 1990); John Rule, *Albion's People: English Society 1714–1815* (London, 1992); and M. J. Daunton, *Progress and Poverty: An Economic and Social History of Britain 1700–1850* (Oxford, 1995). See also the works cited below for Ch. 12. In addition to the bibliographies in these works, see Stanley Pargellis and D. J. Medley, *Bibliography of British History: The Eighteenth Century* (Oxford, 1951), and Lucy M. Brown and Ian R. Christie, *Bibliography of British History 1789–1851* (Oxford, 1977).

Chapter 1: Landscapes and Perspectives

Introductions to the appearance of rural England in past centuries include W. G. Hoskins, *The Making of the English Landscape* (Harmondsworth, 1970), and Oliver Rackham, *The History of the Countryside* (London, 1986). For a detailed mapping of farming types and land use, and a scholarly summary of agrarian structures and development, including the broader relationships of land, industry, labour, markets, and economic development, as well as full bibliographies, see J. Thirsk (ed.), *The Agrarian History of England and Wales*, v, Thirsk (ed.), *1640–1750* (Cambridge, 1984, 1985), and vi, G. E. Mingay, (ed.), *1750–1850* (Cambridge, 1989). For works on rural and other industry see the works cited for Ch. 8, below. An argument that modernization and increased productivity of agriculture was largely the work of seventeenth-century yeomen, and that eighteenth-century landlords simply took increased revenue shares at the expense of tenants, is made in Robert C. Allen, *Enclosure and the Yeoman: The Agricultural Development of the South Midlands 1450–1850* (Oxford, 1992). The smallest landholders, invisible in much of the literature, are the subject of J. M. Neeson, *Commoners: Common Right, Enclosure, and Social Change in England 1700–1820* (Cambridge, 1993). An older and unequalled account of one Midland village, Wigston Magna in Leicestershire, is W. G. Hoskins, *The Midland Peasant: The Economic and Social History of a Leicestershire Village* (London, 1975). See also Ann Kussmaul, *A General View of the Rural Economy of England 1538–1840* (Cambridge, 1993).

Many English and foreign writers in addition to Moritz (see Ch. 1, n. 4) published accounts of England in this period, often presenting diverse observations under the rubric of travel accounts. Two well-known ones from which we quote are those of Daniel Defoe, *A Tour Through the Whole Island of Great Britain* (1724), ed. Pat Rogers (Harmondsworth, 1971) and William Cobbett, *Rural Rides* (1830; many editions). On geographic mobility in the population, see the articles by Armstrong and Huzel in *Agrarian History*, vi. *1750–1850*; Landau (cited below for Ch. 5); and Kussmaul (cited below for Ch. 2). For population estimates, see E. A. Wrigley and R. S. Schofield, *The Population History of England 1541–1871: A Reconstruction* (Cambridge, 1981).

Conflicting images of London are usefully analysed in M. Byrd, *London Transformed: Images of the City in the Eighteenth Century* (New Haven, 1978). For attempts to re-order the provincial city in genteel ways, see Peter Borsay, *The English Urban Renaissance: Culture and Society in the Provincial Town* (Oxford 1989); for London see Sir John Summerson, *Georgian London* (revd edn., London, 1970). M. Dorothy George, *London Life in the Eighteenth Century* (Harmondsworth, 1966), contains much useful information about the darker realities of London life. For an exuberant, and highly readable portrait of London in this period, readers should consult Roy Porter, *London: A Social History* (London, 1994), chs. 5–7. E. A. Wrigley, 'A Simple Model of London's Importance in Changing English Society and Economy, 1650–1750', *Past & Present*, 26 (1967), 44–70 squarely places London's growth in a national and continental context. For London as a death-trap, see John Landers, *Death and the Metropolis: Studies in the Demographic History of London 1670–1830* (Cambridge, 1993). For London crime, see John Beattie (cited below for Ch. 10) and Peter Linebaugh (cited below for Ch. 6).

Chapter 2: Hierarchy

Quantitative estimates of social inequality include L. Soltow, 'Long-Run Changes in British Income Inequality', *Economic History Review*, 2nd ser., 21 (1968), 17–29, which used the unrevised figures of King and Colquhoun; the Lorenz curves we present were constructed from the revised figures given in Peter H. Lindert and Jeffrey G. Williamson, 'Revising England's Social Tables 1688–1812', *Explorations in Economic History*, 19 (1982), 385–408. See also their article on 'Reinterpreting Britain's Social Tables, 1688–1913', *Explorations in Economic History*, 20 (1983), 94–109. The social structure and how it worked is the subject of the book as a whole, but specific groups may be mentioned here. Accounts of the social and political importance of the peerage include T. H. Hollingsworth, J. V. Beckett, *The Aristocracy in England 1660–1914* (Oxford, 1986) and John Cannon, *Aristocratic Century: The Peerage of Eighteenth-Century England* (Cambridge, 1984). The social and economic position of the high court judges (see Ch. 4), who included some notable founders of new peerages, is explored in Daniel Duman, *The Judicial Bench in England 1727–1875: The Reshaping of a Professional Elite* (London, 1982). On gentlemanly honour and daily discipline in the armed forces, see A. N. Gilbert, 'Law and Honour among 18th-Century British Army Officers', *Historical Journal*, 19/1 (1976), 75–87, and N. A. M. Rodger, *The Wooden World: An Anatomy of the Georgian Navy* (London, 1986), ch. 6. For some aspects of landed gentlemen's image of rural England, see John Barrell, *The Dark Side of the Landscape: The Rural Poor in English Painting 1730–1840* (Cambridge, 1980) and Douglas Chambers, *The Reinvention of the World: English Writing 1650–1750* (London, 1996).

On nabobs, see J. M. Holtzman, *The Nabobs in England: A Study of the Returned Ango-Indian, 1760–1785* (New York, 1926) and Michael Edwardes, *The Nabobs at Home* (London, 1991); on profits in the slave trade, R. B. Sheridan, ' "Sweet Malefactor": The Social Costs of Slavery and Sugar in Jamaica and Cuba, 1807–1854', *Economic History Review*, 29 (May 1976), 236–57. The relationship between the greater merchants and the gentry is explored in Nicholas Rogers, 'Money, Land, and Lineage: The Big Bourgeoisie of Hanoverian London', *Social History*, 4 (1979), 437–50. A different perspective is offered by Lawrence and Jeanne Fawtier Stone, *An Open Elite? England 1540–1880* (Oxford, 1984). The changing representation of the social structure and the growing importance of the middling sort is traced in P. J. Corfield, 'Class by Name and Number in Eighteenth-Century Britain' in ead. (ed.), *Language, History and Class* (Oxford, 1991), 101–30, and more recently in the essays in Jonathon Barry and Christopher Brooks (eds.), *The Middling Sort of People* (London, 1995). Paul Langford also stresses the cultural and political importance of the middling, or, as he prefers to term it, the middle, class, in *A Polite and Commercial People: England 1720–1783* (Oxford, 1989). For a detailed account of the lives and demography of the London merchants and tradesmen, see Peter Earle, *The Making of the English Middle Class: Business, Society, and Family Life in London, 1660–1730* (London, 1989). As some of these titles imply, there is considerable debate about when the middling sort became a middle class. (For further readings, see Ch. 12.) Part of this discussion is related to Edward Thompson's formulation of eighteenth-century society in turns of patrician–plebeian reciprocities. See E. P. Thompson, *Customs In Common* (London, 1992), ch. 2, and the recent commentary by Peter King, 'Edward Thompson's Contribution to Eighteenth-Century Studies. The Patrician–Plebeian Model Re-examined', *Social History*, 21/2 (May, 1996), 215–28.

For the structure of agrarian society, see the works cited for Ch. 1. For one example of the constraints of local relationships on the power of landlords and their agents in the early eighteenth century, see David Rollinson, 'Property, Ideology and Popular Culture in a Gloucestershire village, 1660–1740: Westonbirt', *Past & Present*, 93 (Nov. 1981), 70–97. On traditionalist views of smallholders, Neeson (cited for Ch. 1, above), ch. 1; on the large and important social classes of rural farm servants, and the causes of the marked cycles in their prominence in this period, see Ann Kussmaul, *Servants in Husbandry in Early Modern England* (Cambridge, 1981). For an argument about a longer period, K. D. M. Snell, *Annals of the Labouring Poor: Social Change and Agrarian England 1660–1900* (Cambridge, 1985).

Chapter 3: The Politics of Love and Marriage

On marriage among the aristocracy and gentry, Lawrence Stone's work defined the field and is accessible in abridged paperback versions: *The Family, Sex and Marriage in England 1500–1800* (Harmondsworth, 1979); *Road to Divorce: England 1530–1987* (Oxford, 1992), and *Uncertain Unions and Broken Lives* (Oxford, 1995). See also Randolph Trumbach, *The Rise of the Egalitarian Family: Aristocratic Kinship and Domestic Relations in Eighteenth-Century England* (New York, 1978), on the tensions within aristocratic kin arising from marriage. Several historians have taken issue with Stone's interpretation of strict settlement and the growth of affective individualism, from different directions. They include Lloyd Bonfield, *Marriage Settlements, 1601–1740: The Adoption of the Strict Settlement* (Cambridge, 1983), and 'Affective Families, Open Elites and Strict Family Settlements in Early Modern England', *Economic History Review*, 2nd ser., 39 (1986), 341–54; Susan Staves, *Married Women's Separate Property in England, 1660–1833* (Cambridge, Mass., 1990); Eileen Spring, 'The Family, Strict Settlement, and the Historians', *Canadian Journal of History*, 18 (1983), 379–98, and 'Law and the Theory of the Affective Family', *Albion*, 16 (1984), 1–20. For a useful guide to the varieties of family settlements, their place in the law, and the provisional nature of some of the larger social conclusions that have been drawn from them, see John Saville and Barbara English, *Strict Settlement: A Guide for Historians* (Hull, 1983). Ruth Perry, 'Colonizing the Breast: Sexuality and Maternity in Eighteenth-Century England', *Journal of the History of Sexuality*, 2/2 (1991), 204–34 is a critical article on the meaning of aristocratic and bourgeois motherhood.

On plebeian marriage, the best book is John R. Gillis, *For Better, For Worse: British Marriages 1600 to the Present* (New York, 1985). Important insights can also be found in Anna Clark, *The Struggle for the Breeches* (Berkeley and Los Angeles, 1995), which adopts a more jaundiced and tension-ridden view of plebeian marriage than does Gillis. For the wife-sale and rough music, the best authorities are Edward Thompson, *Customs in Common* (London, 1991), ch. 7, and Samuel Pyeatt Menefee, *Wives For Sale* (Oxford, 1981). On clandestine marriages, see Roger Lee Brown, 'The Rise and Fall of the Fleet Marriages', in R. B. Outhwaite (ed.), *Marriage and Society* (London, 1981), 117–36. On bastardy, the standard work is Peter Laslett, Karla Oosterveen and Richard M. Smith (eds.), *Bastardy and its Comparative History* (London, 1980) although there are many articles on the subject, including Nicholas Rogers, 'Carnal Knowledge: Illegitimacy in Eighteenth-Century Westminster', *Journal of Social History*, 23 (1989), 355–75, and Grace Wyatt, 'Bastardy and Prenuptial Pregnancy in a Cheshire Town during the Eighteenth Century', *Local Population Studies*, 49 (1992), 38–50.

Demography forms a critical underpinning to all accounts of sexuality and nuptiality in the eighteenth century. E. A. Wrigley and R. S. Schofield (cited for Ch. 1, above) is indispensable, but important insights into different demographic regimes and their relationship to productive relations can be found in David Levine, *Family Formation in an Age of Nascent Capitalism* (New York, 1977) and *Reproducing Families* (Cambridge, 1987).

Chapter 4: Political Order

The classic, and still useful, account of Britain's political structure is Lewis Namier, *The Structure of Politics at the Accession of George III* (2nd edn., London, 1957). For the early decades of the century, see Geoffrey Holmes, *Party Politics in the Age of Anne* (London, 1967) and W. A. Speck, *Tory and Whig: The Struggle in the Constituencies 1701–1715* (London, 1970). For the persistence of Toryism as a parliamentary force until the mid-century, see Linda Colley, *In Defiance of Oligarchy: The Tory Party 1714–1760* (Cambridge, 1982). The most complete reappraisal of Britain's electoral structure and politics is Frank O'Gorman, *Voters, Patrons, and Parties* (Oxford, 1989), although penetrating insights can be found in John A. Phillips, *Electoral Behavior in Unreformed England* (Princeton, 1982) and his very useful 'The Structure of Electoral Politics in Unreformed England', *Journal of British Studies*, 19 (Feb. 1979), 76–100. On popular Jacobitism, see Paul Kléber Monod, *Jacobitism and the English People, 1688–1788* (Cambridge, 1989) and Nicholas Rogers, 'Riot and Popular Jacobitism in Early Hanoverian England', in Eveline Cruickshanks (ed.), *Ideology and Conspiracy: Aspects of Jacobitism, 1689–1759* (Edinburgh, 1982), 70–88. For efforts to re-establish the vitality of popular politics in the eighteenth century, see John Brewer, *Party Ideology and Popular Politics at the Accession of George III* (Cambridge, 1976); Nicholas Rogers, *Whigs and Cities: Popular Politics in the Age of Walpole and Pitt* (Oxford, 1989); and more recently, H. T. Dickinson, *The Politics of the People in Eighteenth-Century Britain* (London, 1995), and Kathleen Wilson, *The Sense of the People: Politics, Culture and Imperialism in England, 1715–1785* (Cambridge, 1995). For a view that none of this matters, that eighteenth-century England was Anglican, aristocratic, conservative, and hierarchical, a 'confessional state' whose principal conflicts revolved around dynastic and religious strife, see J. C. D. Clark, *English Society 1688–1832* (Cambridge, 1985).

Chapter 5: Harvests and Dearth

For the chronologies of dearth and food riot, see the references for Ch. 9. On many causes of economic seasonality, see T. S. Ashton, *Economic*

Fluctuations in England 1700–1800 (Oxford, 1959). For the effects of demobilization and dearth on different social classes, see D. Hay, 'War, Dearth and Theft in the Eighteenth Century: The Record of the English Courts', *Past & Present*, 95 (May 1982) and R. W. Fogel, 'Second Thoughts on the European Escape from Hunger: Famines, Chronic Malnutrition, and Mortality Rates', in S. R. Osmani (ed.), *Nutrition and Poverty* (Oxford, 1992), 243–86. The latter article is the basis for the French comparisons in this chapter, and should be read with Andrew Appleby, 'Grain Prices and Subsistence Crises in England and France, 1590–1740', *Journal of Economic History*, 39 (1979), 865–87. John Walter and Roger Schofield (eds.), *Famine, Disease and the Social Order in Early Modern Society* (Cambridge, 1989) summarizes and presents findings on the interrelationships of want, migration, disease, and morbidity, and the social and political impact of the last two great dearths of the eighteenth century is fully assessed in Roger Wells, *Wretched Faces: Famine in Wartime England, 1793–1801* (Gloucester, 1988); see also Ch. 7, below. The interrelationships of food supply, disease, and population growth are discussed at many points in Wrigley and Schofield (cited above for Ch. 1). On access to land and its exploitation by smallholders, see Neeson (cited above for Ch. 1), ch. 2, and Snell (cited above for Ch. 2).

For a general overview of the English poor laws, Sidney and Beatrice Webb, *English Local Government*, 10 vols. (London, 1929), vols. 7–9, is still indispensable. Snell (cited above for Ch. 2), has much to say about rural poverty and the changing gender division in the countryside. Snell's use of poor-law examinations as a window to the changing dimensions of poverty has, however, been challenged by Norma Landau, 'Pauper Settlement and the Right to Poor Relief in England and Wales: The 18th-Century Context of the Laws of Settlement', *Continuity and Change*, 6 (Dec. 1991), 375–439, and works cited there. James Stephen Taylor, 'The Impact of Pauper Settlement, 1691–1834', *Past & Present*, 73 (Nov. 1976), 42–74, has the best general account of the intricacies and impact of the settlement laws; see also Landau, 'The Regulation of Immigration, Economic Structures and Definitions of the Poor in 18th-Century England', *Historical Journal*, 33 (Sept. 1990), 541–72, and articles by Huzel and others in *Agrarian History*, vi, *1750–1850* (cited above, for Ch. 1). Peter Dunkley, *The Crisis of the Old Poor Law in England, 1795–1834* (London, 1982) provides an interesting perspective on the paternalist timbre of the poor laws after 1795, although the introductory chapter to E. J. Hobsbawm and George Rudé, *Captain Swing* (London, 1968) gives a more jaundiced view. Much interesting work on the actual operation of the poor law can be found in local studies such as A. F. J. Brown, *Essex At Work 1700–1815* (Chelmsford, 1969), and J. M. Martin, 'Rich, Poor and Migrant in Stratford on Avon', *Local Population Studies* (1978), 40–3. On the evolution of the workhouse, see Anne Digby, *Pauper Palaces* (London, 1978).

Chapter 6: Custom

On the legal meanings of custom and examples from the law reports see C. K. Allen, *Law in the Making* (Oxford, 1964); for its social manifestations in popular ritual and practice, Robert Bushaway, *By Rite: Custom, Ceremony and Community in England 1700–1880* (London, 1992); some of the connections with other areas of social life are cited in Robert Malcolmson, *Popular Recreations in English Society 1700–1850* (Cambridge, 1973). The ambiguities and concordances of custom as law and custom as social practice are the subject of E. P. Thompson, *Customs in Common* (London, 1992), who pioneered the field. A background account of the early-modern state, including its involvement in a wide range of economic regulation, either episodic or more continuous, in the name of social order, is essential to an understanding of the eighteenth-century inheritance. The best succinct account is Penry Williams, *The Tudor Regime* (Oxford, 1979).

Manorial custom and its enforcement in manorial courts in the eighteenth century is explored in Neeson (cited above for Ch. 1); case studies of conflicts over customs (both local, and at the common law) include D. Hay, 'Poaching and the Game Laws on Cannock Chase', in D. Hay, P. Linebaugh, E. P. Thompson, *Albion's Fatal Tree: Crime and Society in Eighteenth-Century England* (London, 1975), 189–254, and Peter King, 'Legal Change, Customary Right, and Social Conflict in Late Eighteenth-Century England: The Origins of the Great Gleaning Case of 1788', *Law and History Review*, 10/1 (Spring 1992), 1–31.

The customs and legally recognized usages of trades, and their place within the inherited corpus of Tudor and Stuart legislation, can be studied in W. E. Minchinton (ed.), *Wage Regulation in Pre-Industrial England* (New York, 1972); D. Hay, 'Masters and Servants, Justice and Judges' (forthcoming); and in scattered evidence in many studies of particular trades, such as woollens and worsteds. For an older instance, see Alfred P. Wadsworth and Julia de Lacy Mann, *The Cotton Trade and Industrial Lancashire 1600–1780* (Manchester, 1931; repr. 1965); for a recent account, which places custom at the heart of industrial relations, see Adrian Randall, *Before the Luddites: Custom, Community and Machinery in the English Woollen Industry 1776–1809* (Cambridge, 1991), and also essays in John Rule (ed.), *British Trade Unionism 1750–1850* (London, 1988) and Rule, *The Experience of Labour in Eighteenth-Century Industry* (London, 1981). On perquisites and embezzlement, and their place in the custom of trades, see Adrian Randall, 'Peculiar Perquisites and Pernicious Practices: Embezzlement in the West of England Woollen Industry, *c.*1750–1840', *International Review of Social History*, 35 (1990), 193–219; Peter Linebaugh, *The London Hanged: Crime and Civil Society in the Eighteenth Century* (London, 1991), esp. pts. 3, 4; and (for a different emphasis) John Styles, 'Embezzlement, Industry, and the Law in England, 1500–1800', in

M. Berg, P. Hudson, M. Sonenscher (eds.), *Manufacture in Town and Country before the Factory* (Cambridge, 1983), 173–210.

The place of the marketing offences in state law and popular belief (with an emphasis on the latter) was reconstructed in E. P. Thompson, 'The Moral Economy of the English Crowd', *Past & Present*, 50 (1971), 76–136, reprinted with an additional essay of commentary on subsequent work in his *Customs in Common*. The practice of the early-modern state is described in John Walter and Keith Wrightson, 'Dearth and the Social Order in Early Modern England', *Past & Present*, 71 (1976), 22–42, and its probable effects on price fluctuations in Fogel (cited above for Ch. 5). The legal standing of the marketing laws, both statute and judge-made law, is explored in D. Hay, 'Moral Economy, Political Economy, and Law', in Adrian Randall and Andrew Charlesworth (eds.), *The Moral Economy and Popular Protest: Crowds, Conflict and Authority* (London, 1997); other chapters in the book deal with extensions of the use of the idea of moral economy to other areas, as does Randall, 'The Industrial Moral Economy of the Gloucestershire Weavers in the 18th Century', in Rule (ed.), *British Trade Unionism*. See also Ch. 7, below.

Chapter 7: The Disruption of Custom, the Triumph of Law

Most of the works cited above for Ch. 6 are relevant to this chapter also. On enclosure, see also the works on agrarian structure cited above for Ch. 1. The prevailing orthodoxy until recently was summarized in J. D. Chambers and G. E. Mingay, *The Agricultural Revolution 1750–1880* (London, 1966). Recent important work includes J. M. Martin, 'Members of Parliament and Enclosure: A Reconsideration', *Agricultural History Review*, 27 (1980), 101–9; id., 'The Small Landowner and Parliamentary Enclosure in Warwickshire', *Economic History Review*, 32 (1979), 328–43; and id., 'Village Traders and the Emergence of a Proletariat in South Warwickshire, 1750–1851', *Agricultural History Review*, 32 (1984), 413–16. See also Michael E. Turner, 'Benefits but at Cost', in George Grantham and Carol S. Leonard (eds.), *Agrarian Organization in the Century of Industrialization: Europe, Russia, and North America* (Grunswick, Conn., 1989), and *English Parliamentary Enclosure: Its Historical Geography and Economic History* (Folkestone, 1980). The arguments that enclosure had both significant benefits to agricultural productivity and little consequence, intended or unintended, for the poor now seem doubtful: on the first, see Allen (cited above for Ch. 1); on the last, Neeson (cited above for Ch. 1); Snell (cited above for Ch. 2), ch. 5; and Jane Humphries, 'Enclosures, Common Rights, and Women: The Proletarianization of Families in the Late Eighteenth and Early Nineteenth Centuries', *Journal of Economic History*, 1 (1990), 17–42. Some of the inconsistencies in the earlier view of uncontentious transition are in fact exhibited in G. E. Mingay, *The Unquiet Countryside* (London, 1989).

On apprenticeship, resistance to machinery, and repeal of the old protective legislation see also the works cited below for Ch. 8; and T. K. Derry, 'Repeal of the Apprenticeship Clauses of the Statute of Apprentices', *Economic History Review*, 1st series, 3 (1931–2), 67–87; and Iowerth Prothero, *Artisans and Politics in Early-Nineteenth-Century London: John Gast and His Times* (Folkestone, 1979). On the final repudiation of the marketing laws by the government and the judges, see D. Hay, 'The State and the Market: Lord Kenyon and Mr Waddington', *Past & Present* (forthcoming 1997).

Chapter 8: New Populations

For perspectives on the historical writing on industrialization see David Cannadine, 'The Present and the Past in the English Industrial Revolution 1880–1980', *Past & Present*, 103 (1984), 131–72. For recent general treatments that cover most issues, including the regional nature of industrial development and industrial decline, readers should consult Maxine Berg, *The Age of Manufactures 1700–1820: Industry, Innovation and Work in Britain* (2nd edn., London, 1994); Pat Hudson, *The Industrial Revolution* (London, 1992); and ead. (ed.), *Regions and Industries* (Cambridge, 1989). The essays in John Rule (ed.), *British Trade Unionism* (London, 1988) and id., *Experience of Labour* (both cited above for Ch. 6), are important, and a detailed local study of industrial relations in a northern coalfield is David Levine and Keith Wrightson, *The Making of an Industrial Society: Whickham 1560–1765* (Oxford, 1991). An important recent study of the major and most ancient industry that informs our own account is Adrian Randall, *Before the Luddites: Custom, Community and Machinery in the English Woollen Industry 1776–1809* (Cambridge, 1991). E. P. Thompson, *The Making of the English Working Class* (revd edn., Harmondsworth, 1968), remains essential reading, as well as an inspiration for a great deal of later work. On the deep sea proletariat see Marcus Rediker, *Between the Devil and the Deep Blue Sea* (Cambridge, 1987). On the place of women and children in industry and the economy, see Ivy Pinchbeck, *Women Workers and the Industrial Revolution 1750–1850* (London, 1930); Berg, *Age of Manufactures*, esp. ch. 7 and her essay in Patrick Joyce (ed.), *The Historical Meanings of Work* (1987); and Bridget Hill, *Women, Work, and Sexual Politics in Eighteenth-Century England* (Oxford, 1989). See also the works cited for Chs. 6 and 7, above.

Our text omits the complex debate over models used to explain the path of industrialization in Britain and Europe. Proto-industrialization, or family-based rural industry, whether in a strictly artisan or putting-out system, has been one of them, complementing (and sometimes contrasted with) the Marxian emphasis on the transformation of the independent producer into a wage-dependent labourer, and accounts of handicraft workshop industry based on a more elaborate division of labour than traditional guild production. Proto-industrialization theory has turned attention to family work strategies and to the symbiosis of agricultural and industrial change. It has been criticized for its teleological and linear bias (as necessarily leading to modern, machine-driven industry) and for failing to address the complex temporality and diversity of industrial modes of work in the early modern period. We have avoided the concept because of these criticisms, although we have been sensitive to some of the issues which it has helped to highlight: dual economies; the relationship of land, production, and demographic growth; gendered divisions of labour; and the customary expectations surrounding work in an age when workers still retained considerable control over the labour process. See F. Mendels, 'Proto-industrialization: The First Phase of the Process of Industrialization', *Journal of Economic History*, 32 (1972), 241–61; Hans Medick, 'The Proto-industrial Family Economy', *Social History*, 1/3 (Oct. 1976), 291–315; F. Mendels, 'Proto-industrialization: Theory and Reality', *Eighth International Congress of Economic History* (Budapest, 1982), section A-2, 69–105; D. C. Coleman, 'Proto-industrialization: A Concept Too Many', *Economic History Review*, 36 (1983), 435–48; Maxine Berg, Pat Hudson, and Michael Sonenscher (eds.) *Manufacture in Town and Country Before the Factory* (Cambridge, 1983), and Maxine Berg, *Age of Manufactures*, ch. 3.

Chapter 9: The Power of the People

The transformation of our perception of the eighteenth-century riot began over three decades ago with Eric Hobsbawm, *Primitive Rebels* (Manchester, 1959) and the work of George Rudé, who saw in the 'crowd' a more rational and respectable body of people than earlier historians had seen in the 'mob'. See Rudé, *The Face of the Crowd: Studies in Revolution, Ideology and Popular Protest. Selected Essays of George Rudé*, ed. Harvey J. Kaye (New York, 1988); and id., *Wilkes and Liberty: A Social Study of 1763 to 1774* (Oxford, 1962); id., *The Crowd in History: A Study of Popular Disturbances in France and England, 1730–1848* (New York, 1964); and id., *Paris and London in the Eighteenth Century: Studies in Popular Protest* (1973). E. P. Thompson, *Making of the English Working Class* (cited above for Ch. 8), was less interested in profiles of occupational standings than in the historical continuities, political and industrial contexts, and the shared values of rioters and gentry, in the context of the food riot and more widely: see his *Customs in Common* (cited above for Ch. 6). Other approaches and local studies include John Bohstedt, *Riots and Community Politics in England and Wales, 1790–1810* (Cambridge, Mass., 1983) and 'Women in English Riots 1790–1810', *Past & Present*, 120 (Aug. 1988), 88–122; A. J. Peacock, *Bread or Blood* (1965) on the 1816 East Anglian riots; W. J. Shelton, *English Hunger and Industrial Disorders* (London, 1973); Adrian Randall, 'Gloucestershire food riots in 1766', *Midland History*, 10 (1986), 72–93; Charles Tilly, *Popular Contention in Great Britain, 1758–1834* (Cambridge, Mass., 1995).

On political and other sources of disorder, see the sources cited above for Ch. 4 and below for Ch. 11; also Geoffrey Holmes, 'The Sacheverell Riots: The Crowd and Church in Early 18th Century London', *Past & Present*, 72, (Aug. 1976), 55–85; Peter Linebaugh, 'The Tyburn Riot against the Surgeons' in D. Hay, P. Linebaugh, E. P. Thompson (eds.), *Albion's Fatal Tree* (London, 1975) and other essays in that volume; Robert Malcolmson, ' "A Set of Ungovernable People": The Kingswood Colliers in the Eighteenth Century', in John Brewer and John Styles (eds.), *An Ungovernable People* (London, 1980), and other essays in that volume; W. Nippel, 'Reading the Riot Act: The Discourse of Law-Enforcement in 18th-Century England', *History and Anthropology*, 1 (1985), 401–26; Nicholas Rogers, 'Popular Protest in Early Hanoverian London', *Past & Present*, 79 (1978), 70–100, and 'Riot and Popular Jacobitism in Early Hanoverian England', in Evelyn Cruikshanks (ed.), *Ideology and Conspiracy: Aspects of Jacobitism, 1689–1759* (Edinburgh, 1982), 70–88; R. B. Rose, 'The Priestly Riots of 1791', *Past & Present*, 18 (Nov. 1960), 68–88.

Some general surveys and larger arguments can be found in Ian Gilmour, *Riot, Rising and Revolution: Governance and Violence in 18th Century England* (London, 1992) (notable as the product of a leading Tory politician with current comparisons in mind); John Stevenson, *Popular Disturbances in England, 1700–1870* (New York, 1979); Roger Wells, 'The Development of the English Rural Proletariat and Social Protest, 1700–1850', *Journal of Peasant Studies*, 6/2, 115–39 (and subsequent debates in that journal) and *Wretched Faces* (cited above for Ch. 5); Andrew Charlesworth, *An Atlas of Rural Protest in Britain 1548–1900* (1983). For the longer background to the place of riot in society see B. W. Quintrell, 'The Making of Charles Ist's Book of Orders', *English Historical Review*, 95 (July 1980), 553–72; David Underdown, *Revel, Riot, and Rebellion: Popular Politics and Culture in England 1603–1660* (Oxford, 1985); and John Walter and Keith Wrightson, 'Dearth and the Social Order in Early Modern England', *Past & Present*, 71 (May 1976).

For sabotage and threats, see E. P. Thompson, 'The Crime of Anonymity', in Hay, Linebaugh, and Thompson (eds.), *Albion's Fatal Tree*, 255–308; on using the criminal law, see Peter King, 'Decision-Makers and Decision-Making in the English Common Law 1750–1800', *Historical Journal*, 27 (1984), 25–58; and D. Hay and F. Snyder (eds.), *Policing and Prosecution in Britain 1750–1850* (Oxford, 1989). For some Celtic comparisons see James S. Donnelly, 'The Rightboy Movement, 1785–1788', *Studia Hibernica*, 17–18 (1977–8), 120–202 and 'The Whiteboy Movement, 1761–1765', *Irish Historical Studies*, 21 (Mar. 1978), 20–54; K. J. Logue, *Popular Disturbances in Scotland, 1780–1815* (Edinburgh, 1978). Ireland is particularly relevant to the response of the state to events in England also: see F. Darvall, *Popular Disturbances & Public Order in Regency England* (London, 1934) and Stanley

H. Palmer, *Police and Protest in England and Ireland, 1780–1850* (Cambridge, 1988).

Chapter 10: War and Peace

The development of the British state in the long eighteenth century is charted in John Brewer, *The Sinews of Power: War, Money and the English State, 1688–1783* (New York, 1989) and in Lawrence Stone (ed.), *An Imperial State at War: Britain from 1689 to 1815* (London, 1994). The construction of a British identity and its relationship to war is traced in Linda Colley, *Britons: Forging the Nation 1707–1837* (New Haven, 1992). Wartime taxation and its social implications is explored in detail in Peter Mathias and Patrick O'Brien, 'Taxation in Britain and France, 1715–1810', *Journal of European Economic History*, 5 (1976), 601–50 and Patrick O'Brien, 'The Political Economy of British Taxation, 1660–1815', *Economic History Review*, 2nd ser., 41 (1988), 1–32.

Basic figures on army and naval recruitment can be conveniently found in Roderick Floud, Kenneth Wachter, and Annabel Gregory, *Height, Health and History* (Cambridge, 1990), tables 2.1 and 2.6; that book also discusses the social provenance of recruits. Naval recruitment is treated in many books, including the old, but still very useful, J. R. Hutchinson, *The Press Gang Afloat and Ashore* (London, 1913). For more recent accounts, see Daniel Baugh, *British Naval Administration in the Age of Walpole* (Princeton, 1965), ch. 5; N. A. M. Rodger, *The Wooden World* (London, 1986), ch. 5; and Nicholas Rogers, 'Liberty Road: Opposition to Impressment in Britain during the American War of Independence', in Colin Howell and Richard Twomey (eds.), *Jack Tar In History* (Fredericton, New Brunswick, 1991), 55–75.

The social ramifications of war in the eighteenth century is a surprisingly unexplored topic. The relationship of war to crime is treated in Douglas Hay, 'War, Dearth and Theft in the Eighteenth Century: The Record of the English Courts', *Past & Present*, 95 (May 1982), 117–60; in John Beattie, *Crime and the Courts in England 1660–1800* (Princeton, 1986), ch. 5; and in Nicholas Rogers, 'Confronting the Crime Wave: The Debate over Social Reform and Regulation, 1749–1753', in L. Davison, T. Hitchcock, T. Keirn, and R. B. Shoemaker (eds.), *Stilling the Grumbling Hive* (New York, 1992), 77–98. Family desertion in wartime is explored in David A. Kent, ' "Gone for a Soldier": Family Breakdown and the Demography of Desertion in a London Parish, 1750–1791', *Local Population Studies*, 45 (1990), 27–42. The broadest and thus far richest treatments of the impact of war are to be found in Roger Wells (cited above for Ch. 5); Clive Emsley, *British Society and the French Wars 1793–1815* (London, 1979) and 'The Social Impact of the French Wars', in H. T. Dickinson (ed.), *Britain and the French Revolution 1789–1815* (London, 1989), 211–28.

Chapter 11: Popular Beliefs and Popular Politics

A useful overview of the now copious literature on Methodism and politics can be found in David Hempton, *Methodism and Politics in British Society,
1750–1850* (Stanford, 1984). On charismatic Methodism after Wesley, see
John Baxter, 'The Great Yorkshire Revival, 1792–1796: A Study of Mass
Revival Among the Methodists', *Sociological Yearbook of Religion in Brit-
ain*, 7 (1974), 46–76 and J. F. C. Harrison, *The Second Coming: Popular
Millenarianism 1780–1850* (London, 1979). Some other religious roots of
late-eighteenth-century millenarianism in London are discussed in D. Hay,
'The Laws of God and the Law of Man: Lord George Gordon and the Death
Penalty', in J. Rule and R. Malcolmson (eds.), *Protest and Survival: The
Historical Experience: Essays in Honour of E. P. Thompson* (London, 1993),
60–111. On Methodism and popular belief, see John Rule, 'Methodism,
Popular Beliefs and Village Culture in Cornwall, 1800–1850', in Robert
D. Storch (ed.), *Popular Culture and Custom in Nineteenth-Century England*
(London, 1982), 48–70. On the initial hostility to Methodism, see John
Walsh, 'Methodism and the Mob in the Eighteenth Century', in G. L.
Cumming and Derek Baker (eds.), *Studies in Church History*, viii. *Popular
Belief and Practice* (Cambridge, 1972), 203–28.

The seminal study of Wilkes and the Wilkite movement is George Rudé,
Wilkes and Liberty (Oxford, 1962). It should be supplemented by John
Brewer, *Party Ideology and Popular Politics at the Accession of George III*
(Cambridge, 1976), ch. 9, and 'The Wilkites and the Law, 1763–1774: A
Study of Radical Notions of Governance', in John Brewer and John Styles
(eds.), *An Ungovernable People* (London, 1980), 128–71. The literature on
anti-slavery is voluminous, but two recent books that address the mobilization of anti-slavery opinion in new ways are Seymour Drescher, *Capitalism and Anti-Slavery* (London, 1986) and Clare Midgley, *Women Against
Slavery: The British Campaigns 1780–1870* (London, 1992). For work on English radicalism, popular politics, and the American Revolution, students
should consult Colin Bonwick, *English Radicals and the American Revolution*
(Chapel Hill, NC, 1977) and two studies by James Bradley: *Popular Politics
and the American Revolution in England* (Macon, Ga., 1986) and *Religion,
Revolution, and English Radicalism* (Cambridge, 1990). Both books provide
important evidence of the provincial dimensions of English radicalism during the American War, as do Kathleen Wilson, *The Sense of the People*
(Cambridge, 1995) and John Money, *Experience and Identity. Birmingham and
the West Midlands 1760–1800* (Montreal, 1977).

Money's book also provides important evidence on the nature of popular loyalism in the 1790s. This subject, and the relative weight of loyalist
versus Radical sentiment in Britain during the French wars, is discussed in
Mark Philp (ed.), *The French Revolution and British Popular Politics* (Cam-

bridge, 1991). The most comprehensive study of English radicalism in the early years of the French Revolution is Albert Goodwin, *The Friends of Liberty* (Cambridge, Mass., 1975). For a pioneering article that chants the changing meaning of radical iconography, see James Epstein, 'Understanding the Cap of Liberty: Symbolic Practice and Social Conflict in Early Nineteenth-Century England', *Past & Present*, 122 (Feb. 1989), 75–118. The critical text for the understanding of popular politics and working-class culture 1790–1832 is E. P. Thompson (cited above for Ch. 8); it is one with which every historian of class and popular politics during the French Wars and beyond has had to engage.

Chapter 12: Class and Power in Hanoverian England

The most useful account of the development of a pluralistic propertied order is Paul Langford, *Public Life and the Propertied Englishman 1689–1798* (Oxford, 1991). Readers interested in middling identities and the shifting language of class should consult John Seed, 'From "Middling Sort" to Middle Class in Late Eighteenth- and Early Nineteenth-Century England', in M. L. Bush (ed.), *Social Orders & Social Classes in Europe since 1500* (London, 1992), 114–35; Jonathan Barry and Christopher Brooks (eds.), *The Middling Sort of People* (London, 1994); and Dror Wahrman, *Imagining the Middle Class* (Cambridge, 1995).

The classic text on working-class formation is E. P. Thompson (cited above for Ch. 8). For useful appraisals, see Harvey J. Kaye and Keith McClelland (eds.), *E. P. Thompson: Critical Perspectives* (Cambridge, 1990). For feminist critiques, see Joan Wallach Scott, *Gender and the Politics of History* (New York, 1988), ch. 4, and Anna Clark, *The Struggle for the Breeches* (Berkeley and Los Angeles, 1995).

For interpretations of the long eighteenth century that differ from the one framed here, see J. C. D. Clark, *English Society 1688–1832* (Cambridge, 1985); John Cannon, *Aristocratic Century: The Peerage of Eighteenth-Century England* (Cambridge, 1984); and Colley (cited above for Ch. 10).

Index

OXFORD

MORE OXFORD PAPERBACKS

This book is just one of nearly 1000 Oxford Paperbacks currently in print. If you would like details of other Oxford Paperbacks, including titles in the World's Classics, Oxford Reference, Oxford Books, OPUS, Past Masters, Oxford Authors, and Oxford Shakespeare series, please write to:

UK and Europe: Oxford Paperbacks Publicity Manager, Arts and Reference Publicity Department, Oxford University Press, Walton Street, Oxford OX2 6DP.

Customers in UK and Europe will find Oxford Paperbacks available in all good bookshops. But in case of difficulty please send orders to the Cash-with-Order Department, Oxford University Press Distribution Services, Saxon Way West, Corby, Northants NN18 9ES. Tel: 01536 741519; Fax: 01536 746337. Please send a cheque for the total cost of the books, plus £1.75 postage and packing for orders under £20; £2.75 for orders over £20. Customers outside the UK should add 10% of the cost of the books for postage and packing.

USA: Oxford Paperbacks Marketing Manager, Oxford University Press, Inc., 200 Madison Avenue, New York, N.Y. 10016.

Canada: Trade Department, Oxford University Press, 70 Wynford Drive, Don Mills, Ontario M3C 1J9.

Australia: Trade Marketing Manager, Oxford University Press, G.P.O. Box 2784Y, Melbourne 3001, Victoria.

South Africa: Oxford University Press, P.O. Box 1141, Cape Town 8000.

LAW FROM OXFORD PAPERBACKS

INTRODUCTION TO ENGLISH LAW
Tenth Edition

William Geldart

Edited by D. C. M. Yardley

'Geldart' has over the years established itself as a standard account of English law, expounding the body of modern law as set in its historical context. Regularly updated since its first publication, it remains indispensable to student and layman alike as a concise, reliable guide.

Since publication of the ninth edition in 1984 there have been important court decisions and a great deal of relevant new legislation. D. C. M. Yardley, Chairman of the Commission for Local Administration in England, has taken account of all these developments and the result has been a considerable rewriting of several parts of the book. These include the sections dealing with the contractual liability of minors, the abolition of the concept of illegitimacy, the liability of a trade union in tort for inducing a person to break his/her contract of employment, the new public order offences, and the intent necessary for a conviction of murder.

HISTORY IN OXFORD PAPERBACKS
TUDOR ENGLAND
John Guy

Tudor England is a compelling account of political and religious developments from the advent of the Tudors in the 1460s to the death of Elizabeth I in 1603.

Following Henry VII's capture of the Crown at Bosworth in 1485, Tudor England witnessed far-reaching changes in government and the Reformation of the Church under Henry VIII, Edward VI, Mary, and Elizabeth; that story is enriched here with character studies of the monarchs and politicians that bring to life their personalities as well as their policies.

Authoritative, clearly argued, and crisply written, this comprehensive book will be indispensable to anyone interested in the Tudor Age.

'lucid, scholarly, remarkably accomplished . . . an excellent overview' *Sunday Times*

'the first comprehensive history of Tudor England for more than thirty years' Patrick Collinson, *Observer*

HISTORY IN OXFORD PAPERBACKS

THE STRUGGLE FOR
THE MASTERY OF EUROPE 1848–1918

A. J. P. Taylor

The fall of Metternich in the revolutions of 1848 heralded an era of unprecedented nationalism in Europe, culminating in the collapse of the Hapsburg, Romanov, and Hohenzollern dynasties at the end of the First World War. In the intervening seventy years the boundaries of Europe changed dramatically from those established at Vienna in 1815. Cavour championed the cause of *Risorgimento* in Italy; Bismarck's three wars brought about the unification of Germany; Serbia and Bulgaria gained their independence courtesy of the decline of Turkey—'the sick man of Europe'; while the great powers scrambled for places in the sun in Africa. However, with America's entry into the war and President Wilson's adherence to idealistic internationalist principles, Europe ceased to be the centre of the world, although its problems, still primarily revolving around nationalist aspirations, were to smash the Treaty of Versailles and plunge the world into war once more.

A. J. P. Taylor has drawn the material for his account of this turbulent period from the many volumes of diplomatic documents which have been published in the five major European languages. By using vivid language and forceful characterization, he has produced a book that is as much a work of literature as a contribution to scientific history.

'One of the glories of twentieth-century writing.' *Observer*

PAST MASTERS

General Editor: Keith Thomas

HOBBES

Richard Tuck

Thomas Hobbes (1588–1679) was the first great English political philosopher, and his book *Leviathan* was one of the first truly modern works of philosophy. He has long had the reputation of being a pessimistic atheist, who saw human nature as inevitably evil, and who proposed a totalitarian state to subdue human failings. In this new study, Richard Tuck shows that while Hobbes may indeed have been an atheist, he was far from pessimistic about human nature, nor did he advocate totalitarianism. By locating him against the context of his age, Dr Tuck reveals Hobbes to have been passionately concerned with the refutation of scepticism in both science and ethics, and to have developed a theory of knowledge which rivalled that of Descartes in its importance for the formation of modern philosophy.

PAST

MASTERS

RUSSELL

A. C. Grayling

Bertrand Russell (1872–1970) is one of the most famous and important philosophers of the twentieth century. In this account of his life and work A. C. Grayling introduces both his technical contributions to logic and philosophy, and his wide-ranging views on education, politics, war, and sexual morality. Russell is credited with being one of the prime movers of Analytic Philosophy, and with having played a part in the revolution in social attitudes witnessed throughout the twentieth-century world. This introduction gives a clear survey of Russell's achievements across their whole range.